MULTIPLE INTELLIGENCES
in the
ELEMENTARY CLASSROOM

A Teacher's Toolkit

MULTIPLE INTELLIGENCES
in the
ELEMENTARY CLASSROOM

A Teacher's Toolkit

SUSAN BAUM,
JULIE VIENS, and
BARBARA SLATIN
in consultation with HOWARD GARDNER

Teachers College, Columbia University
New York and London

Clip art graphics used in the Pathway Guides and Organizers are copyright © Microsoft, Inc.

Figure 7.2 adapted from Sullivan, A. (1999). Entry points to understanding light. In L. Hetland and S. Veenema (Eds.), *The Project Zero classroom: Views on understanding.* Cambridge, MA: President and Fellows of Harvard College (on behalf of Project Zero). Used by permission of publisher.

Figure 9.2, Graphic Representation of the Three-Ring Conception of Giftedness, and the Medieval Task Cards on pages 92–93 are used by permission of Creative Learning Press.

Published by Teachers College Press, 1234 Amsterdam Avenue, New York, NY 10027

Library of Congress Cataloging-in-Publication Data

Baum, Susan.
    Multiple intelligences in the elementary classroom : a teacher's toolkit / Susan Baum, Julie Viens, Barbara Slatin ; in consultation with Howard Gardner.
      p. cm.
    Includes bibliographical references and index.
    ISBN 0-8077-4610-X (pbk. : alk. paper)
      1. Elementary school teaching. 2. Multiple intelligences. 3. Cognitive styles. I. Viens, Julie. II. Slatin, Barbara. III. Title.
    LB1555.B355 2005
    370.15'2—dc22   2005041924

ISBN 0-8077-4610-X (paper)

Printed on acid-free paper
Manufactured in the United States of America

12   11   10   09   08   07   06   05   8   7   6   5   4   3   2   1

Contents

Foreword

Because I am intimately associated with the theory of multiple intelligences, individuals often come up to me and declare proudly, "We have an MI classroom," or "I am working at a multiple intelligences school." It is flattering to be singled out in this manner, so I respond politely with a thank you. But actually, I think to myself, "What are you using MI for? Multiple intelligences cannot and should not be an end in itself."

When developed in the early 1980s, multiple intelligences was a theory of how the human mind evolved over thousands of years and how it functions today. I saw the concept of multiple intelligences as a contribution to psychology and not, except incidentally, as a contribution to education. No one was more surprised than I to see educators throughout the country, and even abroad, working with students of all ages and backgrounds, gaining sustenance from the theory. Although I myself had little formal background in precollegiate education, I naturally became intrigued by some of the educational implications of the theory.

One might describe the literary sequels to a new idea, such as MI theory, in three steps.

1. *Straight exposition of the theory.* Much early writing, including my own initial efforts, was directed at stating the basic ideas of the theory and perhaps suggesting a few implications.
2. *Tracts pushing one or another application of the theory in a univocal manner.* Once the basic theory had become known, many educators carried out projects and wrote works that focused on a specific application: multiple intelligences for gifted students, multiple intelligences in kindergarten, multiple intelligences assessments, multiple intelligences curricula, and the like. These efforts varied widely in interest and quality. Sometimes I learned a great deal from them; at other times I was irked at the superficiality of the applications. Often I wondered whether the writer actually had read my work or simply was imagining what the theory might claim. I finally was stimulated to write directly about misconceptions and misapplications of the theory (Gardner, 1995, 1999b).
3. *More reflective works based on considerable thinking, experimentation, and reflection.* Without question, the present book falls into this third category. The authors each have been steeped for many years in the principal ideas of MI theory, they have undertaken considerable practice themselves, and they have learned from that practice. The audience is the beneficiary of their "trials under fire." The book is clear, not grandiose; authoritative without being authoritarian; up-to-date, and balanced. Shunning a cookbook approach, this volume instead puts forth five distinct and distinctive ways of using MI ideas in elementary schools. It presents sample lessons, as well as a potpourri of organizing questions, activities, simulations, and analyses. I learned much from reading the book and am pleased to have been involved as a consultant.

One can think of the educational process as involving four distinct nodes, as shown in Figure F.1.

Figure F.1.

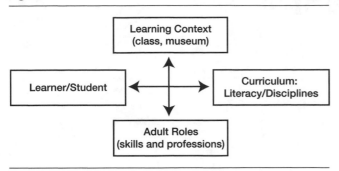

Most of the time, educators focus on the horizontal axis: the solitary student, and the curriculum to be mastered—literacies in the early grades, then disciplinary content and ways of thinking in secondary school. But it is important as well to keep in mind the vertical dimension: the context in which education takes place and the adult skills and roles for which education, broadly conceived, is a preparation.

We might think of the five pathways laid out by the authors as addressing these respective nodes. The Exploration pathway focuses on the relation between the child and the learning environment—which can be a classroom, a museum, a home, or even the community at large. The Bridging pathway addresses the ways in which young children can most readily become literate. The Understanding pathway directs its attention, in turn, to the way in which students master consequential academic content. The Authentic Problems pathway gives students a taste of the kinds of complex challenges and projects that they will confront in the world of work. Finally, the Talent Development pathway searches out those domains and disciplines for which a child may have a special aptitude or hunger, which may be geared toward a role that is highlighted in school or in the larger community.

With the notion of pathways, the authors go well beyond the univocal messages of the second generation of MI books. No longer is there a single or a "right" way to use MI. Rather, educators are encouraged to become familiar with a range of approaches and choose the one that makes most sense in light of their own goals and contexts.

My guess is that most readers initially will try to use the ideas of one pathway, but that, over time, aspects of different pathways will be attempted. In the end, educators will come up with their own blend—their homemade pathway, so to speak. In doing so, educators will realize the most important implication of MI theory: Each of us has the same intelligences, but ultimately each of us will fashion a distinctive MI profile and bring it to bear in the ways that are most productive for ourselves. By the same token, the several pathways are available to anyone; the committed educator eventually will hit on the pathway that most fully satisfies his or her own aspirations. The authors are to be congratulated on having fashioned a thoughtful, penetrating, and useful work that should help many educators become more effective practitioners.

—Howard Gardner

Acknowledgments

We are pleased to acknowledge the following colleagues who have helped us formulate and develop our ideas: Carolyn Cooper, Phyllis Hernandez, the late John Jablonski, Marjorie Leopold, Terry Neu, and Barry Oreck.

A thank you to those whose practices are represented in this book: Kelly Hayes, Plato Karafelis, Jessica Nicoll, Hank Nicols, Kathy Offner, and Christine Ollum.

A note of gratitude to Laurie Paladino for her diligence in helping to prepare the final manuscript, and to Vivian Wheeler for expert editing.

We especially thank Howard Gardner, whose multiple intelligences theory continues to be an inspiration and resource for a great many educators like ourselves. Dr. Gardner also provided invaluable feedback through the several iterations of this book.

We are grateful to the teachers, administrators, and students with whom we have worked over the years; their commitment and special talents made the pathways a reality.

And special thanks to our families—Laurie, Owen, and Benjamin Bailey; Jonathan, Michael, Jennifer, and Kaitlyn Baum; Mark, Sophia, and Shayla Gottlieb; and Scott and Brad Slatin—for their ongoing patience, support, and assistance.

PART ONE

The Basics

CHAPTER 1

Book Basics

The introduction of multiple intelligences (MI) theory in 1983 generated great excitement in the educational community. In marked contrast to the traditional view that individuals possess one general intelligence, it was a provocative new concept claiming the existence of at least seven (now eight) distinct intelligences: linguistic, logical–mathematical, musical, spatial, bodily–kinesthetic, interpersonal, intrapersonal, and naturalist.

Multiple intelligences theory was intended for an audience of psychologists when Howard Gardner introduced it in 1983 in his book *Frames of Mind* (Gardner, 1993c). Although it said little about classroom practice, the theory was received primarily and enthusiastically by educators, who saw in the theory the variety of abilities they regularly observed and recognized in their students.

Since its introduction, MI theory has been used by educators to plan and support programs that draw on an understanding of students as uniquely able individuals. But because it is neither a learning theory nor a curricular model, MI theory does not come with a prescription or set of directions for practice. As a result, its implementation varies widely among the thousands of individuals who use it.

We (the authors) began our collaboration in 1992 when we came together to help a school in New York City implement its vision of developing instructional strategies based on students' strengths. From our extensive work with teachers and schools using MI theory, each of us came into the project feeling strongly that MI theory could make a positive difference for students and teachers. This and subsequent collaborations with dozens of schools confirmed that belief.

HOW THIS BOOK IS UNIQUE

In response to teachers' requests for help implementing MI theory, we developed the Pathways Model presented in this book. Each pathway—Exploration, Bridging, Understanding, Authentic Problems, and Talent Development—assembles a set of MI-inspired approaches and practices, based on a particular goal for using MI theory. And each focuses on one of five overarching goals that we identified among educators using the theory well. The pathways help teachers to name their goals and identify appropriate MI practices.

With dozens of books on multiple intelligences already available, it is reasonable for someone to ask, "Why use *this* book?" *Multiple Intelligences in the Elementary Classroom: A Teacher's Toolkit* is distinct from other resources on the topic in that it fills a gap. To our knowledge, this is the only book that *guides* readers' learning about MI theory and undertaking MI-inspired practices. In that respect it can be used as a professional development guide for a team of practicing educators or as a textbook in a teacher education course. Our work with dozens of rural, suburban, and urban schools enables us to continue to field test and refine the pathways and the professional development strategies we use to share the model with educators. This book represents our best iteration to date of the Pathways Model.

One way to describe our book is by explaining what it is not. It is not filled with activities organized by intelligences or with lesson plans that each use all eight intelligences. Still, between these covers are dozens of activities that teachers can try "as is" or use as a catalyst to create other activities. By the same token, we do not offer a packet of "MI assessments" to be photocopied and applied directly, but we do include examples and consideration of assessments from the perspective of one's purposes and goals for using MI in the classroom.

In *Multiple Intelligences in the Elementary Classroom* those purposes and goals are represented as "pathways." Rather than a collection of MI activities, this book—and the Pathways Model itself—presents collections of MI approaches and activities tied to a particular goal. For example, the goal of the Bridging pathway is to develop students' basic skills by using MI-informed "bridge points" that connect students' strengths to a literacy skill area. The Talent Development pathway focuses on creating opportunities for students to use and build their special talents. In other words, one's goals for using MI theory will activate one or another pathway linked to those goals.

To the question, "What does it mean to be MI-informed?" this book responds with a unique framework. The Pathways Model promotes, first, a well-grounded understanding of multiple intelligences theory and, second, enlightened application of the theory in the classroom.

Putting the pathways into a book is a wonderful way to get the model out to interested educators. However, a book is not the ideal context for professional development. In an effort to enhance readers' experience, we apply—to the extent possible—principles of professional development preferred by teachers with whom we have worked and those characterized in the literature as "best practices" (Darling-Hammond, 1996; McLaughlin, 1996).

The book is organized to encourage two or more individuals to meet together regularly in a team or study group setting. These groups might be pre-existing teams at a school, like grade-level teams, or cross-grade curriculum development teams. Teams may be groups of teachers from different schools that are participating in the same educational initiative or reform effort. Or, a team might be two colleagues who have decided to buddy up informally to work through the book together. Whatever the makeup of the team, regular meetings provide a supportive and interactive context. They emphasize collegiality, provide a safe context to take risks and try out new ideas, and provide regular opportunities to discuss, debrief, and reflect.

Each chapter of this book is organized to allow for independent work, such as experimentation in the classroom, while encouraging groupwork, discussion, and reflection through thought questions and problem-solving activities at the end of each chapter.

This book respects the audience as thinking and thoughtful teachers and students. We do not dictate how to use MI theory; rather, we guide the users' discovery and development of their own interpretations and applications of MI theory. We do not recommend going it alone or simply reading the book rapidly cover to cover, although it is possible to do so. The book is organized to support an ongoing learning process.

HOW THIS BOOK IS ORGANIZED

Part One of the book is composed of three introductory chapters: Chapter 1, Book Basics; Chapter 2, MI Basics: The Theory; and Chapter 3, MI Basics: Moving from Theory to Practice. The current chapter, Book Basics, represents the metaphorical map for our pathways journey. It provides the "whys" and "hows" of MI application and outlines the organization and content of the book.

Chapter 2, MI Basics: The Theory, gives a basic overview of the theory, introducing readers to MI theory and the eight intelligences, in contrast to existing unitary conceptions of intelligence. Chapter 3, MI Basics: Moving from Theory to Practice, presents the key features of MI theory and their implications for teaching and learning practices.

Part Two focuses on the pathways. Chapter 4, Pathway Basics, provides a brief rationale and overview of each of the five pathways: Exploration, Bridging, Understanding, Authentic Problems, and Talent Development. This chapter sets the stage for more intensive study of each pathway.

Each of the subsequent chapters presents one pathway in depth and each includes the following five sections: Pathway Background, Snapshot: One Team's Journey, Putting the Pathway into Action, Thought Questions and Activities, Supporting Materials, and For Further Study. These sections are described below in the order of their appearance in the chapters.

The Pathway Background section includes an explanation of the primary goals of the pathway, its theoretical underpinnings, and its instructional and assessment implications. Learning theories and current understandings of curriculum and instruction on which the pathway draws also are explained. Every Pathway Background section ends with an introduction to the steps of the pathway that play a central role in its implementation.

The Snapshot: One Team's Journey section chronicles the work of a team of teachers implementing MI theory at the fictitious Lincoln Elementary School. Although Lincoln Elementary is a fictitious school, most of the experiences described in the snapshots describe real events, real students, and real teachers applying MI in real schools. Under the Lincoln Elementary School roof, we bring together diverse applications of MI theory drawn from different contexts. By using a fictitious setting we can bring the many real examples together as a coherent narrative.

We locate Lincoln Elementary in "Stratton," a fictitious mid-sized community in the northeastern United States. It serves 400 students and has a growing population of English-language learners. With the support of the principal, the school's 4th-grade team and several specialists have joined together to study MI theory and experiment with MI-informed practices using the Pathways Model.

The Lincoln Elementary team's story weaves its way through this book, providing a detailed and engaging look at all the pathways through one story and cast of characters. Each pathway chapter presents a "snapshot" of the Lincoln Elementary School team and 4th-grade students at a particular moment, as they explore and implement each pathway. The principal characters are 4th-grade teachers Lillian Vega, Sandra Edwards, and David Barnes; English as a Second Language (ESL) instructor Felix Lopez; art teacher Jan Simon; music teacher Paul Evans; resource teacher Carol Rogers; principal Eve Hodet; and 4th graders Yvette DiCarlo and Chris Robinson.

The Putting the Pathway into Action section is our "how to" section and starts with steps for implementing the key features of each pathway. The second subsection, Guiding Your Journey, includes a Pathway Guide and completed Pathway Organizer. The Pathway Guide outlines the steps involved in implementing the pathway. The organizer is a worksheet organized by the key features of the pathway on which one can plan or draft pathway activities. The completed sample organizer provided in the Guiding Your Journey subsection serves as an example and model to help teachers draft their own plans.

The Thought Questions and Activities section follows. Thought questions are meant to provoke readers' consideration of important aspects or issues related to the pathway covered in the chapter. They are meant to be used in a group setting but can be answered by an individual reader as well. Implementation activities provide different ways to explore and experiment with the pathway and to reflect and debrief on these experiences. The thought questions and implementation activities provide interactive and experiential means for users of the book to deepen their understanding of the pathway.

The Supporting Materials section is made up of different types of resources to support work in the pathway: a blank Pathway Organizer suitable for reproduction, any needed materials—such as instructions—to conduct implementation activities, and additional pathway activity examples.

The For Further Study section contains resources to pursue more in-depth study of the pathway.

The book closes with Chapter 10, Conclusion: A Case for the Pathways, which describes research that supports the Pathways Model and each of the five pathways. This concluding chapter provides the solid ground of research-based evidence upon which readers can launch their own pathway journeys with confidence.

HOW TO USE THIS BOOK

This book is meant to be *used*, not just read, to guide an ongoing process of studying and experimenting with MI theory. Although the book can be used individually, it is designed for educators or education students to explore MI theory together as a group. We strongly encourage readers to work with at least one colleague for support. We also suggest moving through the book in order, from beginning to end.

The chapters are ordered purposefully, starting with MI theory and its practical implications. The pathway chapters build on one another in the order they are presented in the book. Therefore, it makes good sense to study them in that order.

How each chapter or pathway is navigated is more flexible. For example, members of a group may work their way through all the pathways together. Or responsibility for different pathway chapters may fall to different subgroups, with each taking the lead for one or more pathways. This is an efficient way to explore all the pathways before making a long-term commitment to any particular one.

Each pathway chapter can be used as a detailed script or a loose guide. A group may choose a particular pathway or two for more in-depth study and experimentation or may choose to explore all pathways with equal intensity. It is our hope that readers will find here the key to translating the promise of multiple intelligences theory into successful and meaningful teaching and learning experiences for themselves and their students.

MI Basics: The Theory

Over the past decade, MI theory has been a popular basis for reform efforts among individual teachers and entire schools. Many educators use MI theory because it validates what they already know and do. They believe that their students represent a diversity of cognitive strengths and ways of learning, and they use diverse practices in response. MI theory also is popular because it is compatible with the philosophies and approaches already in place in many schools (for instance, whole language, cooperative learning, hands-on math).

MI theory is used as a lens through which educators reflect on their practices in order to extend what they currently do well and to better meet the diverse needs of their students. MI theory provides a useful vocabulary for collegial discussion and for conversations with parents, and helps teachers and parents understand, celebrate, and use their students' and children's unique ways of knowing (Kornhaber & Krechevsky, 1995).

Understanding MI theory well is fundamental to its thoughtful and appropriate application. MI theory is not a learning theory or a specific educational approach; it must be translated into classroom practice. There is no single right way to apply it, nor any specific way prescribed or endorsed by Howard Gardner. Applying MI theory well, therefore, requires understanding the theory thoroughly and then deciding and planning how to implement it.

This chapter aims to support readers' deepening understanding of MI theory so they can move on confidently to its thoughtful application. The next section, an overview of MI theory, serves as a starting point in our MI pathways journey.

VIEWS OF INTELLIGENCE

Multiple intelligences theory was introduced against the backdrop of the traditional—and widely held—view of intelligence as a unitary trait that can be adequately measured by an IQ test (Gardner, 1993c). Psychometrics was the first formal scientific approach to intelligence. It is still the primary lens through which the general public perceives intelligence. It remains focused on the measurement and the heritability of intelligence (Fraser, 1995; Gould, 1981; Herrnstein & Murray, 1994).

The IQ view of intelligence, rooted in benign if not benevolent purposes, has a long history of misuse in the service of racist analyses of intelligence and as "evidence" for the lesser intelligence or inferiority of certain groups (Gould, 1981).

> Since the turn of the century, psychometric intelligence has been defended and disputed; it is the theory upon which some have built and against which others have reacted, and it continues to play a significant role in the intelligence discourse. (Viens, Chen, & Gardner, 1997, p. 122)

Psychometric intelligence can be traced to French psychologist Alfred Binet. At the request of the French Ministry of Education in the early 1900s, Binet and his colleague Theodore Simon developed a test that effectively identified children at risk for school failure (Binet & Simon, 1916). However, it was almost immediately used as the basis for a psychometric measurement of general capabilities or intelligence. Since that time, intelligence tests have been heavily weighted toward the types of highly predictive abilities measured in Binet's test, such as verbal memory and reasoning, numerical reasoning, and appreciation of logical sequences.

In 1912 the German psychologist Wilhelm Stern devised the intelligence quotient, or IQ, which represents the ratio of one's mental age to one's chronological age, as measured by intelligence tests. Lewis Terman (1916), an American psychometrician, is credited (or blamed!) for popularizing the IQ test in the United States in the 1920s. Terman introduced the Stanford-Binet IQ tests, the first paper-and-pencil, group-administered versions of the intelligence test.

Largely because of Terman's work, the intelligence test quickly became a standard part of the American educational landscape. Since that time, conventional wisdom has equated intelligence with IQ. Moreover, Terman's work played a significant role in the development of the belief that intelligence is inherited and unchanging.

Most testing before 1935 was based on the conception of intelligence as a general ability. Using a statistical technique called factor analysis, which he had developed, Charles Spearman found that variables such as test scores, teacher rankings, and sensory discrimination scores could be analyzed to demonstrate positive correlations.

Factor analysis mathematically extracts the common factor among intercorrelated tests, identifying the latent sources of underlying variation in the test scores, known as factors. Each factor represents a distinct, underlying ability. For Spearman, the common factor in his study—the underlying attribute the tests measured—was general intelligence, or g (Spearman, 1927). His g represented one underlying mental energy on which all mental activities drew. With the inclusion of Spearman's conceptualization, conventional wisdom asserts that intelligence is one general capacity, measured by a test, inherited from one's parents, and fixed from birth.

In recent years IQ tests have seen declining use. Legal battles have encouraged public schools to back away from them. For the most part IQ testing today is limited to cases where there is a problem (say, a suspected learning disability) or for a selection procedure (entry into a gifted program). However, the line of thinking to which psychometric intelligence gave rise maintains a powerful presence. Most directly, all academic measures are thinly disguised intelligence tests. Most pervasively, the traditional view of intelligence has been internalized by the American public, consequently becoming a determining force in teaching, learning, and assessment practices in schools.

The traditional view of intelligence has played a significant role in driving standard school fare, preserving an antiquated emphasis on the same narrow set of language and math skills as reflected on those early test items. Core curricula and determinants of "good" or "smart" students find their roots in this long-held view of intelligence.

The psychometric view of intelligence has long had its critics, particularly when IQ tests first hit the U.S. educational scene in the 1920s. The influential American journalist Walter Lippman took Terman to task in a series of debates that were published in the *New Republic*. He criticized the superficiality of the test items, the risks of assessing intellectual potential through a single brief method, and possible cultural biases in the tests. Yet, nothing really changed. As Gardner (1999b) notes:

> So long as these tests continued to do what they were supposed to do—that is, yield reasonable predictions about people's success in school—it did not seem necessary or prudent to probe too deeply into their meanings or to explore alternative views of what intelligence is or how it might be assessed. (p. 13)

Theoretical critics of the IQ test included those who still maintained a psychometric view of intelligence. Louis L. Thurstone (1938) claimed that intelligence was multidimensional and was reflected in seven factors or primary mental abilities: verbal comprehension, word fluency, number facility, spatial visualization, associative memory, perceptual speed, and inductive reasoning. J. P. Guilford (1967) claimed up to 150 separate factors in his "structure of intelligence" model. Modern factor analysts have posited hierarchical patterns of group factors, with g still explaining part of the variance in all tests. Vernon (1971), Cattell (1987), Horn (1986), and Carroll (1993) all proposed structures with g at the top, followed by other factors at lower levels.

Critics of the psychometric view point out that it has focused on measurement and does not help us understand the processes or development of intelligence, leaving out cognitive and developmental psychology altogether (Viens et al., 1997). Moreover, intelligence tests include only a small range of human abilities, primarily those in language and mathematics (Bornstein & Sigman, 1986; Gardner, 1993c; Sternberg, 1985, 1995).

In the past few decades, theories of intelligence have become more complex, acknowledging that previous theories have looked merely at particular aspects of intelligence. This growing complexity of theories is evident in the work of neo-Piagetians such as Robbie Case (1985, 1986). Recent theories draw comprehensively on a range of theoretical sources, including psychology, anthropology, sociology, and education. They define intelligence more broadly than before, beyond factors and test scores, and try to explain its operation in the real world. Three theories are representative of this newer breed of intelligence theory: Sternberg's triarchic theory, Ceci's bioecological approach, and Gardner's theory of multiple intelligences.

Robert Sternberg's (1985, 1988) triarchic theory proposes three subtheories: componential, experiential, and contextual intelligence. Each refers to information-processing mechanisms through which individuals carry out intelligent behavior. The componential subtheory tries to identify underlying processes of behavior in which individuals engage to fit with the environment. The experiential subtheory deals with the role of experience. The contextual subtheory treats intelligent activity necessary for particular environmental contexts. Sternberg also posits three central processes: knowledge-acquisition components, tapped when learning how to perform tasks; performance components, used in the act of performing tasks; and metacomponents, engaged to plan, monitor, and evaluate task performance.

Sternberg (1997) notes, "Intelligence comprises the mental abilities necessary for adaptation to, as well as shaping and selection of, any environmental context." He explains:

> Among the core mental processes that may be key in any culture or other environmental context are (a) recognizing the existence of the problem, (b) defining the nature of the problem, (c) constructing a strategy to solve the problem, (d) mentally representing information about the problem, (e) allocating mental resources in solving the problem, (f) monitoring one's solution to the problem, and (g) evaluating one's solution to the problem. (p. 1031)

The key elements of Steven Ceci's bioecological approach include cognitive processes, knowledge, domain, cognitive complexity, and IQ. According to Ceci (1990) and as summarized in Viens, Chen, and Gardner (1997):

> Cognitive processes are mental processing mechanisms that constrain an individual's intelligence. Knowledge refers to rules, information, and the like that are garnered through cognitive processes. A domain is a set of organized knowledge (juggling, computer programming, and carpentry are domains of knowledge). Domains organize "bits" of knowledge, which can be part of different domains. Cognitive complexity refers to an individual's ability to engage cognitive processes efficiently within knowledge structures. IQ is a score derived from an intelligence test. According to Ceci, IQ is a measure of only one type of intelligence. (p. 115)

Ceci's model represents the contextualist view of intelligence, focusing on dimensions outside the individual as critical to intelligence: school, other people, technology, culture, historical era, and others. Like Sternberg's triarchic theory, Ceci's includes information-processing components, experience, and—most significant—context. He argues against general intelligence, claiming that low-level mental processing is affected by knowledge and experience. Like Gardner, Ceci posits biologically based multiple cognitive potentials (Ceci, 1990; Ceci & Liker, 1986).

MULTIPLE INTELLIGENCES THEORY

It was in his own work in neuropsychology and child development that Gardner began to question the traditional view of intelligence. In the 1970s and 1980s he worked in two contexts studying the nature of human cognitive capacities. At the Boston University Aphasia Research Center, Gardner conducted studies to understand the *patterns* of abilities exhibited by stroke victims who suffered from impaired language and other cognitive and emotional trauma. At Harvard Project Zero, he worked with ordinary and gifted children to understand the *development* of cognitive abilities. He observed something different, not explained by the psychometric view of intelligence.

The daily opportunity to work with children and with brain-damaged adults impressed me with one brute fact of human nature: People have a wide range of capacities. A person's strength in one area of performance simply does not predict any comparable strengths in other areas.

In most cases, however, strengths are distributed in a skewed fashion. For instance, a person may be skilled in acquiring foreign languages, yet be unable to find her way around an unfamiliar environment or learn a new song or figure out who occupies a position of power in a crowd of strangers. Likewise, weakness in learning foreign languages does not predict either success or failure with most other cognitive tasks. (Gardner, 1999b, p. 31)

Based on his work with these two groups Gardner (1999b) reached a conclusion.

The human mind is better thought of as a series of relatively separate faculties, with only loose and nonpredictable relations with one another, than as a single, all-purpose machine that performs steadily at a certain horsepower, independent of content and context. (p. 32)

Gardner found that most theories of intelligence looked only at problem solving and ignored the creation of products. They also assumed that *their* notion of intelligence would be apparent and appreciated anywhere, regardless of cultural values and beliefs. In this respect, Gardner distinguished his theory of intelligence from others by defining intelligence as the ability to solve problems or to create products that are valued within one or more cultural settings. Gardner (1999b) has since refined the definition of intelligence, which now describes intelligence as:

. . . the biopsychological potential to process information that can be activated in a cultural setting to solve a problem or fashion a product that is valued in one or more community or cultural settings. (pp. 33–34)

MI theory challenges the notion of IQ in at least three significant ways. MI maintains that: (1) several intelligences are at work, not just one; (2) intelligence is expressed in our performances, products, and ideas, not through a test score; and (3) how the intelligences are expressed is culturally defined. Gardner's definition claims that intelligence represents potential that will or will not be brought to bear, depending on the values, available opportunities, as well as personal decisions made by individuals of a particular culture.

This definition locates intelligence in what people can do and the products they can create *in the real world*, in contrast to the implied intelligence indicated by a test. It suggests a qualitative expression, a description, of an individual's collection of intelligences, rather than a single quantitative expression of a set of narrowly defined paper-and-pencil tasks.

The Eight Intelligences

- Linguistic
- Logical–mathematical
- Musical
- Spatial
- Bodily–kinesthetic
- Interpersonal
- Intrapersonal
- Naturalist

IDENTIFYING INTELLIGENCES: THE EIGHT CRITERIA

If there are qualitatively different ways to express intelligence, how does one characterize each of these separate faculties? To determine and articulate these separate faculties, or intelligences, Gardner turned to the various discrete disciplinary lenses in his initial investigations, including psychology, neurology, biology, sociology, anthropology, and the arts and humanities. He and his colleagues looked at the many abilities individuals demonstrate and the diverse roles they assume. They asked, "What are the basic biological faculties responsible for these abilities that we observe around us every day?"

Gardner's new view of intelligence gave rise to a list of eight criteria used to identify these basic biological faculties. That is, rather than relying primarily on the results of psychometric instruments, Gardner laid out eight criteria that require different kinds of evidence, from brain research, human development, evolution, and cross-cultural comparisons, for a candidate ability to be considered an "intelligence." With varying amounts and quality of research on the different candidate abilities, Gardner and his colleagues asked whether an ability met the set of criteria "reasonably well." If it did, it was designated an intelligence. If it did not, it might be set aside, or recast and reinvestigated against the criteria.

These criteria have served as the primary means of identifying a set of intelligences that captures a reasonably complete range of the types of abilities valued by human cultures (Gardner, 1993c). Only abilities that satisfy all or a majority of the criteria are selected as intelligences. Gardner initially identified seven such intelligences. An eighth intelligence, naturalist, has since been added. A ninth, existential ability, is under consideration (see Gardner, 1999b, pp. 47–66). We now introduce each of the criteria, using examples from the current list of intelligences.

The Criteria for Identifying an Intelligence

- Potential isolation by brain damage (neurological evidence)
- Evolutionary history and evolutionary plausibility
- Identifiable set of core operations
- Susceptibility to encoding in a symbol system
- Recognizable endstate and distinctive developmental trajectory
- Existence of savants, prodigies, and other individuals distinguished by the presence or absence of specific abilities
- Support from experimental psychological tasks
- Support from psychometric findings

Potential Isolation by Brain Damage

This criterion calls for neuropsychological evidence that one intelligence can be isolated from others at the basic brain level. The extent to which a specific ability is destroyed or spared as a result of brain damage, as with stroke patients, gives us a great deal of information about the basic nature of abilities.

> Every stroke represents an accident of nature from which the careful observer can learn much. Suppose, for example, one wants to study the relation between the ability to speak fluently and the ability to sing fluently. One can mount arguments indefinitely about the relatedness or the independence of these faculties, but the facts of brain damage actually resolve the debate. Human singing and human language are different faculties that can be independently damaged or spared. Paradoxically, however, human *signing* and human speaking are similar faculties. Those parts of the brain that subserve spoken language in hearing people are (roughly speaking) the same parts of the brain that subserve sign language in deaf people. So here we encounter an underlying linguistic faculty that cuts across sensory and motor modalities. (Gardner, 1999b, p. 30, emphasis in original)

The relative autonomy of musical intelligence is strongly indicated by cases of brain injury in which musical ability is preserved, but other abilities, such as language, are lost. The existence and independence of the musical and linguistic intelligences are supported by the identification of brain centers that mediate linguistic and musical processing. Specific areas of the brain have been identified as playing major roles in music perception and production.

Evolutionary History and Plausibility

Evolutionary evidence is central to any understanding of human cognition or intelligence. The existence of an intelligence is indicated by the extent to which some evolutionary antecedents can be determined in other species. For example, the highly developed spatial capacities of other mammals can be mined for evidence of a spatial intelligence. Recent work in evolutionary psychology looks at the contemporary workings of human capacities and tries to infer the selection pressures that led to the development of a particular faculty.

We see evidence in early humans for the identification of a naturalist intelligence, that is, the understanding and use of flora and fauna. Evolutionary evidence for musical intelligence is drawn from its apparent unifying role in Stone Age societies, as well as its link to other species (think of birdsong). All identified societies have demonstrated evidence of some form of musical activity within their culture.

Identifiable Set of Core Operations

While the first two criteria come from the biological sciences, this criterion and the next are based on logical analysis. Although specific intelligences operate in rich contexts, usually in combination with other intelligences, it is helpful to isolate capacities that seem "core" to an intelligence. These capacities are likely to be triggered by relevant internal or external types of information. For example, linguistic intelligence includes the core operations of phonemic discrimination, a command of syntax, sensitivity to the pragmatic uses of language, and acquisition of word meanings. The core operations of spatial intelligence include sensitivity to large-scale, local three- and two-dimensional spaces, while the core operations that trigger musical ability include sensitivity to pitch, rhythm, and timbre.

Susceptibility to Encoding in a Symbol System

Human beings spend a great deal of time learning and using different kinds of symbol systems. Our primary communications occur through symbol systems such as written and spoken language, mathematical systems such as logical equations, and picturing (e.g., charts, graphs). Over time people developed these symbol systems to communicate information in an organized and accurate manner. Indeed, symbol systems seem to have arisen to code those meanings to which human intelligences are most sensitive. Therefore, a fundamental characteristic of intelligence seems to be a susceptibility to embodiment in a symbolic system. Musical notation is another example of a distinct symbol system.

Recognizable Endstate and Distinctive Developmental Trajectory

This is the first of two criteria that come from developmental psychology. Intelligences are not demonstrated "in the raw." Rather, they operate within different domains and "adult endstates." For example, musical intelligence is expressed in several endstates, including musician, composer, and sound engineer, within the *domain* of music.

Individuals exhibit their intelligences after proceeding through a developmental process, most likely specific to that endstate. Both the musician and the sound engineer will develop musical intelligence along the developmental path needed for their respective endstates. In a sense, intelligences have their own developmental histories. Thus, an individual who wants to be a softball player must develop her abilities in ways distinct from those of the aspiring dancer. Other people must follow distinctive developmental paths to become, for instance, clinicians or clergy, each with well-developed interpersonal intelligence.

It is important to assume a cross-cultural perspective, because an intelligence may be brought to bear in cultures that exhibit quite different roles and values. Both the clinician in American culture and the shaman in a tribal culture are using their interpersonal intelligences—but in different ways and for somewhat different ends (Gardner, 1999b, pp. 38–39). Like other intelligences, a developmental scale (ranging from novice to expert) can be articulated for a developing naturalist.

Existence of Savants, Prodigies, and Other Individuals Distinguished by the Presence or Absence of Specific Abilities

Individuals who have unusual profiles of intelligence offer another area to explore in identifying intelligences. These profiles often include high-level ability in an isolated area, suggesting that the particular ability may be an intelligence. Savants, prodigies, and autistic individuals exhibit a high level of ability in one area, whereas their other abilities are typically ordinary (savants and prodigies) or severely impaired (autistics). Many autistic children, for example, possess outstanding abilities in areas such as calculation, musical performance, and drawing. At the same time they demonstrate severe impairments in communication, language, and sensitivity to others.

Like autism, prodigious ability tends to show up in domains that are rule governed and that require little life experience; examples are chess, mathematics, representational drawing, and other forms of pattern recognition and reproduction. Prodigies also demonstrate relative weaknesses in other domains. Each of these groups—savants, autistics, prodigies, and gifted children—provides evidence about which abilities have a biological basis and operate relatively independently.

Support from Experimental Psychological Tasks

Traditional psychology is the source of the last two criteria. Using experimental psychological tasks, researchers can understand the extent to which two operations are related by observing how well individuals can carry out activities from the two operations simultaneously. If one activity does not interfere with the successful completion of the other, then we can assume that the activities draw on distinct capacities. For example, most individuals are able to walk while they talk; in that case, the intelligences involved are separate. On the other hand, most people find it hard to talk while working on a crossword puzzle or listening to a song with lyrics, because linguistic intelligence comes to the fore in both tasks. Studies of transfer or task interference can help us to identify discrete intelligences.

Support from Psychometric Findings

A high correlation between certain subtests of standardized tests suggests a single intelligence at work, while a low correlation suggests separate intelligences. Therefore, one may say that much current psychometric evidence is a criticism of MI theory, presenting a correlation in scores among various tasks that suggests a general (*g*) or unitary intelligence. However, as psychologists have broadened their definition of intelligence and added to their measuring tools, psychometric evidence has emerged favoring MI. Recent studies of spatial and linguistic intelligences strongly suggest that these two areas are relatively separate, having at best only a weak correlation. Similar measures of musical acuity can be teased apart from other tasks, thus supporting the identification of a separate musical intelligence. And studies of social intelligence have revealed a set of capacities different from standard linguistic and logical intelligences.

These eight criteria are still in use as new candidate intelligences are considered. For example, the realm of the spiritual as typically defined does not satisfactorily meet the criteria for designation as an intelligence, so at this time it is not considered an intelligence. Evidence for an existential intelligence is more persuasive but not yet conclusive. Existential ability refers to the human inclination to ask very basic questions about existence: Who are we? Where do we come from? It finds a home in mythology and philosophy and among issues that are infinite or infinitesimal. At this time there is no satisfactory brain evidence for the existence of an independent existential intelligence in the nervous system. It is also debatable whether existential abilities are not an amalgam of logical and linguistic intelligences (Gardner, 1999b).

The criteria have served well as the principal means of identifying a set of intelligences that captures a reasonably complete range of abilities valued by human cultures. By keeping the criteria in active use, MI theory can be, and has been, modified to reflect our increasing understanding of the ways in which people are intelligent. MI theory offers the most accurate description to date of intelligence in the real world, and it continues to be a helpful articulation and organization of human abilities.

THE EIGHT INTELLIGENCES

Currently eight intelligences—eight qualitatively independent ways to be intelligent—have been identified. All the intelligences differ not only neurologically, but in the symbol systems that they apply, the tools they call on, the core or subabilities included, and how they are utilized in the real world. Each of the intelligences is described below according to the following categories: key abilities, subabilities, endstates or domains, strategies or products, and everyday uses. Definitions of these descriptors follow below.

Key to Descriptors

Key Abilities are broad abilities central to the specific intelligence.

Subabilities are the more specific abilities within each of the intelligences.

Roles or Domains refer to societal niches that emphasize the particular intelligence. For example, the journalist role requires a great deal of linguistic intelligence. Domains refer to the disciplines of the real world, activities that are valued and at which we can improve. (Endstates are realized in domains.)

Strategies or Products. Although strategies or products are the result of particular combinations of intelligences, their development typically relies most heavily on a specific intelligence.

Everyday Uses. We use our multiple intelligences in combination for everyday activities. This category describes routine contexts in which a particular intelligence is drawn on heavily.

NOT refers to misconceptions regarding the intelligence.

Linguistic Intelligence

Linguistic intelligence is the capacity to use language—your native language, and perhaps other languages—to express what's on your mind and to understand other people. Poets really specialize in linguistic intelligence, but any kind of writer, orator, speaker, lawyer, or a person for whom language is an important stock in trade highlights linguistic intelligences. (Gardner & Checkley, 1997, p. 12)

Key Abilities of Linguistic Intelligence

- Involves perceiving or generating spoken or written language.
- Allows communication and sense making through language.

- Includes sensitivity to subtle meanings in language.

Subabilities

expressive language
invented narrative or storytelling
descriptive/instructional language
reporting
poetic use of language
wordplay

Roles or Domains that Require Significant Linguistic Intelligence

novelist
comedian
lawyer
journalist
preacher
coach
poet
teacher
dispatcher

Strategies or Products that Emphasize Linguistic Intelligence

script
word game
instructions/manuals
novel
newspaper
discussion
theater
debate/speech
lyrics/libretto

Everyday Uses of Linguistic Intelligence

reading the paper
writing a letter
participating in a meeting

Linguistic Intelligence Is NOT—

bilingualism (but might include facility in learning languages)
being talkative/liking to talk

Logical–Mathematical Intelligence

People with highly developed logical–mathematical intelligence understand the underlying principles of some kind of a causal system, the way a scientist or a logician does, or can manipulate numbers, quantities, and operations, the way a mathematician does. (Gardner & Checkley, 1997, p. 12)

Key Abilities of Logical–Mathematical Intelligence

- Enables individuals to use and appreciate abstract relations.
- Includes facility in the use of numbers and logical thinking.

Subabilities

numerical reasoning (calculations, estimation, quantification)

logical problem solving (focusing on overall structure and relationships, making logical inferences)

Roles or Domains that Require Significant Logical–Mathematical Intelligence

math teacher
scientist
engineer
architect
computer programmer
construction
budget analyst
accountant
knitting

Strategies or Products that Emphasize Logical–Mathematical Intelligence

graph
spreadsheet
flowchart
timeline
equation/proof
invention
computer program
business plan
logic puzzle

Everyday Uses of Logical–Mathematical Intelligence

reading the bus schedule
solving puzzles
managing the family checkbook

Logical–Mathematical Intelligence Is NOT

oriented only to numbers (it also includes non-numerical logical relations)

Musical Intelligence

Musical intelligence is the capacity to think in music—to be able to hear patterns, recognize them, remember them, and perhaps manipulate them. People who have a strong musical intelligence don't just remember music easily—they can't get it out of their minds, it's so omnipresent. Now, some people will say, "Yes, music is important, but it's a talent, not an intelligence." And I say, "Fine, let's call it a talent." But, then we have to leave the word *intelligent* out of *all* discussions of human abilities. You know, Mozart was damned smart! (Gardner & Checkley, 1997, p. 12)

Key Abilities of Musical Intelligence

- Involves perceiving and understanding patterns of sound.
- Includes creating and communicating meaning from sound.

Subabilities

music perception
music production
composition or notation

Roles or Domains that Require Significant Musical Intelligence

musician
choreographer
music critic
conductor
disc jockey
piano tuner
composer
sound engineer
cheerleader

Strategies or Products that Emphasize
Musical Intelligence

>   composition/songwriting
>   critique/analysis
>   jingle
>   recital/performance
>   sound effects
>   musical/opera
>   dance set to music
>   soundtrack/accompaniment
>   recording/sampling

Everyday Uses of Musical Intelligence

>   appreciating a song on the radio
>   playing a musical instrument
>   distinguishing different sounds of the car, such
>   as "hearing" engine trouble

Musical Intelligence Is NOT—

>   engaged by playing background music

Spatial Intelligence

Spatial intelligence refers to the ability to represent the spatial world internally in your mind—the way a sailor or airplane pilot navigates the large spatial world, or the way a chess player or sculptor represents a more circumscribed spatial world. Spatial intelligence can be used in the arts or in the sciences. If you are spatially intelligent and oriented toward the arts, you are more likely to become a painter or a sculptor or an architect than, say, a musician or a writer. Similarly, certain sciences like anatomy or topology emphasize spatial intelligence. (Gardner & Checkley, 1997, p. 12)

Key Abilities of Spatial Intelligence—

*   Involves perceiving and transforming visual or three-dimensional information in one's mind.
*   Allows for re-creation of images from memory.

Subabilities

>   understanding causal or functional relation-
>   ships through observation

>   use of spatial information to navigate through
>   space
>   sensitive perception or observation of visual
>   world and arts
>   production of visual information or works of art

Roles or Domains that Require Significant
Spatial Intelligence

>   gardener
>   sculptor
>   surgeon
>   mechanic
>   housepainter
>   carpenter
>   photographer
>   dancer
>   athlete

Strategies or Products that Emphasize
Spatial Intelligence

>   graph/chart
>   painting
>   blueprints
>   diagram
>   film/TV program
>   map
>   sculpture
>   model
>   invention

Everyday Uses of Spatial Intelligence

>   finding one's way in an unfamiliar town
>   giving or using directions
>   playing chess or checkers
>   decorating one's home
>   arranging a flower garden

Spatial Intelligence Is NOT

>   necessarily visual (blind people need excellent
>   spatial abilities)

Bodily–Kinesthetic Intelligence

Bodily–kinesthetic intelligence is the capacity to use your whole body or parts of your body—your hands, your fingers, and your arms—to solve a problem, make something, or put on some kind of a production. The most evident examples are people in athletics or the performing arts, particularly dance or acting. (Gardner & Checkley, 1997, p. 12)

Key Abilities of Bodily–Kinesthetic Intelligence

- Allows use of one's body to create products or solve problems.
- Refers to the ability to control all or isolated parts of one's body.

Subabilities

athletic movement
creative movement (including responsiveness to music)
body control and fine motor abilities
generating movement ideas (as in choreography)

Roles or Domains that Require Significant Bodily–Kinesthetic Intelligence

dancer
athlete
actor
coach
artisan
mime
sculptor
sign language interpreter
surgeon

Strategies or Products that Emphasize Bodily–Kinesthetic Intelligence

dance performance
mime
performance art
play
weaving
painting/other art product
sports/games
crafting jewelry

Everyday Uses of Bodily–Kinesthetic Intelligence

playing on a softball team
getting into and standing in a crowded subway car

brushing one's teeth
fixing something

Bodily–Kinesthetic Intelligence Is NOT

necessarily demonstrated by a physically active child
unstructured release of energy through physical activity

Interpersonal Intelligence

Interpersonal intelligence is understanding other people. It's an ability we all need, but is at a premium if you are a teacher, clinician, salesperson, or politician. Anybody who deals with other people has to be skilled in the interpersonal sphere. (Gardner & Checkley, 1997, p. 12)

Key Abilities of Interpersonal Intelligence

- Is a sensitivity to the feelings, beliefs, moods, and intentions of other people.
- Involves the use of that understanding to work effectively with others.
- Includes capitalizing on interpersonal skills in pursuit of one's own ends.

Subabilities

assumption of distinctive social roles (e.g., leader, friend, caregiver)
ability to reflect analytically on the social environment or other people
taking action (e.g., political activist, counselor, educator)

Roles or Domains that Require Significant Interpersonal Intelligence

educator
counselor
community organizer
diplomat
activist
social scientist/researcher
management consultant
religious leader
negotiator/arbitrator

Strategies or Products that Emphasize
Interpersonal Intelligence

tutoring/teaching
improvisational theater
role play
community action
moral dilemmas
action research
peer mediation
community service
leadership role

Everyday Uses of Interpersonal Intelligence

retail transactions
asking or giving directions
interactions with co-workers
parenting

Interpersonal Intelligence Is NOT

a preference for working in a group
being well-liked
being polite
possessing "social graces"
being ethical or humane

Intrapersonal Intelligence

Intrapersonal intelligence refers to having an understanding of yourself, of knowing who you are, what you can do, what you want to do, how you react to things, which things to avoid, and which things to gravitate toward. We are drawn to people who have a good understanding of themselves because those people tend not to screw up. They tend to know what they can do. They tend to know what they can't do. And they tend to know where to go if they need help. (Gardner & Checkley, 1997, p. 12)

Key Abilities of Intrapersonal Intelligence

- Enables individuals to form a mental model of themselves.
- Involves drawing on the model to make decisions about viable courses of action.

- Includes the ability to distinguish one's feelings, moods, and intentions and to anticipate one's reactions to future courses of action.

Subabilities

self-understanding
the ability to self-reflect analytically
articulating that understanding through other
types of expression or intelligences (poetry,
painting, song, etc.)
using that self-knowledge well toward personal
or community goals

Roles or Domains that Require Significant
Intrapersonal Intelligence

therapist
poet
motivational speaker
psychologist
artist
activist
musician
philosopher
spiritual leader

Strategies or Products that Emphasize
Intrapersonal Intelligence

genealogy
portfolio/reflections
sermon
poem
journal/diary
action plan
artwork
autobiography
musical composition

Everyday Uses of Intrapersonal Intelligence

job/career assessment
religious practices
therapy

Intrapersonal Intelligence Is NOT

preferring to work alone and/or in isolation

Naturalist Intelligence

Naturalist intelligence designates the human ability to discriminate among living things (plants, animals) as well as sensitivity to other features of the natural world (clouds, rock configurations). This ability was clearly of value in our evolutionary past as hunters, gatherers, and farmers; it continues to be central in such roles as botanist or chef. I also speculate that much of our consumer society exploits the naturalist intelligence, which can be mobilized in the discrimination among cars, sneakers, kinds of makeup, and the like. The kind of pattern recognition valued in certain of the sciences may also draw upon naturalist intelligence. (Gardner & Checkley, 1997, p. 12)

Key Abilities of Naturalist Intelligence

- Includes the ability to understand the natural world well and to work in it effectively.
- Allows people to distinguish among and use features of the environment.
- Is also applied to patterning abilities.

Subabilities

observational skills
pattern recognition and classification
knowledge of the natural world
employing that knowledge to solve problems and fashion products (e.g., farming, gardening, hunting or fishing, cooking)

Roles or Domains that Require Significant Naturalist Intelligence

florist
fishing
chef
botanist
farming
environmental educator
biologist
forest ranger
sailing

Strategies or Products that Emphasize Naturalist Intelligence

plants/flowers
field notes
surveys of flora/fauna
animal husbandry
nature walks
studies/experiments
"Outward Bound"
creating classification systems (for natural or nonnatural phenomena)

Everyday Uses of Naturalist Intelligence

cooking
gardening
enjoying scenery
organizing CDs or other collection

Naturalist Intelligence Is NOT

limited to the outside world

THOUGHT QUESTIONS AND ACTIVITIES

Thought Questions

- How would you define intelligence from a multiple intelligences perspective? How does or doesn't that map onto your existing understanding of intelligence?
- What are the multiple intelligences? How are they expressed in life?
- What do you consider your personal areas of strength? How do you see them informing your teaching at this time? How might they limit your classroom offerings?

Implementation Activities

Activity 1. Identify questions or specific interests that have emerged among your group after reading about MI theory above. Identify related materials—books, articles, videotapes—to review and share.

Activity 2. Study intelligences "in practice." Choose several adult roles or domains, list underlying intelligences at work for each, and elaborate on how each intelligence operates. For example, the role "surgeon" calls for a high degree of naturalist intelligence, as well as the bodily–kinesthetic ability to use the surgical tools well and the spatial intelligence to map out the surgical area. Some might add strong interpersonal abilities as a necessary characteristic.

On another tack, consider how alternative intelligences could be tapped to accomplish the tasks of a specific domain or endstate. For example, a chef needs a great deal of naturalist intelligence to understand the nuances of the ingredients at work and their interactions.

Activity 3. Take the opportunity to consider the intellectual profiles of members of your team. Reflect on, write about, and/or discuss in what types of activities they excel, how individuals solve the same problems differently, what types of problems they like to solve, vocations and avocations, and the like.

Consider completing a questionnaire or survey (see Figure 2.1 under Supporting Materials). Keep in mind that MI surveys or assessments are only readings of one's *perceived* strengths or preferences among intelligences. They serve best as a catalyst for further discussion about one's strengths and weaknesses and as clues for observation. Each participant should complete the graph. Reflect on the profiles drawn from these surveys.

Activity 4. It is useful to question MI surveys and the information they cull. Your group might discuss the following points:

- Do you think the survey accurately reflects your strength areas? How so?
- What is the evidence in your everyday life that leads you to agree or disagree with the survey results?
- How does the complexity of intelligences in the real world limit the usefulness of such surveys?

- Review the descriptions of the intelligences. Compare them with the survey items. Does the survey jibe with the descriptions? Do you think the survey accurately describes or portrays the intelligences?
- What items might you add to the survey (or would you ask yourself) to more accurately assess each intelligence?

SUPPORTING MATERIALS

See Figure 2.1 on next page for a copy of the Personal MI Graph.

FOR FURTHER STUDY

Gardner, H. (1993c). *Frames of mind: The theory of multiple intelligences (10th anniversary ed.).* New York: Basic Books.

Tenth anniversary edition of the original book that introduced multiple intelligences theory. The most comprehensive presentation of the origination of multiple intelligences theory and of each of the original seven intelligences. A primary resource for those interested in the theoretical and empirical research base of the theory and the rationale and workings of each of the intelligences.

Gardner, H. (1999b). *Intelligence reframed: Multiple intelligences for the 21st century.* New York: Basic Books.

Gardner's most recent work about multiple intelligences theory. Chapter titles include: Are There Additional Intelligences? Is There a Moral Intelligence? and Issues and Answers Regarding Multiple Intelligences. The book includes detailed description of the naturalist intelligence and a valuable comprehensive listing of resources about MI theory.

Viens, J., & Kallenbach, S. (2004). *Multiple intelligences and adult literacy: A sourcebook for practitioners.* New York: Teachers College Press.

A guide for educators in adult basic education, English for Speakers of Other Languages (ESOL), and GED/adult diploma programs. This resource offers a variety of ways to support students' reflection around their multiple intelligences strengths, interests, and learning strategies. It includes several reproducible MI self- and group reflection activities.

Figure 2.1. Personal MI Graph

Activity/ability	Linguistic	Logical–Mathematical	Musical	Spatial	Bodily–Kinesthetic	Interpersonal	Intrapersonal	Naturalist
Be family "accountant"								
Do logic puzzles								
Sing								
Speak in public								
Read biographies								
Do crossword puzzles								
Keep a diary								
Give advice and support								
Spend time outdoors								
Act in theatrical productions								
Write songs								
Do crafts								
Build or renovate								
Read or write poetry								
Take photos								
Take care of kids								
Study maps								
Do volunteer work in the community								
Be able to say no								
Do sports								
Dance								
Draw or paint								
Garden or farm								
Play musical instrument								
Sculpt or carve								
Add your own								
Add another								
TOTALS								

CHAPTER 3

MI Basics:
Moving from Theory to Practice

In Chapter 2 we introduce MI theory and the eight intelligences in contrast to existing unitary conceptions of intelligence. The present chapter bridges MI theory to practice by interpreting its key features into everyday classroom applications.

KEY FEATURES OF MI THEORY

At least seven distinguishing features of MI theory have implications for educational practice. Each is presented below.

A Definition of Intelligence Based on Real-World Intelligence

MI theory's definition of intelligence sets it apart from the conventional understanding of intelligence: "Intelligence is a biopsychological potential to process information that can be activated in a cultural setting to solve problems or create products that are of value in a culture" (Gardner, 1999b, pp. 33–34). MI theory's definition of intelligence locates intelligence in real-world problem solving and product making and accounts for the cultural dimension of what counts as intelligence. In contrast to the "implied" view of intelligence of IQ tests, MI theory is based on an understanding of how people's intelligences really operate.

A Pluralistic View of Intelligence

There exists a plurality of intelligences, each with its own symbol system and ways of knowing and processing information. This is in distinct contrast to the traditional view of intelligence, which asserts the existence of one general intelligence that is put to use

to solve any problem, no matter what the task or domain. Using the criteria outlined in the previous chapter, eight distinct intelligences have been identified.

All Eight (or More) Intelligences Are Universal

MI theory posits that intelligence originates biologically. The eight intelligences have been identified across all known cultures. As human beings, all individuals have potential in all of the intelligences. Indeed, this propensity might be considered a significant contributor to what makes us human. In practice, this feature reminds us that every student in every classroom brings to bear a collection of all eight intelligences, each to varying degrees of strength.

Intelligences Are Educable

As a constant interaction among biological and environmental factors, intelligences are educable; they change and grow. According to MI theory, the more time an individual spends using an intelligence and the better the instruction and resources, the smarter the individual becomes in that area. Translated into practice, this key feature reads: "All children can learn." It also works against pigeonholing or excluding individuals according to certain intelligences.

Individuals Possess Unique Profiles of Intelligence That Develop and Change

Although MI theory claims a biological basis for intelligence, it does not suggest that intelligence is purely genetic and inherited. From the perspective of "nature" in the nature–nurture debate, we are all at promise for all the intelligences. How and to what extent the intelligences manifest themselves depend to a significant degree on "nurture." An individual's intelligences develop and change based on interaction with the environment (people, resources, etc.).

Cultural, societal, and individual factors shape how much one sees of a particular intelligence and how it is manifested. For example, in the case of linguistic intelligence, writing might dominate in one context and storytelling in another. A child in the first context whose mother is a reporter, and whose home is filled with books, a computer, and writing implements, might have better developed writing abilities than a child without those environmental supports.

Each Intelligence Involves Subabilities

No one is merely "musically" or "linguistically" intelligent. One's musical intelligence might be demonstrated through the ability to compose clever tunes or to hear and distinguish instrument parts in a song. In the case of linguistic intelligence, ability might emerge through the expressive language of a poem, the descriptive language of a presentation, or the closing arguments in a courtroom. These distinctions within intelligences are important for teachers to keep in mind when developing activities and assessments for their students (Hatch, 1997).

Intelligences Work in Combination, Not Isolation

In the form of biopsychological potential, the intelligences are relatively autonomous. In their expression, however, the intelligences work together in the context of a domain or a discipline, which are social constructs. A domain is a culturally organized and valued activity "in which individuals participate on more than just a casual basis, and in which degrees of expertise can be identified and nurtured" (Gardner, 1999b, p. 82). Computer programming, car mechanics, gardening, photography, historical research, archeology, speechwriting, and soccer are just a few examples of domains. The intelligences are the raw material we bring to bear in solving problems or fashioning products. The domain or discipline is the context that defines the problem and within which intelligences are brought together.

For example, a violinist needs musical intelligence to be successful, but only in combination with interpersonal abilities, such as communication with other musicians in the orchestra; intrapersonal abilities, such as translating the emotion of the piece; and bodily–kinesthetic abilities, such as the physical act of playing the instrument. Put simply, the musical domain generally requires high levels of musical intelligence, but other intelligences must be tapped in order to permit successful performance in this domain.

Similarly, no intelligence is isolated to a specific domain. For example, spatial intelligence is not used only in the visual arts. Particular intelligences are applied across many domains. In the case of spatial intelligence, these abilities come to the fore in the arts, as well as in sailing, gardening, and even surgery. An individual's strength in a particular intelligence may manifest itself in one (or more) domains and not in others. Someone with a high level of spatial ability, for instance, may have little ability or interest in the artistic domain and may be attracted to more-scientific applications of spatial intelligence embedded in, say, biology or topology.

IMPLICATIONS OF MI THEORY FOR PRACTICE

We have said that there is no "right" way to apply multiple intelligences theory. It is a descriptive theory of intelligence, not a pedagogical framework. Indeed, there is a sizable gap between MI theory as a psychological claim about how the brain works and any sort of educational prescription (Gardner, 1995). Not surprisingly, then, the introduction of MI theory has resulted in numerous interpretations and applications.

For many educators, MI theory confirms what they have always believed: Students possess a range of abilities that standard school fare neither acknowledges nor develops. Therefore, it was with enthusiasm that educators initially accepted the challenge of creating and implementing applications for MI theory. In the dozen years since the first applications emerged, educators' enthusiasm has not waned; if anything, it has intensified. There are hundreds of MI-based programs in this country and many others internationally.

Much of the early work pertaining to MI theory was conducted at Harvard Project Zero, a research organization co-directed by Howard Gardner. One of its research endeavors, Project Spectrum, was a 9-year initiative that began in 1984 to investigate MI theory in early education (Chen, Krechevsky, & Viens, 1998; Krechevsky, 1991). Project Zero, and in particular Project Spectrum, has provided a research and development wing, and often a catalyst, for the many developing MI-based programs and "MI schools."

Most MI-based programs have been initiated to create opportunities for students across a range of intelligences or to create more individualized or personalized education by addressing students' strengths. To identify students' particular areas of strength and interest, many programs create new, authentic forms of assessment that account for a broader spectrum of abilities (Chen et al., 1998; Kornhaber & Krechevsky, 1995).

Many MI-based programs have been conceived with a more specific educational purpose or programmatic goal in mind, such as reaching children in at-risk situations, justifying arts programs, promoting project-based or interdisciplinary curriculum, or developing school-wide talent enrichment programs (Gardner, 1993a; Kornhaber & Krechevsky, 1995).

Using MI-informed approaches usually involves an iterative process between curriculum/instruction and assessment. MI theory helps teachers frame activities so that many entry points into the subject matter are available to students. Teachers use the knowledge they have accumulated about students' intelligences and preferences to inform subsequent instruction. Teachers who offer different pedagogical approaches and allow exploration of differing perspectives create the possibility of reaching more students more effectively.

We have said earlier that intelligences normally do not work in isolation; every task or problem requires competence in certain areas. It is in culturally defined domains that our unique combinations of intelligences are brought to bear. Therefore, intelligences are likely well used and best observed in the context of domains rather than intelligence-specific activities or curriculum. Domains, rather than single intelligences, become a useful tool for considering how to use and assess students' intelligences authentically in the classroom. To tap as well as assess students' logical–mathematical abilities, teachers might have students design a bridge and build a model (perhaps as part of a larger project—for example, creating a model of a city).

When assessing students' abilities, teachers using MI theory focus on student strengths and look at a broader range of abilities (Chen et al., 1998; Kornhaber & Krechevsky, 1995). Uses and goals of their assessments vary. For some, assessment involves informal or formal observations at learning centers, or specially designed performance assessments. Assessments take place during projects or other activities, or are themselves special events, such as presentations and exhibitions (Gardner, 1993d). Information culled from assessments is not only reported but also put to several uses: to build on student strengths in subsequent instruction and curriculum, to bridge to student weaknesses, to assign or group children in enrichment groups or for projects, and to celebrate student talent.

Assessment should be multifocal, tapping not only one context but several. For example, to assess linguistic abilities teachers may use a variety of real performances such as a story, report, or play, rather than a short-answer test. Likewise, assessment of spatial abilities may include domain-based activities such as reading and creating maps, designing bridges, doing a photography project, or creating a mural. Using domains to think about integrating MI into assessment helps to keep the assessment authentic as well as "intelligence fair"; in other words, it assesses what it is claiming to assess.

Much like MI-informed curriculum and instruction, MI-informed approaches to assessment include using the theory to frame options by which students can demonstrate their mastery and understanding of the material. MI practices also have led to the use of standard and video portfolios as tools to demonstrate and report students' understandings (Faculty of New City School, 1994; Gardner, 1993a; Kornhaber & Krechevsky, 1995).

REFINING OUR UNDERSTANDING OF MI THEORY

Although it is true that there is no single right way to apply MI theory, common theoretical, terminological, and practical pitfalls lead to misconceptions about and misapplications of MI theory. We address several of these concerns below.

Superficial or Limited Understanding of the Defining Tenets

In order to *practice* MI theory well, one needs to *understand* MI theory well. Conversely, superficial knowledge of the theory or outright misunderstanding can lead to applications that are contrary to those the theory might suggest. For example, while acknowledging a plurality of intelligences suggests enhancing instructional practices in some way to account for them, it is not a directive to teach everything in eight different ways. Understanding that intelligences do not work in isolation helps avoid separating intelligences in the classroom artificially or labeling students by one intelligence or the other.

Imposing Educational Positions onto MI Theory

Unfortunately, positions on various issues or educational practices have been erroneously ascribed to or closely associated with MI theory or Howard Gardner himself. MI theory does not incorporate positions on gifted education, special education, interdisciplinary curriculum, or other key educational issues (Gardner, 1995).

One such example is tracking. Multiple intelligences theory does not take any position on tracking; however, the existence of several intelligences that can be isolated in theory has led to the erroneous assumption that MI theory suggests grouping children by ability within specific intelligences. In actuality, many educators using MI are strongly opposed to tracking. A superficial understanding of MI theory, as well as confusing ostensibly MI-based practices with implications of the theory, can easily lead to this type of misunderstanding.

Confusing MI-Based Practices with Other Practices

MI theory has been confused theoretically and used interchangeably with other, sometimes similar approaches and practices. Therefore, distinguishing MI theory from like-minded or complementary approaches is a useful way to deepen one's understanding of the theory.

Learning style approaches in particular have been confused with MI theory. Yet the psychological construct of MI theory is fundamentally different from that of learning styles. Intelligence refers to our psychobiological potential to process certain kinds of information in certain kinds of ways. It is a capacity that resides in each person, and each intelligence can be used in a variety of domains (Krechevsky & Seidel, 1998).

Learning styles refer to how individuals take in information; and they have a variety of frameworks. Some describe organizational preferences (sequential versus random) or perceptual content (abstract ideas and feelings versus concrete experiences and objects). Others that are based on multisensory styles refer to auditory, visual, tactile, and kinesthetic learners. Learning styles also refer to environmental preferences or variables such as light, sound, kinds of furniture, time of day, room temperature, and working together or alone.

In contrast to learning styles, the intelligences possess distinct developmental trajectories that lead to adult endstates—valued roles in the community. Thus, to nurture valued roles and domains, we nurture particular intelligences: "One can be a tactile or auditory learner and still become an accountant or a botanist. However, if one has not developed strong logical–mathematical or naturalist intelligences, success in those professions will be limited" (Krechevsky & Seidel, 1998, p. 23).

Unlike learning styles, each intelligence is geared toward certain types of content. For example, musical intelligence is engaged when one hears music or picks up a clarinet and plays. However, musical intelligence is not summoned only through musical sounds; it can be activated, as well, by reading a score or watching the rhythmic movement of windshield wipers in the rain. We also can relate certain products to certain intelligences; a shell collection, a soufflé, and an analysis of life in a desert all involve the naturalist intelligence.

To help distinguish between learning styles and intelligences, consider the example of having heard or read a poem. Learning style refers to how you *received* or took in the poem, auditorily (hearing it) or visually (reading it). How you received the "information" (in this case, the poem) is distinct from how you used your intelligences to process and understand it. To make sense of the poem, you may have drawn on one or more intelligences: linguistic intelligence in constructing meaning directly from the words; spatial intelligence, if the poem evoked a vivid image in your mind's eye; and/or intrapersonal intelligence, if the poem inspired an emotional response.

Both learning styles and MI theory are used to differentiate teaching and learning and can work in complementary fashion. But one needs to be careful about applying MI-based labels in stylistic fashion, such as saying, "He's my spatial learner." As typically used, learning styles cut across all content areas. However, there is little authority for assuming that an individual who evinces a style in one milieu or within one context will necessarily do the same in another.

Confusing Related Terminology

Since the term *multiple intelligences* can be confused with related, but not synonymous, terms, misapplications arise. The terms *domain*, *subject area*, and *interest* sometimes are used interchangeably with the intelligences.

An intelligence is the ability of the brain to deal with particular types of information, the biopsychological potential we bring to bear on any given task or activity. A domain, or discipline, is an organized set of activities within a culture in which individuals participate on more than a casual basis and in which certain levels of expertise exist and others can be developed. Gardening, musical performance, chess, and dance are all examples of domains.

Any *domain* uses several intelligences, which, except for the rare anomaly, manifest themselves in combination rather than in isolation (Gardner, 1995). For instance, the domain of dance embod-

ies bodily–kinesthetic intelligence, and it includes a great deal of spatial intelligence as well. Other intelligences that might be engaged include intrapersonal intelligence (in the dancer's interpretation) and interpersonal intelligence (in relating to the audience or other troupe members). Bodily–kinesthetic intelligence also comes to the fore in the domains of gardening, basketball, and surgery. While an intelligence is the intellectual cognitive potential, a domain is the sphere or activity where intelligences come together, where human beings engage their unique combinations of intelligences. This suggests that the intelligences employed depend also on the strengths and interests an individual brings to the task, in addition to the intelligences the domain is most likely to require.

Another term, *subject area*, refers to the familiar, school-designated separations between areas of study. Language arts, mathematics, social studies, science, and physical education are all subject areas. While each subject area might call on some intelligences more heavily than others, each does not represent or emphasize one intelligence. Nor should one particular intelligence be a subject area. (As noted previously, intelligences generally do not manifest themselves in isolation.) Moreover, a subject area can involve more than one domain. In short, a subject area is not an intelligence, and an intelligence should not be a subject area.

By definition, there is a difference between strength in an intelligence and an *interest*. Intelligences are mental abilities that result in ways of thinking that come easily to individuals and in which they excel. Interests are activities to which individuals are drawn, but in which they do not necessarily excel. In practice, the eight intelligences have been used as categories of individual interest or of strengths *and* interests, with no discrimination between the two.

How an individual pursues an interest most likely depends on his or her own profile of intelligences. Interest in stamp collecting may be based on naturalist intelligence for some whose primary interests are collecting and organizing the stamps. The pursuit for those who like to examine the artwork and aesthetic designs of the stamps is of a more spatial bent.

From the perspective of the classroom, the issue of interest versus ability sparks a central consideration of assessment. Teachers assessing students' "multiple intelligences" need to contemplate whether they intend to assess student ability, interest, or both. In some cases, the distinction matters little. For example, if a teacher's goals in using MI theory relate to giving children opportunities across different domains, then assessing students' MI strengths becomes less germane, as does the distinction between interest and ability. On the other hand, gifted education or talent development programs focus more on ability in specific domains, employing performance assessments or observation frameworks to assess level of ability. (Of course, among those talented students interest or passion underlies the motivation to develop their domain-based abilities.)

Considering MI as an End Rather Than a Means

Because the intelligences are defined by the types of things human beings puzzle over, make, and do, MI theory does have implications for the content of what is taught. However, in and of themselves the intelligences do not constitute a suitable goal of education for at least two reasons. First, intelligences are best thought of as the tools individuals use to engage in any activity or domain. Second, intelligences rarely work in isolation; therefore, teaching "spatial" or "bodily–kinesthetic" is an artificial separation of how intelligences actually operate.

For instance, it makes sense to have interest or ability groups set in domains, such as a photography minicourse, a "World of Bugs" interest group, or a chess club, rather than to set aside "intrapersonal" time or a special "spatial intelligence" class. As another example, the interpersonal and bodily–kinesthetic intelligences might come to the fore during a community service project or a dance class, in combination with other intelligences extant in that domain or that individual students bring to the activity.

Multiple intelligences theory is a tool, a means, that educators use to proceed from their overarching goals to applications. Therefore, it is crucial to ask, "To what end am I using MI?" Addressing that question will help sort out a number of issues about what constitutes an appropriate MI-informed practice.

Confusing MI Theory with Practices Touted as "MI-Based"

Without both a careful reading of MI theory and a thoughtful analysis of one's purposes in using it, misapplications can ensue. Although most topics can be approached effectively in a number of ways, MI theory does not suggest that all concepts or subjects be taught by using all of the intelligences for every lesson. In fact, it is unlikely that all topics can be approached, practically, conceptually, or effectively, through all the intelligences, or need to be. Also, almost any approach to teaching or instructional activity will involve more than one intelligence. Teaching about molecular change through a movement exercise, for instance, involves, at a minimum, spatial and bodily–kinesthetic intelligences.

In some cases MI theory has been applied very superficially. Random body movements or running about the classroom has been called part of a "hands-on MI program." Playing background music while children do mathematics also has been dubbed "doing MI." Still, unless one's focus and thinking is on the music—for example, following the contours of a melody—musical intelligence is not brought to bear.

Moreover, no single intelligence represents "doing MI." Weekly art activities do not constitute a multiple intelligences curriculum. Some "MI programs" consist of using materials of the intelligences; for example, drawing pictures and singing lists often are used as mnemonic devices. Like exercise or background music, mnemonic devices are fine ideas for the classroom, but they do not represent substantial engagement of the intelligences.

No Definitive Profiles of Intelligence Exist (and There Is No Need for Them)

The practice of direct evaluation of students' intelligences, including grading them, as a "reading" of MI theory is particularly worrisome. There seems little point in grading individuals on how "spatial" or how "linguistic" they are. Such practice is likely to open the door to a new form of tracking and labeling children. Moreover, an individual may not be particularly gifted in any one intelligence; it is the particular combination of skills that stands out. If multiple intelligences are not the goals of education, then neither should their evaluation be.

It is also vital to remember that any attempt at assessing student intelligences is a "best guess," and no matter how comprehensive or rigorous, it should always be administered cautiously and used judiciously. Why so? It is simply not possible to assess an individual's intelligences definitively and with reliability. All that we can assess with certainty is performance on some kind of task. We can assess a student's ability to play chess, but she still cannot be deemed "spatially intelligent." We can say she has demonstrated some spatial ability, but she may well have exploited other intelligences as well.

The more a *range* of tasks is assessed, the more valid a statement about a strength becomes. Different individuals demonstrate different abilities with each intelligence. If a child demonstrates spatial abilities through chess, while another child may be a skilled artist, the former child's spatial abilities will be overlooked by an assessment of spatial ability through art activities only.

Even if a representative sample of tasks for that intelligence was monitored, we could assume only that every task was solved using the particular intelligence in question. Perhaps some of the activities were not "intelligence fair"—that is, they did not call primarily on that intelligence for success. Or perhaps the individual found a way to solve the problem using other intelligences. Only carefully designed experiments—not a simple or clear-cut task—can result in accurate inferences about mind or brain mechanisms.

Perhaps more to the point, there is probably no need to generate definitive profiles of students' intelligences. This is not to suggest that teachers refrain from observing students with an eye toward their apparent strengths, but rather that they exercise caution with respect to characterizing students' intellectual profiles. Grading intelligences or tracking students according to intelligences seems particularly contrary to a classroom set up for a range of expressions. Such "personal stereotyping" may result in a narrow, limiting view of a child (Gray & Viens, 1994). Perhaps using eight labels is preferable to using one. All the same, labeling can be harmful and should be treated carefully. Look for special strengths, but do not attach permanent labels (Hatch, 1997).

MI YESTERDAY, TODAY, AND TOMORROW

In what seem to be ever-increasing numbers and sophistication, MI theory is being applied in schools around the globe. Even so, many fear that it is just another educational fad that will go the way of "open classrooms" and "individual differences." Will MI theory be around tomorrow?

Most likely, we think; and our reasons are several. First, although MI theory was introduced 20 years ago, new MI resources and programs continue to appear. Second, MI theory has become an accepted theory of intelligence, while traditional conceptualizations are under increasing attack. Third, as a theory and not a prescription or recipe, MI theory is a vehicle for thinking adults to use in configuring their own educational settings. Therefore, it does not suffer from overreliance on one particular set of materials and approaches, which becomes old hat and finds itself on a shelf with other discarded materials.

MI theory continues to exist in the form of research and development as well. Researchers at Harvard Project Zero recently have conducted studies to look systematically at the development of MI practices and at schools using MI practices. The Adult Multiple Intelligences (AMI) Study is the first multisite MI research project in adult basic education. Findings suggest that MI theory can be a generative tool for teachers of low-literacy adults as well as adults with limited English skills (Kallenbach & Viens, 2002). AMI findings resonate with K–12 research suggesting that MI theory is a validating, useful, and flexible organizing framework for educators (Kornhaber & Krechevsky, 1995).

Project SUMIT (Schools Using Multiple Intelligences Theory) at Project Zero was a national study of schools that implemented MI theory for at least 3 years. It sought to identify, document, and promote effective models of MI application. Project SUMIT researchers identified several "Compass Points" for using MI theory effectively: a supportive culture, teacher readiness, and use of MI to foster high-quality student work (Kornhaber, Fierros, & Veenema, 2004).

MI theory continues to evoke and renew inspiration in both new and veteran teachers as (1) an articulation of how they think about students and (2) a valuable tool for teaching the way they want to teach. Over 20 years of MI research and practice, together with a great many initiatives in progress, have produced a plethora of ideas on which educators can draw for their own settings. Perhaps more important, there is a robust and ever-growing band of colleagues with whom to share the many possibilities for the application of multiple intelligences in the classroom.

SNAPSHOT: ONE TEAM'S JOURNEY

Lincoln Elementary School is located in Stratton, a mid-sized city in the northeastern United States. Its student population numbers 400 and includes a burgeoning population of English-language learners. The school's 4th-grade team includes the classroom teachers, Lillian Vega, Sandra Edwards, and David Barnes, who have been joined on their MI initiative by Felix Lopez, the ESL specialist; Jan Simon, the art teacher; Paul Evans, the music teacher; and Carol Rogers, a resource teacher.

At Lincoln Elementary, MI theory has been in the air for some time. The 4th-grade team members are intrigued with the theory's potential for their classrooms and subjects and want to know more about what using MI theory would really mean. What would it look like? The team articulates its main questions as: What does MI mean for us? And *is* MI for us?

The group studied the theory and its educational implications over 6 weeks. They started by finding appropriate resources and assigning themselves readings, which they shared and discussed at their meetings. They also read about and debated issues of translating MI theory to practice. These conversations moved them to review MI-based applications in MI activity books.

The team found two activities particularly valuable in deepening their understanding of MI theory and its implications for their own classrooms. One was to consider their own "profiles of intelligences," using an informal reflection survey as a starting point (see the Supporting Materials section of this chapter). They were not surprised to realize how closely their teaching strategies seemed to align with their own strengths and preferences.

The second experience was called the Novice/Expert Activity (see Supporting Materials), which they conducted at a meeting of the full faculty. The teachers were asked to demonstrate their understandings of a particular topic in their self-described "novice" areas, and then in their "expert" areas. In effect, the teachers experienced how students might feel when asked to develop and demonstrate understanding in ways that do not come easily, versus ways in which students are competent and confident and feel comfortable learning and expressing themselves. The dramatic differences between their two final products—one completed in a strength area, the other in a novice area—gave the teachers pause regarding how they asked their own students to develop and demonstrate understanding.

This insight validated Jan's desire to build more art process into the regular classroom activities. The simulation, in combination with the self-assessment activities, helped Lillian see that, more often than not, she was asking students to understand through *her* intellectual preferences—writing and drawing—not necessarily their own.

The teachers felt strongly that MI theory validated how they conceptualized and understood intelligence and the diverse strengths students bring to bear in learning. From their conversations, implications and potential uses of MI theory emerged that connected with their goals for their students and for themselves as teachers. By its conclusion, the 6-week experience was seen by the team as the first of many "outings" on their multiple intelligences journey.

BEFORE PUTTING THE PATHWAYS INTO ACTION: BUILDING UNDERSTANDING OF MI THEORY

There is no particular or *necessary* process for building deeper understanding of MI theory, although most groups or individuals pursue a combination of readings, discussion, and hands-on activities. Weekly meetings provided an ongoing context for the Lincoln Elementary team to begin their MI study. In any inquiry it is important to carve out a regular schedule to meet as mutually interested and supportive colleagues. Once MI theory emerges as important among a group of colleagues, a regular meeting place and time should be established. Seemingly mundane issues of this sort become the backbone of sustaining work together in typically hectic lives.

Like most groups that decide to explore MI theory, the Lincoln Elementary team started by reading a combination of materials. The members began with the more theoretical and psychology-oriented texts, then moved to more practice-based works. These varied materials are important in attaining a deep understanding of MI theory and the "lay of the land" of possible MI approaches and practices. Assigning different readings and rotating discussion leaders make these initial study activities more like collegial sharing sessions, more refreshing and efficient than having everyone read the same material at the same time.

Studying MI theory commonly leads practitioners to reflect on their own intelligences. They use informal, multiple choice checklists (Armstrong, 1994), lists of intelligence "indicators" (Campbell, 1994; Viens & Kallenbach, 2004), and/or more open-ended inventories of how they make professional and personal use of the intelligences in their lives. They follow these with analyses and comparisons of their teaching as related to their own proclivities and interests. The discovery of a close relationship between one's personal profile and teaching is a very common "a-ha moment" for individuals exploring MI theory. Often it becomes a starting point for teachers' experiments and applications of MI theory in their classrooms. That is, they start to fill the MI gaps in those classrooms.

THOUGHT QUESTIONS AND ACTIVITIES

Thought Questions

- What do you consider the most important features of MI theory? The most provocative features?
- How might using MI theory change your practices?
- Under lively debate is whether you should teach students *about* MI theory, sharing with

them the language of the theory and engaging them in activities such as MI self-reflection. What is your opinion? How might it help students or harm them? What goals could be addressed by using MI theory in this way?

Implementation Activity

The Novice/Expert Activity implemented by the Lincoln Elementary School teachers (see Snapshot section) is designed to help you consider what happens when individuals are allowed to communicate and learn in a manner that is aligned with an area of strength as opposed to an area of weakness. Instructions for the activity are available in the Supporting Materials section that follows. About 25 participants and a facilitator are needed, and the activity takes about 90 minutes. After completing the activity, consider the following questions:

- What does this activity reveal about learning and assessment?
- Can you predict which of your current students would appear "smarter" if they expressed or developed their understanding in alternative ways?
- What practical implications does this activity suggest for classroom use?

SUPPORTING MATERIALS

Novice/Expert Activity
(Baum, 1994)

This activity is designed to help you consider what happens when children are allowed to think, communicate, and learn in a manner that is aligned with their unique profile of intelligences. About 25 participants are needed, also tables and additional space where one of the groups can work. The directions are for the facilitator. Participants should not read the directions before engaging in the activity.

Discuss how each individual has preferred modes of solving a problem and developing products. Some individuals are at their best when they can visualize a solution and communicate it through the visual arts.

Others may prefer the performing arts, writing, or engineering and design. In this activity you will rate your self-efficacy, perceived ability, or level of development in each of the following domains: writing, drawing, performing arts, and engineering (model building). Each person ranks their level of talent or expertise in the above four domains, with "1" being most expert and "4" being most novice. A facilitator needs to record the number of responses for each group because this information will be needed to form groups later on. When the participants have finished their rankings, tally the information on a board or overhead. Record and share totals with the participants. You may choose to use a chart like the one shown in Figure 3.1.

1. There are two parts to this simulation. The first involves grouping the participants into novice groups (#4, least-preferred domain). The second involves grouping the participants into expert groups (#1, most-preferred domain). The ideal number of participants in each group is between four and ten. If a group is too large, consider splitting it in half or having some participants switch to the next least- or most-favored domain.

2. Tell the participants to imagine themselves in 5th grade working on group projects. The class has been studying the Middle Ages, and each group is required to create a product that demonstrates four aspects of life in the feudal system. The object is to create a product that explains at least four of the feudal social classes and their relationships to one another.

3. The participants first work together in their novice or least-preferred domains (#4), using that form of expression to create their product (see Figure 3.2). The group will pass the assignment if the rest of the class can recognize the four social classes of the feudal system it portrayed.

4. Assign an observer to each group. Observers can be recruited from groups that have large numbers of members. Allow each group 10 to 15 minutes to complete its product. The observer records the time spent on the task, the group dynamics, any avoidance behaviors, the level of enthusiasm, the group's standards for success, and any other observations.

5. When the time is up, each group must share its product in the following way: The performing arts group performs in front of the audience, and the drawing group shares its transparencies on the overhead projector. Both of these groups must ask the audience to try to identify the four social classes in the feudal system as illustrated in their products. (The performing arts group may use words, songs, etc., in its performance.) A person from the writing group reads the written product, and the builders display their product at the front of the room with the audience identifying the aspects of the feudal classes. After the products are presented, the observers from each group share their observations.

6. The group process is repeated. This time the participants are grouped into their most-preferred or expert (#1) area. The instructions are the same. The observers remain with their initially assigned area so that they are able to compare the process when par-

Figure 3.1. Novice/Expert Activity Tally Sheet

Expert (#1)	Total	Novice (#4)	Total
Drawing		Drawing	
Writing		Writing	
Building		Building	
Acting/Performing Arts		Acting/Performing Arts	

Figure 3.2. Novice/Expert Activity Group Directions

Group	Materials	Products
Writing	paper and pencil	Must be written down
Drawing	transparencies, markers	Must be illustrated without verbal explanations
Building	LEGO™ bricks	Must build items that are recognizable without verbal explanations
Acting/Performing Arts	space outside the classroom	Must be performance

ticipants are working in an area of strength as compared with working as a novice or in a least-preferred area. More time may be needed, as the groups will tend to be more elaborate and have higher standards for success.

7. Upon completion of the products, have the groups share their work and the observers present their findings, as in the previous group activity. This time the observers need to emphasize the differences between the novice and expert groups in terms of process and product.

8. Debrief the activity. It is crucial to conduct a discussion with the participants in which their experiences in both activities are compared. You may want to cover the following aspects: the role of the group, creativity, enthusiasm, time on task, noise level, quality of the product, level of detail, and level of knowledge. Have participants share how they used their strength areas in both their expert and novice areas (e.g., Did the non-drawers spend much time talking before drawing? How much time did the expert drawers spend talking?).

Notes to the Facilitator. You are likely to find that the second set of products is superior to the first. It appears that the second group knows more about the feudal system than the first group. In reality, the knowledge level does not change. What does change is the avenue in which the participants are allowed to express their knowledge of the feudal system. In the first activity, the groups are restricted or constrained by their ability to draw, write, build, or perform. For instance, they may know that serfs plowed the fields, but do not know how to draw a plow or do not remember enough about a plow to sketch one successfully. In the second group, however, the more talented artists can draw anything successfully.

In most cases, the role of the group is supportive in the first experience. The group will see the benefits of working with other novices when first learning or trying something new. In the second experience, the members of the group are more independent and confident, and may prefer to work on their own.

Creativity is used differently. In the first activity, it is used to avoid the task or to find clever ways to compensate for lack of talent. In the second experience, the creativity is demonstrated in the enhancement and quality of the product. Participant enthusiasm is usually much higher.

On occasion, participants in the second experience feel pressured to be perfect because they have admitted that they are "expert" in this area. In the first experience, they perceive the expectations to be much lower, while in actuality the criteria for passing remain the same. As will become evident, the time on task increases greatly when students are working in their talent area. Likewise, the quality of the products in the second experience will be far superior to those in the first. In fact, all participants will seem exceptionally talented. Interestingly, because the participants feel more competent and knowledgeable, they will go beyond the minimal expectations of the assignment. You can use Figures 3.3 and 3.4 on the next page to guide the discussions.

FOR FURTHER STUDY

Gardner, H. (1993d). *Multiple intelligences: The theory in practice.* New York: Basic Books.

   A collection of essays moving from the theory of multiple intelligences to implications for practice.

Gardner, H. (1999b). *Intelligence reframed: Multiple intelligences for the 21st century.* New York: Basic Books.

   Gardner's most recent work about multiple intelligences theory. Related chapter titles include: Myths and Realities About Multiple Intelligences, Issues and Answers Regarding Multiple Intelligences, and Multiple Intelligences in the Schools. Also includes a valuable comprehensive listing of resources about MI theory.

Kornhaber, M. L., Fierros, E. G., & Veenema, S. A. (2004). *Multiple intelligences: Best ideas from research and practice.* Boston: Pearson Education.

   Practical guide based on information from more than 40 schools. This Project Zero-based team identified six critical "Compass Point Practices" that relate to effective integration of MI theory in elementary school. Six case studies are used to illustrate the Compass Point Practices.

Figure 3.3. Debriefing the Novice/Expert Activity

	Experience 1	Experience 2
Role of Group		
In which situation did you rely more on your group as a necessary support?	_____	_____
In which experience did you feel more independent?	_____	_____
What conclusions can you draw?	_____	_____
Time on Task		
In which experience were you actively involved over time?	_____	_____
Quality of Product		
Which condition resulted in the better product and showed more skill or talent?	_____	_____
Elaboration		
Which experience resulted in a product that showed more attention to detail?	_____	_____
Knowledge		
In which product did it seem the participants had more knowledge?	_____	_____
Creativity		
In which case was creativity used to: Compensate for lack of skill or comfort? Enhance the quality of the product?	_____	_____
Intelligences Used		
How were strengths used to compensate for weaknesses?	_____	_____
How were strengths used in expert activities?	_____	_____
Stress		
Which condition caused more stress for you?	_____	_____
Why? What are the implications of this?	_____	_____

Figure 3.4. Domain Expert Summary Sheet

Writers

Have no problem using language or words to communicate their knowledge of the topic. They can play with words in creative ways to achieve their desired goal.

Artists

Attend to and remember visual details and have no problem re-creating images on paper. Their knowledge and creativity are shown in the visual product. In short, they can use drawing to communicate what they know rather than just "tell" what they can draw.

Engineers

Notice naturally how things are put together and how they work. Have no difficulty getting their hands to create working models and prototypes. Their understanding of the content begins with this focus. Their creativity will find new methods of conceptualizing the problem, since they will not be limited to what they know how to build.

Performing Artists

Have enjoyment of and flair for the dramatic and have a natural stage presence. Understand how to use voice, mood, dialogue, and timing to communicate their message to the audience. Their creativity allows them to find innovative ways to integrate music, dance, set design, and props to enhance their performance. Such additions reflect deeper understanding of the concepts they are dramatizing.

PART TWO

The Pathways

CHAPTER 4

Pathway Basics

It is not uncommon to hear educators request packets of MI lessons or activities to implement in their classrooms. Because the theory resonates strongly with teachers' understanding of how students think and learn, it is reasonable for teachers to assume that utilizing activities that come under the banner of "MI lessons" will satisfactorily engage MI theory in the business of learning. From this perspective, implementing MI theory means teaching to the intelligences, one of several misconceptions about MI theory that we discussed in Chapter 3. Applying MI theory is not about making the intelligences the end goal or about teaching everything in eight different ways. Rather MI theory is a means to an end. The starting block is the set of goals toward which the theory will be applied. It is fundamental to identify goals first, and then consider how MI can assist in their attainment.

That is where the pathways come in. Educators develop or choose a specific MI-informed approach and cluster of activities that serve their purposes and address their goals. Any given set of "MI activities" is not likely to address—at least not adequately and certainly not precisely—the goals set for practice. That is the role of the pathways: guiding the development of MI applications that "fit the bill" and satisfactorily addressing the goals that educators set.

WHAT IS THE PATHWAYS MODEL?

The Pathways Model is an approach that links MI to a set of five educational purposes to which MI-informed activities can apply. The pathways evolved as scores of MI activities and approaches were reviewed and organized according to overarching

goals. The five pathways represent the main goals claimed by dozens of educators for their application of MI theory. The goals include identifying students' profiles of intelligences, using MI to promote literacy, designing curriculum opportunities using MI that promote understanding, engaging students in authentic activities where they are able to use their expertise to solve problems and develop products, and identifying and nurturing students' gifts and talents.

Part Two of this book will introduce you to the five pathways and describe how to implement them in the classroom. In this chapter, we provide a brief overview of the pathways and foreshadow how the teachers in our fictitious Lincoln Elementary School explored the pathways and implemented them in their classrooms.

The Five Pathways

The five pathways are named to align with the purposes they serve: Exploration, Bridging, Understanding, Authentic Problems, and Talent Development.

The Exploration pathway focuses on enriching the classroom environment to give students experiences across diverse domains, and to provide a context for teachers to observe students in action and informally assess their strengths and interests. That is, the enriched learning environment of the Exploration pathway invites teachers to learn about their students with a fuller perspective. Familiarity with students' abilities and interests is the first step in planning personalized educational experiences, ones that tap students' own ways of learning.

The Bridging pathway emphasizes a purposeful application of students' areas of strength to support literacy development and skill mastery. The strategies suggested in this pathway use the collection of multiple intelligences as a tool to engage students in learning by tapping into areas they enjoy and in which they are successful. This pathway is also based on the assumption that using a variety of "entry points" into literacy learning motivates different kinds of learners to become engaged in the content.

Teachers who work with children experiencing difficulties in the basic literacies have found the Bridging pathway particularly relevant to their goals. It suggests "remediation" that focuses on students' strengths at least as intently as such programs typically focus on their deficits. The Bridging pathway is used both with individual students, using strategies specific to a child's identified strengths and interests, and with groups of children, using diverse strategies targeting different types of learners.

In the Understanding pathway, MI theory is used to enhance and diversify how topics and concepts are approached. Students are given opportunities to access and understand material, as well as to demonstrate their understanding, in ways that align with their areas of strength and interest.

The pressure of coverage has been blamed for students' lack of deep understanding of concepts. That limited understanding is exacerbated by a view of education that assumes all students learn the same way. Both these factors have led to an overreliance on the written and spoken word as the *modus operandi* in the classroom. From a multiple intelligences perspective, linguistic approaches alone cannot possibly provide all students with meaningful ways into the curriculum. The Understanding pathway supports the design of entry points into learning and exit points for assessment that draw on the range of intelligences.

The Authentic Problems pathway uses MI theory as a framework for implementing authentic, problem-based learning experiences. In essence, this pathway tries to simulate the real-world experience of intelligences in action by providing real or realistic problems to solve. In these learning situations, students assume the role of the practicing professional and use authentic means to solve problems and develop products. In the classroom, they become budding engineers, sculptors, actors, or poets, and their products are used to communicate their creative solutions to problems they encounter. Learning becomes relevant through real-world contexts. Basic skills are developed in authentic situations.

The Talent Development pathway focuses on developing programs that identify and nurture students' talents. Seeing many children every day, teachers regularly notice those who exhibit special abilities, but they usually have no resources to help the students follow through. This pathway creates the context to assist promising students on their journey from novice to expert in a particular domain. Staff can organize clubs or special classes; teachers can arrange purposefully designed experiences, such as internships, to nurture these abilities. Students are afforded an opportunity—sometimes their only opportunity—to enjoy, succeed, and excel in school. This pathway disregards grade-level expectations by seeking increasingly more advanced challenges as the learner demonstrates interest and readiness. It promotes self-actualization in ways that help students define and celebrate their talents, and may even help students make decisions about careers and advanced schooling.

Using the Pathways

How each school uses the pathways may vary. Depending on the needs of a particular school setting, different pathways may be appropriate. Perhaps a team wants to offer students MI-informed experiences and identify students' areas of strengths through these enhanced environments (Exploration). Or they may want to start by building on their students' strengths to improve their literacy development (Bridging). The team may decide that the best place to start is by enhancing the ways students can engage in key areas of study (Understanding) or by teaching through projects (Authentic Problems). Finally, teachers may be motivated by students' lack of opportunities to discover and nurture their special talents, and decide to develop those opportunities (Talent Development). Whichever pathway is chosen, it will help practitioners home in on the pathway and particular MI-based approaches that speak to their goals.

The pathways should not be confining. They are meant to help educators focus on the most appropriate MI implementation strategies for their goals, and more specifically, on the most appropriate place to begin their MI journey. It is more often the case than not that people cross the boundaries of pathways, moving between and among them as their goals require.

Crossing of pathway boundaries also occurs because the pathways are not mutually exclusive. Elements of some pathways are found in others. For example, the Exploration pathway emphasizes informal assessment of students' strengths, which is also a central element of the Talent Development pathway. Pathways can be used in parallel and in combination. Each is distinct by virtue of its primary purpose.

Moreover, the pathways are not distinguished by the particular activities they include. There are not specific activities for each of the pathways; rather the distinction is in how they are used. For example, the geodesic dome activity we will describe later can be applied in any of the pathways. In the Exploration pathway, a teacher may use it to see whether any student shows particular ability in that area. Or the building of the dome may be an initiating activity in the Bridging pathway for students to engage in writing procedural narratives. This same building activity can be an entry point in the Understanding pathway, where the goal is to see meaning in formulas or to test the reasons for a triangle in engineering and design. Building geodesic domes may have a fitting place in the Authentic Problems pathway, where students create scale models of their new school playground. Finally, the activity may be used as an identification activity for a talent development program in engineering and design.

Activities or experiences originating from one pathway may engage other pathways. The geodesic dome activity may incidentally become an Exploration activity for those students new to this type of activity or domain. Moreover, the teacher may plan to observe or may spontaneously notice one or more students exhibiting a high level of ability or interest in the activity; they may be engrossed, or they may create a structure that is more complex than the one produced by following the directions. By keeping an open mindset, the teacher may employ more than one pathway at the same time. In some cases, as in the example above, it simply happens; in others, a multiple-pathway perspective is planned.

Rarely do goals fit a designated category. Assume that a school, among its many goals, wishes to align its curriculum with standards. It decides to begin MI work by applying it to a standards-based curriculum. No single pathway addresses standards. Teachers may use the Bridging pathway as a guide to help students master literacy standards while they apply the Authentic Problems pathway to create real-world contexts for other standards. The Understanding pathway is tapped to identify diverse ways to approach specific standards and to assess students' mastery of them.

Getting started with the Pathways Model involves the following steps:

- Identify the educational goals appropriate for the school or classroom.
- Select the pathways that align most closely with the goals.
- Work as a team.

SNAPSHOT: ONE TEAM'S JOURNEY

The Lincoln Elementary School team members have just completed a 6-week study of multiple intelligences theory and a review of their current practices. They feel they are "MI-ready," with a solid understanding of MI theory, a grade-level team-meeting structure in place, support from their principal, a belief that all children can learn, and a firm commitment to find ways to ensure that all students in their school do so.

The whole team is meeting now to firm up plans for pursuing their MI effort. At previous meetings they agreed that the possibilities for applying MI theory were overwhelming, and that they needed a starting point. They also realized that they had both mutual goals for using MI theory and distinct individual goals for their practices. Sandra heard from a teacher friend in New York about something called the "Pathways Model" for applying MI theory. She managed to track down some materials and shared them with her colleagues before the meeting.

At the meeting all agree that the pathways offer a way to explore possible applications of MI theory and a way to ensure that they keep their "eyes on the prize," as Felix puts it. The others concur; the pathways should help keep their MI applications focused on their goals. They decide to come to the next meeting with specific ideas about how they will begin their MI journey.

PUTTING THE PATHWAYS INTO ACTION

The Lincoln Elementary teachers decided to explore the pathways sequentially. They felt that it made the most sense because they had minimal experiences with multiple intelligences theory and didn't quite understand how the pathways worked. Reading about a pathway, grappling with the thought questions, and testing the activities helped them to develop an in-depth understanding of the purposes of each pathway and how MI related to each purpose.

Their discussions concerning the Exploration pathway led them to question their own practice and to evaluate the resources in their rooms. They asked themselves: To what degree were they allowing the expression of multiple intelligences? Were they creating opportunities to view students at their personal best? The teachers were surprised to discover that one particular student, Chris, had extraordinary spatial abilities, and they couldn't wait to use this knowledge to provide appropriate learning experiences for Chris.

Embarking upon the Bridging pathway enabled the team to explore how building activities could help Chris with his writing. They also explored other bridging opportunities, such as using moral dilemma activities to teach persuasive writing. When the Lincoln Elementary School team began to see the positive results brought about by incorporating students' strengths into learning experiences, they decided to extend this approach in the Understanding pathway. Here they dabbled with a variety of entry and exit points that motivated students to engage deeply in activities. The students experienced the ideas of interdependence and a class structure as they assumed the roles of characters from the Middle Ages.

As the end of the year approached, the team wanted to try something totally new where they could observe students applying basic skills and individual areas of expertise to a real-world problem. The Authentic Problems pathway provided them with a structure to implement problem-based learning. They were amazed at how motivated their students were as they started their own computer graphics business, and at what extraordinary talents some of their students displayed in their individual roles in the company. The teachers recognized the potential some of their students displayed in particular areas and agreed that the students' talents needed nurturance. When the school committee on talent development suggested implementing enrichment clusters the following year, the team was elated.

Reflecting on all they had learned during the year, the team felt satisfied and looked forward to starting anew in September. They felt that this second year would be a time to refine the skills that they had learned and continue their journey along the pathways.

THOUGHT QUESTIONS AND ACTIVITIES

Thought Questions

- Are there particular pathways that align with how you are already considering or applying MI? Which ones? How so?
- Is there a specific pathway that is particularly intriguing to you or that seems like the "best" way to apply MI theory?
- Which of your goals, or of the school-wide goals, could be addressed through MI theory and the pathways?

Implementation Activity

Think about different applications of MI theory and how they relate to the key goal(s) for each of the pathways: enhancing the environment while identifying students' strengths, bridging strengths to literacy development, enhancing students' understanding, using authentic problems, and creating talent development opportunities. Then consider and list individual and school-wide goals, mission or vision statement, mandates, and so on. As a preliminary exercise, map out and discuss which pathways seem to make the most sense in light of the items on the list.

FOR FURTHER STUDY

Multiple intelligences: Theory to practice in New York City schools [manual and video guide]. (1999). New York: New York City Board of Education.

This six-module videotape series and accompanying study guide introduce MI theory and present each of the five pathways in practice. Although the "pathways" terminology is not used, the materials were developed for the New York City Board of Education based on the Pathways Model and in collaboration with the authors of this book, Susan Baum, Julie Viens, and Barbara Slatin.

CHAPTER 5

The Exploration Pathway

The primary goals of the Exploration Pathway are to offer students access to diverse learning experiences and to create an environment set up to uncover students' cognitive strengths, interests, and unique profiles of strengths. MI theory is used as a tool to develop Exploration-minded learning experiences and to fashion an effective approach to identifying and describing students' strengths and interests.

PATHWAY BACKGROUND

MI theory posits that individuals use different, unique blends of intelligences to solve problems and fashion products. In the school context, MI theory validates teachers' intuitive notion that children learn and are smart in different ways. The Exploration pathway rests on the premise that offering students a variety of meaningful experiences across the spectrum of intelligences, over time and in different contexts, gives them a chance to explore and discover their preferred ways of knowing. It also gives teachers the opportunity to note students' strengths and when—under what conditions—they are at their personal best, as well as to collect and document that information to put to future pedagogical ends.

Exploration Experiences

Exploration pathway learning experiences are developed with the goal of creating learning opportunities that call on a range of intelligences or combinations of intelligences. An environment is created where students are invited and encouraged to try new types of experiences; where they can explore favored domains or even challenge areas; and where their strengths or unique combinations of intelligences are supported and used to help them learn. To that end, the Exploration pathway does not *require*—but certainly can result in—the creation of a separate Exploration curriculum or Exploration area where the Exploration pathway goals are foregrounded.

Journeying with MI theory on the Exploration pathway usually results in expanding the types of experiences that are offered in the regular curriculum. In most cases, teachers on the Exploration pathway integrate new units, activities, choices, instructional strategies, and/or resources into their regular curricular offerings. Along with these new learning experiences, teachers bring the Exploration observational mindset to the academic learning goals of the regular curriculum. In other words, assessing student learning of the subject matter is still foregrounded, but identifying students' strengths and interests gets into the picture, more in the background.

Many educators also have created freestanding exploratory activities and added them to the classroom repertoire for the sake of integrating particular kinds of experiences or observation opportunities into their setting.

Excellent examples of exploratory activities can be found in children's museums, science museums, and discovery centers, which offer exciting avenues for students to learn and create in authentic ways and for adults to "catch them in action." These contexts offer a variety of materials and experiences, with areas for free play, experimentation, simulations, hands-on applications, and domain-specific role play. In one area children may be building structures of their own design, while in another they are taking the role of paleontologists, uncovering and classifying dinosaur bones. Gardner (1999b) says of such museum contexts:

In these settings, children can proceed at their own pace and direct their energies wherever they like. There is no need to focus on language or logic and there's no explicit teacher or curriculum. As Frank Oppenheimer, the founder of San Francisco's Exploratorium, once quipped, "Nobody flunks museum." (p. 185)

And in the same way, nobody flunks Exploration. Following the example of the children's museum, Exploration-minded teachers offer centers, open the doors to the "science lab," or make available a range of musical instruments. The expectations (like those at children's museums) are no more specific than to allow children to take this open invitation for discovery—playing with ideas, messing around, or simply wondering.

The children and teachers enter into stand-alone Exploration experiences as they would into a children's museum: in a "discovery" frame of mind. Children explore ideas and domains; they learn about their likes, dislikes, strengths, and challenges. While children are involved in these free explorations, teachers focus not on success or failure, but on where and how students direct their energies, what turns them on, what keeps them coming back, or in what context they "lose themselves."

Exploration development may include integrating children's museum experiences—and other community resources—into the regular curriculum, rather than seeing them as stand-alone Exploration experiences. Project Spectrum, at the Harvard Graduate School of Education's Project Zero, developed what were called *resonant learning experiences* to create links between the preschool curriculum, children's museum exhibits, and activities that were conducted at home. In that case, the museum exhibits and extension activities served to enhance the regular curriculum as well as provide a context for Exploration experiences and observations (Chen, Krechevsky, & Viens, 1998).

To whatever degree the Exploration pathway is implemented within or outside of the regular curriculum, the outcome should be that children have opportunities to explore and use their multiple intelligences in a variety of ways, combinations, and contexts. Through the Exploration pathways lens, teachers are able to know what makes each child unique and how he or she best learns.

Exploration Assessment

Assessment on the Exploration pathway means gathering information about students to get to know them as individuals and as learners by collecting and documenting evidence of their strengths and interests. Exploration assessment can be considered the lens through which we observe students and examine the products of their efforts.

The Exploration pathway is *not* intended to label students by one or another intelligence, which is limiting in its own right. Rather, Exploration activities involve discovering the context in which students are most engaged, enjoy themselves and learning, and are at their personal best.

According to MI theory, our intelligences are latent until engaged in certain contexts or experiences; particular environments engage particular intelligences (in specific ways). Therefore, assessments of students' intelligences need to be tightly contextualized. Assessing students when they are actively engaged in authentic experiences, in terms of the roles they take, the problems they solve, and the products that result, is highly instructive in understanding students' intelligences (Chen et al., 1998; Krechevsky & Seidel, 1998).

Observing students in informal situations is also informative. How they resolve conflicts in the lunchroom or on the playground, what they choose to do with their time, and their reactions and responses to other real-life events are related to their intelligence profiles. For example, over the course of a few weeks a student is observed frequenting the music room before school. In language arts, he chooses to put a poem to music as an end-of-unit project. In a geography lesson, he uses rhythm instruments to represent geographic features, such as an archipelago. The teacher's hunch is that this student might be at his personal best when music is involved in an activity.

An important thing to remember regarding assessment from the perspective of the Exploration pathway is that the intelligences serve as a lens through which one can observe students and describe their unique problem-solving profiles. Curriculum activities double as Exploration activities because teachers layer an Exploration lens onto their academic assessments. That is, they not only assess students' performance related to the learning goals; they also observe students for signs of strengths. This picture of each student changes and gets increasingly detailed over time. Each observation deepens teachers' understanding about the uniqueness of their students and provides clues about how to design appropriate learning experiences.

Steps Along the Exploration Pathway

The goals and processes involved in the Exploration pathway can be summarized by its four primary steps.

- Examining the learning environment for existing and overlooked Exploration opportunities.
- Providing students with learning experiences across a range of domains.
- Gathering and documenting evidence of students' strengths.
- Analyzing the information gathered about student strengths to identify under what conditions they are at their personal best.

These steps and related procedures are described in detail in the Putting the Exploration Pathway into Action section. They are shown graphically in Figure 5.1.

Figure 5.1. Exploration Pathway Graphic

SNAPSHOT: ONE TEAM'S JOURNEY

This snapshot of the Lincoln Elementary School 4th-grade team's initiative to apply MI theory centers on their study and use of the Exploration pathway. Present at this team meeting are: Lillian Vega, 4th-grade teacher; Jan Simon, art teacher; and Felix Lopez, ESL specialist.

When we last checked in, the Lincoln Elementary team had just completed its study of MI theory and had agreed to use the Pathways Model to shape its applications of the theory. The team had focused on the Exploration pathway and discussed the kinds of opportunities that already were offered to their students. By today's meeting the team's list includes storywriting, improvisation and acting, a variety of computer programs, art experiences, and creative movement.

Today, as their meeting time approaches, Lillian Vega looks forward to sharing some recent classroom events. She has acknowledged that she offers very few activities in which students can exercise their naturalist intelligence or certain types of spatial intelligence, namely, the engineering or architectural domains. Lillian sees these areas as definitely germane to the class's current study of the Middle Ages, and she remarks that these are likely areas of strength for at least a few students in her classroom. Lillian recognizes that, because she does not feel comfortable working within these domains herself, she rarely uses them.

Lillian is concerned that without experiences in those areas, students with related strengths will not get the very types of learning opportunities with which they are most likely to connect. At the previous meeting, her colleagues had responded by helping Lillian develop a plan to integrate design and construction of scale models of ancient structures into her unit. Jan had offered to integrate building activities into the students' art sessions, and Lillian had decided to attend the art sessions herself, using her prep time for what she sees as a professional development opportunity.

At the previous meeting, Lillian, Felix, and Jan had brainstormed briefly a list of abilities they thought students might demonstrate while involved in building activities. At the meeting's end, Lillian left the room carrying borrowed blocks, to begin the basic building activities suggested by her colleagues.

Today Lillian shares how those blocks have drawn some students in like magnets, especially her student Chris. "What are we doing with *these*?" he had asked excitedly, already placing one block on top of another. Lillian reports how he eagerly accepted the invitation to build with the blocks and, shortly thereafter, impressed everyone with the elaborate structure he created. "Chris has already become a classroom expert with the blocks," Lillian shares with her colleagues, "and the other kids keep coming to him for technical support!"

Lillian has noticed that Chris tends to participate more in group discussions, especially when they are about building projects. She wonders whether his recent willingness to volunteer for a speaking role in a student-produced video is related to the comfort and success he experienced with the building activities. Lillian notes that Chris has been very involved in the technical aspects of the project, especially the videotaping. And even though he doesn't consider himself an actor, and reading and memorizing scripts are difficult tasks for him, Chris is willing to practice until he gets it right.

As she leaves the meeting, Lillian's head is filled with questions: How else can she include engineering and architecture in the unit? In what other ways should she tap her students' spatial abilities? She is thinking about map making for an upcoming unit or creating a building center in her classroom with help from Felix, who is a weekend carpenter.

PUTTING THE EXPLORATION PATHWAY INTO ACTION

Putting the Exploration pathway into action involves enhancing the learning environment so that students can engage in a range of domains. In the enhanced environment that results, we can observe students in action across many contexts. Through MI-colored lenses, we are able to see our students differently, often in new and exciting ways. And, like the teachers at Lincoln Elementary, we can uncover their talents, strengths, and interests using the Exploration pathway.

Examining the Learning Environment

The journey along the Exploration pathway begins with an examination of the learning environment, commencing with identifying opportunities for both existing and overlooked exploration activities. The resources in the room, the school, and the community help to provide exploration activities that tap a wide variety of intelligences.

Survey the kinds of resources you have available, taking stock of the books, materials, center areas, media, and technology in your classroom. Ask yourself what sorts of tools, and which domains, your students have access to. For example, you might note your rich supply of materials for storytelling, such as pencils, paper, tape recorders, dress-up clothes, a drama corner, a storytelling area, computers with appropriate software. You also might note the minimal resources at students' disposal for musical exploration. (Note that you also may decide that their musical exploration happens adequately in music class.)

Once you have surveyed the different aspects of your learning environment, you can begin to identify the intelligences that are given adequate room for expression in different ways across different domains, and which intelligences could be addressed more inclusively in your setting. Are there particular intelligence areas or domains that you avoid? What are your areas of weakness and are they absent, or nearly so, from your classroom?

This examination helps determine the extent to which the learning environment invites students to draw on a range of intelligences, and helps educators identify which intelligences are most readily brought to bear and which are more unavailable for students to use in their settings.

After you have identified the resources available, you need to ask yourself which kinds of instructional strategies you use and which learning experiences you offer. As you are thinking about your instructional style, analyze which intelligences are encompassed and how. Do you enact a range of intelligences or do you, for example, primarily use language to get your points across? Do you diversify or do you tend to stick to the same teaching strategies across subjects and activities?

The next step is to examine the learning activities you offer and the projects, products, and other work your students complete. After identifying the assortment of learning activities and student work undertaken in your setting, ask yourself whether one type of activity or product—such as writing—is heavily weighted, or whether students have opportunities to communicate knowledge by tapping into a range of intelligences or using different symbol systems.

If you already know something about your students and their strengths and interests, you might ask yourself whether the learning environment supports their particular proclivities. Consider what resources might attract these students and engage their strengths. Another tack involves thinking about those students you have found "hard to reach." Might this be a matter of making the classroom more inclusive of areas in which these students are comfortable and/or skilled? What might those areas be?

Providing Students with Learning Experiences Across a Range of Domains

Once you have examined your learning environment, you are ready to enhance it with opportunities for your students to explore their intelligences. One approach involves adding new experiences to the existing curriculum, and the other requires explorations outside the regular curriculum.

The first approach enhances the existing curriculum by integrating activities that fill the gaps you previously identified. Lillian Vega added building activities to her unit on ancient Greece. Consider different kinds of instructional strategies as well, such as using simulations or integrating the arts.

You might offer different options for students' final products, moving beyond writing assignments to include options such as debates, models, photo essays, or interpretive dances. Enriching the unit by adding resources such as kits, artifacts, works of art, guest speakers, and field trips, as well as using resources available in the community, will allow students to engage in new ways.

The second approach to providing exploratory opportunities is to offer activities outside the regular curriculum. Interest centers and special whole-class activities are two ways to provide these freestanding explorations.

In interest centers, students interact with tools and activities related to a particular domain or theme. One 3rd-grade teacher developed a "pop-up" center focused on paper engineering (see Figure 5.2). Students developed and used their paper engineering skills to create cards, pop-up pages, and books.

Interest centers often inspire student-initiated projects that may extend to other domains. In this class, several of the students established a pop-up greeting card company. Related activities included writing poetry, developing advertisements, bookkeeping, and sales.

Interest centers also can be connected to the existing curriculum (McInerny, Berman, & Baum, 2005). For example, one group of students was invited to create a pop-up book about endangered species, a topic within their science curriculum.

Whole-group lessons also can be used for freestanding explorations. In one instance, a 5th-grade teacher conducted a lesson on how to create a storyboard, knowing that filmmakers use them to conceptualize story lines and sketch out their ideas. Storyboarding is an excellent example of an authentic experience through which students can explore a new domain and exercise their intelligences and through which teachers can observe those intelligences at work.

This teacher chose storyboarding as an authentic and different way for her students to use their spatial abilities. She thought the idea of filmmaking would excite students with related strengths and engage oth-

Figure 5.2. Pop-Up Interest Center

ers who had not demonstrated abilities or interest in spatial activities before. (See the Supporting Materials section in this chapter for the storyboarding activity.)

Gathering Information About Students' Strengths

A primary goal of the Exploration pathway is to know students in terms of the intelligences they favor and the domains that engage them, and to identify those contexts in which students are shown in their best light. There are a variety of ways to learn about students, such as observing them, collecting their work, and asking them to complete surveys and to reflect on their work and experiences.

Observing Students. Observation is the single most effective way to gather information about students' strengths. Observations can be divided into two categories: planned observations and spontaneous observable moments. During any given activity many things are happening, only some of which are relevant to the goals of Exploration. Things to look for that may tell you something about your students' strengths and interests include

- choices they make when given options,
- roles they take when working together to complete a task,
- how they handle unanticipated problems,
- particular problem-solving strategies offered by each child,
- what excites them or captures their attention,
- when they lose or gain interest in a task, and
- different ways they communicate ideas, understandings, thoughts, and feelings to others (including physical actions as well as what they say).
(Krechevsky & Seidel, 1998)

On any given day, many observable events surface that are worthy of documentation. You may notice a student resolving an argument on the playground, helping a friend with a computer problem, composing melodies on the keyboard, designing a movement routine in gym class, or showing off a collection of butterflies. These events or student responses, although unplanned, provide valuable information about the students. You may want to have a clipboard handy or some other easily accessible means to record these observations.

To ensure that you get to know your students in a variety of contexts when they are engaging different intelligences, you also need to plan observation events. Choosing particular activities or events to observe will help you conduct more systematic observations of all your students.

In selecting an event to observe, take into account what you already know about your students and what you still want to find out. Lillian Vega knew she had not seen her students in the context of building because she had not previously offered them the opportunity. Therefore, not only did she expand her unit activities to include building, but she focused her observations on these activities.

To narrow your focus, you may decide to choose an activity with an eye toward observing particular kinds of abilities. Or you may focus on a particular student or two who have escaped your observations thus far or present a particular puzzle for you.

Lillian chose to observe an event that elicited bodily–kinesthetic and spatial intelligence in the context of architecture. She took written notes on how participating students engaged in the activity. Lillian particularly noticed Chris's response, targeting him for future observations to see if a pattern would emerge.

Observation includes documentation. Employ the documentation strategies that work for you. The specific method you choose also will depend on what you are observing or documenting. Most observations require some note taking. Record your observations in journals, in logbooks, on index cards, or on stick-on notes. Photographs and videotapes can support your notes, especially when describing performances and products.

Using observation checklists can help you to document specific behaviors when you know what an activity will likely elicit. Figure 5.3 lists behaviors that are often apparent when an activity is tapping a student's strength area.

These behaviors can apply to any activity. Sometimes it is helpful to adapt them to the particular activity or domain you are targeting. Figure 5.4 il-

Figure 5.3. Observable Signs of Student Strength

The student ...

    Follows directions independently.

    Demonstrates ease in completing the task.

    Produces superior work.

    Assumes a leadership role.

    Loses track of time and is totally engaged in the activity.

    Asks for additional challenges.

    Adds interesting details to the product.

    Asks sophisticated or insightful questions.

Figure 5.4. Student Behaviors to Observe— Geodesic Dome

Student behaviors to observe during geodesic dome activity:

    Follows the visual direction sheet independently.

    Demonstrates ease working with building materials.

    Assumes leadership roles by helping others build their domes.

    Asks to build other structures using his/her own design.

    Adds details to the basic dome structure.

    Generates many uses for the dome.

lustrates a revised version of the generic list of observable behaviors in Figure 5.3, tailored for use with the geodesic dome activity. (See the Supporting Materials section for instructions for the geodesic dome activity.)

Student Products. Careful analysis of student products can reveal information about strengths. A student's poem may reveal self-knowledge (intrapersonal intelligence), sensitivity to the human condition (interpersonal intelligence), a connection with nature (naturalist intelligence), or musicality (musical intelligence).

The storyboard in Figure 5.5 suggests a student's spatial awareness, perspective, understanding of camera angles, and even a concern with how she might be perceived by others.

Student Surveys. You can get to know your students simply by asking them about their preferences and self-described strengths and interests. Many checklists, surveys, and self-assessments that get at

this type of information are available in the popular press (Campbell, 1994; Renzulli, 1997b; Viens & Kallenbach, 2004). "My Way" (Kettle, Renzulli, & Rizza, 2002) is an example of one such tool. This instrument is an inventory that helps students determine the kinds of products they are interested in creating.

Having your students complete and analyze these assessments adds important information to your documentation. However, these tools should not be treated as formal assessments of intelligences, but as supplements to your observations and as a starting point for students' reflections on their preferred intelligences. They should be used in an ongoing way, so that students explore what domains, activities, or ways of thinking come most easily to them or in which they are most engaged. Their purpose is not to achieve a definitive score across intelligences, but to add to your understanding of the students, as well as to involve students in self-reflection.

Student Reflection Activities. Reflection activities provide another way for students to explore and identify their strengths and preferences. Constructing autobiography cubes (see Supporting Materials) or personal mobiles are both excellent prompts for students to gather information about themselves, their preferences, and their passions and strengths. Dialogue journals provide a context for student–teacher conversations about strengths and interests.

MI self-assessments should be reviewed carefully for their characterizations of each intelligence. Such review clarifies your own or the team's reading of each intelligence and checks the tools for faulty characterizations. For example, interpersonal and intrapersonal intelligences often are described erroneously as preferring to work in groups or alone, respectively. "Talking" with one's hands, being talkative, and talking to oneself are not signs of bodily–kinesthetic, linguistic, or intrapersonal intelligences, yet each has been on one observation sheet or another. You may do well to create your own self-assessments, perhaps building on existing forms.

Analyzing the Information

In order to make sense of the information you gather, you need to compile and organize your data

Figure 5.5. Storyboard Example—Humpty Dumpty

for each student. Use a system such as file folders, loose-leaf notebooks, binders, portfolios (Stefanakis, 2002), or computer files. After several observations per student, you may begin to note the emergence of particular patterns. It is valuable to reflect on your findings and to share them with others who know the student. Their insights will provide more information. For example, when Lillian Vega described Chris's skill in building, Jan Simon commented that Chris showed similar skills in many art activities. Lillian and Jan planned to work together to provide appropriate experiences for Chris and others with similar strengths.

Use the following questions to help identify the patterns in your collected data:

- During which activities is the student at his or her personal best?

- Which intelligences consistently display over time and in different contexts?
- Can you identify a pattern when examining the choices this student has made?
- What are the student's interests, and how does he or she engage in these interests? Do the interests support the other patterns that you have noted?
- Does the information from journals and checklists support the patterns observed?
- Do the sources reveal the student's strengths in a particular domain or intelligence?
- In which circumstances and which domains does this student appear to demonstrate cognitive strength, motivation, or passion?
- When and under what conditions is this student "smart"?

- In which specific ways do things seem to make the most sense for the student?

The patterns you identify should not be used to label a student as characterized by one intelligence or another. The patterns you identify should remain at a certain level of specificity. For example, rather than saying, "Sophia is an interpersonal child," one might observe her and conclude that Sophia is an adept negotiator in the housekeeping corner, where she uses her extraordinary linguistic and interpersonal skills to persuade others to follow her lead.

After review, summarize any emerging patterns that you have noticed thus far. As you collect more information, you will continue to refine your understanding of individual students. Lillian recorded her hunch about Chris's spatial abilities, which led her to create additional activities with a strong spatial component. Observing Chris during these activities enabled her to fine-tune her understanding of his abilities and ultimately helped her to support his learning.

Guiding Your Journey

The materials provided here to guide your journey on the Exploration pathway include the Exploration Pathway Guide and the Exploration Pathway Organizer. The guide and the organizer consist of four sections, one aligned with each of the key features of the Exploration pathway. You do not have to use all four, just those related to your purposes. For example, if you want to focus solely on creating an MI-rich learning environment, then think about using the first two sections. The Pathway Guide, shown in Figure 5.6, provides questions to prompt your thinking as you complete the accompanying Organizer. Figure 5.7 shows Lillian's organizer. You will find a full-page, reproducible blank organizer in the Supporting Materials section (see Figure 5.8).

THOUGHT QUESTIONS AND ACTIVITIES

Thought Questions

- How is multiple intelligences theory applied in the Exploration pathway?

- What are the promises and challenges of pursuing the Exploration pathway?
- Teachers today are accountable to a multitude of standards, tests, and content coverage in a limited time frame. In this climate, how do we justify or fit in Exploration pathway goals and activities?
- There is a growing emphasis on providing differentiated instruction so that we meet the needs of all learners in the classroom. How might pursuing the Exploration pathway address differentiation?

Implementation Activities

Activity 1. Analyze your own classroom environment using the Exploration Pathway Organizer and the Exploration Pathway Guide. Are there areas or particular students whose strengths are not being addressed?

Activity 2. Consider small steps within the context of your classroom, goals, units, and so on, to fill a gap area or increase resources for student use in the classroom. Get help from your teammates regarding ways you can develop your abilities in an area in which you do not feel comfortable or competent. Check the resources at the end of this chapter for more ideas.

Activity 3. Plan an interest center designed to give your students exploratory activities in a particular domain or area not traditionally covered in the regular curriculum. In your design include authentic materials for children to explore, task cards, and audiovisual materials (audio- and videotapes). If possible, team up and actually make an interest center.

Activity 4. Observe one or two students across several activities in different contexts during the course of a week. Try to look in many places, not just academics. Observe the students in purely social situations, if possible. Gather several observation notes, and from these consider the students in terms of an emerging profile of intelligences. At your next meeting discuss your observations. Any surprises?

Figure 5.6. Exploration Pathway Guide

Exploration Features	Things to Think About
Examining the learning environment for both existing and overlooked Exploration opportunities. *Do the resources in the room allow for the expression of multiple talents?* 	• What kinds of resources are in my room? • Do I have materials that appeal to the naturalist, artist, scientists, etc.? • Do I have centers that appeal to different strengths and talents? • Do I watch students when involved in both assigned tasks and free-choice opportunities? • What is missing?
Providing students with learning experiences across a range of domains or intelligences. *What learning experiences do I typically employ?* *What else can I do to engage more students?* 	• What kinds of teaching strategies do I use? Can I vary my approach? • What are the typical products I offer the class to show their understandings? Are there specific kinds of products missing? • Do I enrich the curriculum by exposing students to new topics and areas of interest through interest centers, speakers, field trips, etc.? • What more can I do to fill gaps?
Gathering and documenting evidence of students' strengths. *How will I learn about my students' strengths, abilities, and interests?* 	• What Exploration activities do I offer that I can observe? • What kinds of tools are available for me to assess strengths, abilities, and interests? • How can I document this information? • How can this information help me to adapt the classroom to meet the needs of more students?
Analyzing the information gathered about students to identify under what conditions they are at their personal best. 	• Comment on findings for key students to use in future pathways.

Figure 5.7. Sample Completed Exploration Pathway Organizer

Examining the learning environment for both existing and overlooked Exploration opportunities. *Do the resources in the room allow for the expression of multiple talents?* 	• *In my classroom:* Writing materials, art supplies, books, two computers, and software programs • *In my building:* The art and music teachers have materials for my use. Felix knows about building. • *In my community:* Museum, local theater group, science center • Other resources: *What more do you need to better accomodate the individual needs of your students?* Blocks and other building materials. Microscope.

Providing students with learning experiences across a range of domains or intelligences.

What learning experiences do I typically employ?

What else can I do to engage more students?

Learning experiences I typically employ:

☐ Lecture   ☐ Simulations
☐ Text   ☐ Project/problem-based learning
☒ Cooperative learning   ☐ Jigsaw groups
☒ Readiness groups   ☐ Interest groups
☐ Technology   ☐ Web quest
☐ Arts integration   ☐ Learning games
☐ Other

I use cooperative learning and readiness groups. I think using interest-based groups would be helpful.

Instructional strategies I typically use. (In other words, what is your teaching style and does it favor students with certain learning styles? Explain.):

Storywriting, improvisation, and acting; computer programs, art experiences, and creative movement.

Am I favoring certain strengths?

Verbal and performing arts. Nonverbal activities are missing.

Gaps:

Naturalist and spatial intelligences seem to be shortchanged. I would like to use more simulations and arts-integrated activities in the future.

Gathering and documenting evidence of students' strengths.

How will I learn about my students' strengths, abilities, and interests?

How will I learn about my students' strengths, abilities, and interests?

☐ Interest survey   ☐ Interview   ☐ My way
☒ Observation   ☐ Other

I will give the students opportunities to use blocks in building activities and observe their facility with the blocks.

How will you document your findings?

I will take notes and photographs of my observations, especially noting which of my students are the most engaged.

I am keeping my observations and photos of Chris's work in a portfolio.

Analyzing the information gathered about students to identify under what conditions they are at their personal best.

I've noticed when Chris gets to act like the expert, he is much more participatory, especially when discussion involves building. I've noticed that Chris has been volunteering for more things. Chris gets totally engaged when dealing with technical aspects of a project, especially videotaping. Jan confirms my hunch about Chris's spatial talents in art class.

Comment on findings for key students to use in future pathways.

I am considering ways to expand my units to include more spatial kinds of activities such as map making. Maybe I can create a building center. I will ask Felix for suggestions for Chris. Jan will help to find activities and learning experiences to integrate the visual arts.

Activity 5. Conduct one or more of the activities in the Supporting Materials section: geodesic dome, storyboarding, the autobiography cube, and To Float or Not to Float. Using the checklist provided, observe your students as they participate in the activities. Document your observations and bring them to the next session to discuss what you observed and your hunches about the students' strengths.

Activity 6. Developing observation checklists can help you identify student strengths in particular domains. Modify the checklist in Figure 5.3 to use with an Exploration activity of your choice. (See Figure 5.4 for an example of how the checklist was modified for the geodesic dome activity.) Try it out and report back to the group.

SUPPORTING MATERIALS

Figure 5.8 is a full-page, reproducible version of the Exploration Pathway Organizer for your use in planning Exploration activities for your own setting. The following section includes more Exploration activities for you to consider: the geodesic dome activity, the storyboarding activity, the autobiography cube activity, and To Float or Not to Float.

Additional Exploration Examples

Geodesic Dome Activity

Exploration Pathway Connection. Conducting this activity provides a context for observing the expression of a range of different intelligences, in particular spatial and bodily–kinesthetic, and perhaps interpersonal, intelligences.
Behaviors to observe:

- Follows the visual direction sheet independently.
- Demonstrates ease in working with building materials.
- Assumes leadership roles by helping others build their domes.
- Asks to build other structures using his or her own design.

- Adds details to the basic dome structure.
- Generates many uses for the dome.

Materials Required
- Direction sheet
- 60 toothpicks for each participant
- 26 mini-marshmallows per participant, plus extras for eating (get the kind that will harden)

Procedure. Guide the students step-by-step as outlined in the Student Instructions (Figure 5.9). Allow students to move ahead of the rest of the group and note when they want to, which may be indicative of abilities in spatial and bodily–kinesthetic intelligences. Advise the students that the dome is built from the top down and remains basically flat until step 10. For some participants, the dome may resemble a rooftop after step 2. This is not a problem. Just continue to remind them that the dome is built out, not up.

Geodesic Dome Activity Extensions. Leave extra building materials (toothpicks and marshmallows) out as a center activity and observe who continues to design structures over time. Continue to observe who visits the center and what products emerge. At the center you could add challenges such as:

- Using two domes to create a sphere,
- Recording the shapes that appear in the dome, and
- Representing the shapes in terms of triangles and having the students invent equations to represent the areas and perimeters of the shapes in terms of triangles or other combinations of shapes using tangrams and other patterning activities.

Make sure this activity is conducted on a day that is *not* hot and humid; otherwise the marshmallows will become too sticky, will not harden, and will be impossible to manipulate.

Storyboarding: The Real Story of Humpty Dumpty

Exploration Pathway Connection. Implementing the storyboarding activity gives students an

Figure 5.8. Exploration Pathway Organizer (blank).

Examining the learning environment for both existing and overlooked Exploration opportunities.

Do the resources in the room allow for the expression of multiple talents?

☐ in my classroom:

☐ in my building:

☐ in my community:

☐ other resources:

What more do you need to better accomodate the individual needs of your students?

Providing students with learning experiences across a range of domains or intelligences.

What learning experiences do I typically employ?

What else can I do to engage more students?

Learning experiences I typically employ:

☐ Lecture   ☐ Simulations
☐ Text   ☐ Project/problem-based learning
☐ Cooperative learning   ☐ Jigsaw groups
☐ Readiness groups   ☐ Interest groups
☐ Technology   ☐ Web quest
☐ Arts integration   ☐ Learning games
☐ Other

Instructional strategies I typically use (in other words, what is your teaching style and does it favor students with certain learning styles? Explain.):

Am I favoring certain strengths?

Gaps:

Gathering and documenting evidence of students' strengths.

How will I learn about my students' strengths, abilities, and interests?

☐ Interest survey

☐ My way

☐ Observation

☐ Interview

☐ Other

How will you document your findings?

Analyzing the information gathered about students to identify under what conditions they are at their personal best.

Comment on findings for key students to use in future pathways.

Figure 5.9. How to Construct a Geodesic Dome

1. Take 1 marshmallow and 5 tooth-picks.

2. Put a marshmallow on the end of each toothpick.

3. Connect each marshmallow with the toothpicks.

4. Add 3 toothpicks to each marsh-mallow

5. Join the toothpicks. (Attach "neighboring" toothpicks with one marshmallow.).

6. Put marshmallows on single toothpicks.

7. Connect all marshmallows with the toothpicks.

8. Add 2 toothpicks to each marsh-mallow.

9. Connect toothpicks (neighboring toothpicks "hold hands").

10. Connect all marshmallows with toothpicks to form a GEODESIC DOME. It is at this point that the dome takes shape. Up until now, it is basically flat.

opportunity to use spatial and logical–mathematical abilities in a new domain. Other intelligences may emerge.

Materials Required. A sheet of 8½ × 11 or larger paper, folded in two rows of three, creating six frames.

Procedure. Teacher says, "Let's make a movie." Describe how filmmakers plan their films. Have an overhead of a storyboard, a handout of a storyboard, or a comic strip (which is an example of a story-board) so the students will get the idea. To explain how filmmakers use shots to help them plan the focus for each scene, have the students experiment with the idea of long shots, medium shots, close-up shots, and special effects shots. Have them take a 3-inch square of paper and tear a little hole in the middle. Using their squares, have them look at the wall at the far end of the room and notice how they can see the whole wall. This is called a long shot. Next have them look through the hole at the person next to them and notice how limited the view is. Special effects shots, where the objective is for something to look really large or really small, can be demonstrated by having students crouch down and slant their square up, or stand on a chair and look down.

Tell students they must decide what kind of shot or focus they want for each scene in their story.

Student Instructions

1. Fold a piece of 8½ × 11 paper into sixths (first in half horizontally, then in thirds).
2. Have the students remember the nursery rhyme "Humpty Dumpty" and note that it never says whether Humpty is male or female. Tell them since they are the filmmakers, they can decide all the details of the story.
3. Frame 1: Start the first frame by having students brainstorm the setting—where they want the story to take place, season, time of day. Have them decide what the wall will be made of and, for older children, what kind of shot they want. A long shot is preferable, so that the viewer can get a sense of the whole scene. Have them draw frame 1 incorporating the details they have chosen.

4. Pick a few samples and read back frame 1 according to the details drawn in by the student. For instance, one student drew the Great Wall of China and Humpty had on a Chinese hat. The teacher read the picture: "It was a bright sunny day in China with no clouds in sight. Humpty was perched on the Great Wall. He could see the whole countryside below. The ancient wall of steel-gray stone wandered through the hills until it disappeared." It is important for the teacher to model good language and descriptive vocabulary.

5. Frame 2: This time the scene should focus on the motivation of Humpty and how he (or she) is feeling. Have several of the more verbal students role-play Humpty while the rest of the class interviews him about his reasons for being on the wall, how he got there, how he will get down, and so on. This time the students should discuss the kind of shot necessary to focus in on Humpty. Most will choose a close-up because the emphasis is on Humpty and his thoughts. Have students draw their scene and again "read" back some.

6. Frame 3: This should show the action or explain what causes the fall. Students who are spatial often use special effects shots to describe the happening. Notice how the setting is related to what causes the fall. For instance, if the wall is at the seaside, a wave might push Humpty over the edge.

7. Continue in the same manner for the rest of the frames, using the following suggestions:
   a. Frame 4: This is the Rescue Mission ("all the King's Horses," etc.), or where Humpty ended up as a result of the fall. Some students will create rescue teams based on their scenario, and others will extend the story of where Humpty fell, as into a dark black hole. The rescue may not come until later.
   b. Frames 5 and 6: Complete the story. The student whose Humpty wore the Chinese hat had Humpty fall upside down into his pointed hat, which became an egg holder. Some creative

chefs rescued Humpty but then turned him into egg-drop soup. Another student had the story take place by the seashore. When Humpty fell, he landed underwater. He was just about to be eaten by Charlie the Tuna when Charlie remembered he was on a low-cholesterol diet. Humpty floated to the top and was rescued.

8. When the storyboard is finished, plan how the movie will be made. A simple idea is to use a transparency for each frame or to divide a transparency into sixths. Show one frame at a time, with student or teacher providing narration.

The Autobiography Cube

Exploration Pathway Connection. This activity was developed for use with adults (Viens & Kallenbach, 2004). It provides a hands-on way for students to engage in self-reflection about their own interests and strengths. In MI language, it allows them to tap intelligences other than linguistic, intrapersonal, and interpersonal to reflect on and describe their own strengths.

Procedure. On a three-dimensional paper cube they build, students make a collage of pictures and words that reflect their talents and interests.

Start by giving each student a 12 × 16 piece of construction paper. Have the students divide their papers into twelve 4 × 4 squares; fold the papers along these lines; and mark six of the squares with an *x*, as shown in Figure 5.10.

Have the students draw or find pictures, 4 × 4 or smaller, that show their interests, strengths, and special people, events, and activities in their lives. (You might want to have a class discussion or MI reflection activity before your students make these cubes.) Students glue or tape the pictures onto the six unmarked squares, as if making a collage. You might suggest that they add descriptive words as well, using letters cut out of magazines or writing in the words by hand. These can be glued or taped onto the cube as well. Then students refold the paper along the original crease lines.

Figure 5.10. Autobiography Cube Diagram

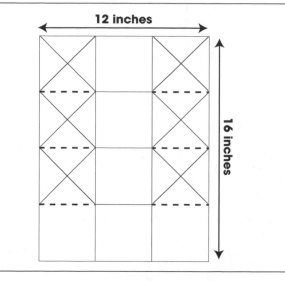

Cut six 4-inch slits in the cube, as indicated by the dotted lines in Figure 5.10. Fold in the undecorated sides to form a cube. Secure the sides of the cube with clear tape. Have the students present their cubes to the rest of the class. Encourage them to discuss what their cube sides represent.

To Float or Not to Float (Baum & Hébert, 1994)

Exploration Pathway Connection. This activity can help you to identify students who are strong in logical–mathematical intelligence. Specific behaviors to watch for include:

- Students make careful observations
- Students generate many questions about what they observe
- Students ask "what if" questions (demonstrating that the student is engaging in problem finding)
- Students can invent their own hypotheses and develop their own experiments to test them, including how to control for alternate hypotheses
- Students draw conclusions about their observations and develop their own theories
- Students return to the activity or an extension or elaboration of the activity over time to continue their own inquiry

- Students record data or observations systematically with pictures, numbers, or words

Materials Required

- Raisins
- Clear plastic cups
- Cans of clear soda at room temperature
- Water
- A lab notebook
- Proposal forms

Procedure

1. Divide the participants into science teams of three or four. Give each team a ½-cup of water, a ½-cup of clear soda, and about 6 to 10 raisins.
2. Instruct the participants to place a few raisins in both the water and the soda and observe what happens.
3. Discuss observations and then have participants generate any and all possible questions about their observations (i.e., the raisins will dance up and down in the soda, but sink in the water).
4. Ask the participants to decide on questions that can be answered by designing their own experiment.
5. Have participants fill out a proposal form for future experiments.

Sample Proposal Form

My problem: I wonder if other things will bob up and down in the soda?
My hunch: I think other things that are wrinkled and sugary will bob.
What I will need. Cups, clear soda, grapes, prunes, rice, dried fruits, gum, spaghetti
What I will do. Drop each in soda and observe what sinks, floats, or bobs up and down. Look for patterns.

If a student does submit a proposal, teachers need to help the student find the necessary materials, provide space and time to conduct the experiment, and encourage the student to share his or her findings.

FOR FURTHER STUDY

Chen, J., Isberg, E., & Krechevsky, M. (Eds.) (1998). *Project Spectrum: Early learning activities* (Vol. 2 in *Project Zero Frameworks for Early Childhood Education*, H. Gardner, D. H. Feldman, & M. Krechevsky, eds.). New York: Teachers College Press.

> A collection of activities developed for learner centers and based on multiple intelligences theory. Each activity description includes a list of key abilities that guides observation of children while they are engaged in the activities.

Johmann, C. A., & Rieth, E. J. (1999). *Bridges! Amazing structures to design, build, and test.* Charlotte, VT: Williamson.

> The nuts and bolts of bridges as youngsters build a cofferdam, design a bridge to cross wide expanses, test the strength of triangles versus squares, hang a suspension bridge, and more. Includes anecdotes about famous bridges, engineers, architects, and inventors; ideas to think about, and challenges to solve problems. Grade level: 2-6.

Krechevsky, M. (1998). *Project Spectrum: Preschool assessment handbook* (Vol. 3 in *Project Zero Frameworks for Early Childhood Education*, H. Gardner, D. H. Feldman, & M. Krechevsky, eds.). New York: Teachers College Press.

> One of three in a series from Project Zero's Project Spectrum at Harvard. It gives performance assessments for young children aligned to the multiple intelligences. This is an excellent resource for teachers looking for freestanding exploration activities with a detailed assessment component.

McGreevy, A. (1982). *My book of things and stuff: An interest questionnaire for young children.* Mansfield, CT: Creative Learning Press.

> An interest questionnaire specifically designed for young children. Includes more than 40 illustrated items focusing on the special interests of 6- to 11-year-olds. Contains a teacher's section, an interest profile sheet, sample pages from a journal, and bibliographies of interest-centered books and magazines. Grade level: K–6

McInerney, M., Berman, K., & Baum, S. (2005). *Creating interest development centers: Opportunities for choice, challenge, and differentiation.* Mansfield Center, CT: Creative Learning Press.

> A guide for effective use of interest centers in the classroom, this book includes six complete interest centers. Activities use entry and exit points based on MI theory. Topics include knights and castles, quilts, meteorology, storytelling, and heroes. See the For Further Study section in Chapter 5 of this book for more resources about interest centers.

Multiple intelligences: Theory to practice in New York City schools [manual and video guide]. (1999). New York: New York City Board of Education.

> This six-module video series with accompanying study guide is based on the Pathways Model described in this book. Module 2 focuses on the Exploration pathway, and the videotape provides excellent examples of its application in New York City public schools.

Renzulli, J. (1997b). *Interest-a-lyzer family of instruments, grades K–12: A manual for teachers.* Mansfield Center, CT: Creative Learning Press.

> Manual on the six interest-assessment tools that constitute the Interest-A-Lyzer "family of instruments." Discusses the importance of assessing student interests and provides suggestions for administering and interpreting these instruments in the school setting. Grade level: K–12.

Sabbeth, A. (1997). *Rubber band banjos and a java jive bass: Projects and activities on the science of music and sound.* Mansfield Center, CT: Creative Learning Press.

> How sounds are made and how humans hear them, how instruments create music, and how to make musical instruments. Step-by-step instructions and illustrations guide young readers through dozens of projects and experiments involving music and sound. Grade level: 3-8.

Salvadori, M. (1990). *The art of construction: Projects and principles for beginning engineers and architects.* Mansfield Center, CT: Creative Learning Press.

> With historical examples from caves to skyscrapers, takes students through the principles of engineering and architecture. Project suggestions using household items give students a hands-on understanding of all aspects of structure and design. Grade level: 5-12.

Stefanakis, E. (2002). *Multiple intelligences and portfolios: A window into the learner's mind.* Portsmouth, NH: Heinemann.

> Uses the case of one school and several of its students to elaborate on the idea of describing students through their multiple intelligences and using portfolios to document and demonstrate students' multiple intelligences profiles.

Waterfall, M. & Grusin, S. (1989). *Where's the me in museum? Going to museums with children.* Arlington, VA: Vandamere Press.

> This book is an excellent guide for thinking about experiencing different types of museums and discovery centers with young children.

CHAPTER 6

The Bridging Pathway

Embarking on the Bridging pathway means choosing to use multiple intelligences to help students master the basic skills of literacy and math. In this case, MI theory offers a framework to use students' strengths to connect cognitively to areas that may be more problematic for them. Through careful scaffolding, teachers guide children from using one symbol system or intelligence to accomplishing tasks in another. This strengths-based approach is meant to improve students' literacy achievement and also serves to increase their motivation and academic self-efficacy, as well.

PATHWAY BACKGROUND

This pathway is based on two assumptions. First is the notion that students achieve better when allowed to pursue learning from a position of strength. The other is the acknowledgment that using a multiple intelligences approach can enhance the learning process.

A Focus on Strengths

While the notion of recognizing and emphasizing students' strengths is not new and may seem obvious, it contradicts typical educational practice. For too long, educational efforts have focused on students' weaknesses, especially in reading and writing. Much time and money have been allocated to the remediation of these underdeveloped skills—often to the exclusion of identifying and nurturing students' strengths. Instructional strategies usually begin with performing language-based activities such as reading, listening to explanations or directions, or brainstorming. In fact, most of what happens in schools is language-based, an environment that is difficult for students with strengths in other intelligences.

The situation is exacerbated because of an increasing emphasis on literacy instruction. Instruction in all domains often becomes a "secret" language arts lesson, where the authentic methods of the domain are relegated to the back burner. Even state tests assess mastery and understanding of concepts in all domains through some writing activity.

The practice of focusing on weaknesses contradicts current learning theory. Cognitive psychologists insist that successful learning is dependent on students' ability to regulate their own learning (Zimmerman, Bonner, & Kovach, 1996). Self-regulation involves students' control over how they attend to information, seek out information, interpret that information, organize and file it into memory, and retrieve it as needed. Self-regulation occurs most naturally when learning is processed through students' strengths and interests (Baum & Owen, 2003; Baum, Owen, & Oreck, 1997; Chen, Krechevsky, & Viens, 1998; Corbo, 1997; Renzulli, 1994). Under these conditions, student performance is optimal because learning is personalized. For example, students with strong artistic ability seem to learn easily when arts processes are integrated into the content area (Baum et al., 1997). (Remember the results of the novice/expert activity described in Chapter 3 when the team participated first as novices, then as experts.)

MI Theory and Learning

Multiple intelligences theory can help to explain individual differences in how students learn. Each symbol system attracts certain people and influences both memory and attention. As Gardner (1999b) points out, neuropsychological evidence indicates the presence of distinct kinds of memories. Some of us may be excellent at remembering names, dates, definitions, and the like (linguistic), but have difficulty remembering tunes or complex melodies (musical).

Similarly, the ability to remember a sequence of dance steps (bodily–kinesthetic) may be more pronounced in some of us than our facility to recall shapes, faces, and visual images (spatial). Because students have different combinations of abilities, they are attracted by different kinds of content, such as music, photographs, dramatic readings, or mathematical formulas. Thus, a guided imagery activity to start a lesson will attract children strong in spatial intelligence. They will be more likely to focus and sustain attention than in other circumstances. Likewise, using a mathematical formula to represent how to organize one's time will make much sense to those strong in logical–mathematical intelligence.

Using a multiple intelligences framework to understand individual differences in how students learn can assist in explaining why some students are successful and others are not. These observations can contribute to instructional strategies that tap individual students' intellectual strengths and allow them to be successful in developing literacy.

Consider the young performing artists in a classroom. They are usually the ones who are talkative and constantly in motion. Such students often become attentive, active participants in learning when they have a chance to perform using their interpersonal and bodily–kinesthetic intelligences as a starting point to the lesson and learning objective.

Suppose the objective were teaching punctuation. Allowing these students to become punctuation marks and to show dramatically how the meaning of a sentence can be altered through the use of punctuation is one way of teaching a literacy skill through bridging from personal strengths to the targeted skill. Another elementary student, talented in music but a laborious reader, confides that he pretends words in the sentence are like notes on a staff: "I just make the words flow."

Bridging involves passing through three points: the initiation, scaffolding, and end points. The *initiation point* involves selecting an activity that draws on intelligences and domains different from the skill area. At the *scaffolding point*, the teacher crafts a learning experience that bridges to the targeted skill. At the *destination point*, students' mastery of the targeted skill is assessed.

Lessons that *finish* rather than *begin* with linguistic or mathematical activities are particularly effective for some students. For example, students whose strengths are in the spatial realm may fare better with writing if allowed to draw a picture first. One teacher tapped into his students' musical intelligence to approach the counterintuitive idea that the larger the denominator, the smaller the value. Students listened for the differences in length between half notes, quarter notes, eighth notes, and so on. They could hear that the half notes were longer than the quarter notes and that both were longer than the eighth notes. From there, the teacher bridged to the mathematical idea that ½ is larger than ¼ (although 2 is smaller than 4), and ¼ is larger than ⅛, and so on. The destination point activity required students to compare fractions and whole numbers on paper and to identify their relative values (and order by value from lowest to highest). More activities around this skill follow as determined by students' performances on the end point activity.

The work of the Bridging pathway involves building cognitive bridges that enhance students' learning processes, including their ability to attend to, organize, understand, and apply the targeted idea or skill. Bridging strategies can effectively engage reluctant students, as well as those students who do not perform well through traditional methods.

When students are encouraged to use alternative intelligences to master basic skills, they have more opportunities for success. In turn, these successes result in improving students' academic self-efficacy, or confidence in themselves as learners (Bandura, 1986). This more positive self-perception motivates students to exert more effort in areas that are more problematic for them.

Bridging Assessment

Because this pathway focuses on using a multiple intelligences approach to engage students in the learning process—especially with regard to promoting student literacy and mastering basic skills—

assessment is twofold. Teachers assess whether the learning objectives were mastered; then, they analyze whether certain kinds of learning experiences produced a positive effect on the components of learning—attention, memory, comprehension, and communication. In both cases, assessment should inform future instruction. The information gleaned should provide clues about how individual students learn and how to structure an environmental context in which all students can be successful.

Steps Along the Bridging Pathway

The major steps in the Bridging pathway are:

- Targeting a literacy or math skill,
- Identifying domains and intelligences for the lesson's initiating activity, and
- Establishing the *bridge points* (initiating activity, scaffolding, and destination point).

The bridge points are defined as follows:

- *Initiating activity*—an activity that is based on a student's strength and is likely to capture her attention and initiate the learning sequence.
- *Scaffolding*—the instructional support provided by the teacher that takes the learner from the initiating activity to the destination point (learning objective). Scaffolding can include questions, prompts, steps, organizers, or discussions that guide the student to mastery of the learning objective.
- *Destination point*—the student's demonstration of his level of mastery of the learning objective for assessment purposes.

Figure 6.1 provides a visual representation of the Bridging pathway.

SNAPSHOT: ONE TEAM'S JOURNEY

The Lincoln Elementary School team members are excited as they start to discuss the Bridging pathway. Having previously read about it, they agree that the Bridging pathway is particularly appropriate for

Figure 6.1. Bridging Pathway Graphic

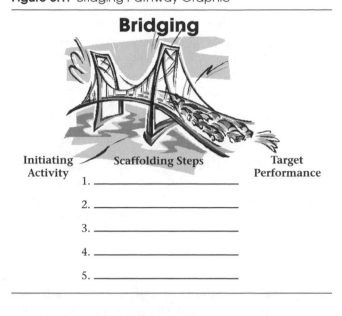

them because the ideas presented can help them to develop new strategies to improve their students' literacy skills.

Bridging I: Starting with a Student's Strengths

Present at the first Bridging pathway meeting are 4th-grade teachers Lillian Vega, David Barnes, and Sandra Edwards. They start the meeting with the question: "How might we use the Bridging pathway?" They center on Chris, having noticed that he is an expert builder. They talk about ways they can use his strength to develop initiating activities in academic areas where he is challenged: reading, oral discussion, and writing. They remark that Chris often seems to be daydreaming during class discussions, rarely appears interested in the topics under discussion, and almost never joins in the discussion.

Sandra suggests that they may be able to incorporate design and engineering activities into the curriculum as an initiating activity to bridge to writing. They brainstorm ways that building activities can bridge to writing. First, they list attributes of building activities and then match them to similar attributes of writing. Their links are shown in Figure 6.2.

The team decides to see what happens if it uses a building activity to bridge to writing procedural narratives. Sandra finds an engineering activity that could

Figure 6.2. Building and Writing Connections

Building Activities	Writing Activities
Buildings need a structure to stand.	Stories have particular structures to "stand" (make sense).
Construction of a building requires specific procedures.	One purpose of writing is a procedural narrative.
Engineering and architecture have particular vocabulary words that describe ideas.	A repertoire of vocabulary words enhances writing.
Buildings can be elaborate and constructed with attention to detail	Descriptive writing requires attention to detail.

be fun for all the students. The students are challenged to build a paper tower—a structure that can support a stack of books—using 20 sheets of paper and one roll of cellophane tape (see Supporting Materials). By allowing all students to participate, the teachers think they can identify other students who could benefit from spatial activities like engineering challenges.

Lillian is hopeful that this activity can be used to improve Chris's ability to write procedural narratives. Although Chris tends not to have ideas for writing, she believes he would be able to analyze the paper structure and elaborate on the elements and procedure used in solving the engineering problem involved. David also remarks that the idea of a structural design in engineering and architecture can be likened to the need for structure in writing. He suggests that Lillian point out to Chris that just as the frame of a building provides its form, so can an outline or web provide the structure for a story.

When Lillian brings the activity to her class, Chris's group builds a structure that holds 20 books—the most of any group. Following the activity, Lillian is pleased to see Chris assume a leadership role in writing the damage report.

> Our structure used four towers of paper. We rolled five sheets of paper in each tower and held the towers together with the tape. The tower held ten books with no problem, but when we added the eleventh, one of the towers started to twist. There was too much torque. The towers were not even and not tight enough. Next time we will roll the paper tighter and make sure the towers are all even. We need to think about where to put the towers so that the books balance better.

Lillian is impressed as Chris gives the report, but asks him to explain one discrepancy: "According to your report the structure supported only 11 books. Is this so?" Chris snatches the report, rereads it, and returns to his seat to correct it. The second version includes the sentence. "As we added books 12–20, the tower really started to lean. It fell at number 21."

Lillian is pleasantly surprised that Chris can express his ideas on paper. She makes sure to compliment the team on their excellent writing. Lillian then takes out an earlier piece of Chris's writing in response to an article about becoming president. That piece consisted of three simple sentences, containing basic vocabulary with no elaboration or evidence of higher level thinking. "If I were President I would make many laws. People would like me and I would get rich. I would be a good president." This had been typical for him. Writing is simply not his strength.

At the next team meeting Lillian and her teammates reflect on the striking difference in Chris's two pieces. They agree that the later piece of writing followed an experience in which Chris was totally engaged. He used his superior spatial and bodily–kinesthetic intelligences to solve the problem. He observed details of the experiment as he analyzed the problem and generated ways to solve it through seeing and doing. The visual and bodily–kinesthetic images Chris gleaned from the activity provided the context for using language and facilitated his ability to find the appropriate words to describe the experience.

The writing about the President had followed a class discussion about an article discussing the President's approval rate. After reading the article, the children discussed why the President would receive a favorable or unfavorable rating. The teacher then asked the students to write about what they would do to get a good rating if they were the President. Chris had never really been engaged with the prewriting exercise, he did not key into the details, and he was not able to generate the appropriate language from the scant information he had stored in his memory.

Reflecting on Chris's Bridging Experience

Chris's success with the engineering activity has led to new respect from his classmates, who now view him as an expert builder. His view of himself as a talented engineer allows him the confidence or self-efficacy to set other goals and develop self-regulation strategies to achieve success in other areas requiring his linguistic intelligence, which is more problematic for him (Baum & Owen, 2003).

By studying those situations where Chris demonstrates effective learning strategies, his teachers begin to note a pattern. Chris seems very different when the activity requires spatial and bodily–kinesthetic intelligences. His talent as an engineer provides evidence that Chris has strong abilities in those areas. These intelligences are also paramount in activities such as video production, which offers students with strong spatial abilities an avenue for visual planning and communication.

We have noted that Chris volunteered to have a speaking role in the social studies video project. Visualizing himself as the actor, Chris used bodily–kinesthetic cues to remember and add meaningful expression to the written lines, a great aid in improving his verbal comprehension. Once his teachers began to understand this pattern, they were able to plan strengths-based activities to improve his skills in language arts.

Planning Backwards from the Target Skill

At a subsequent meeting the team discusses the 4th-grade language arts standards, one of which involves writing persuasive essays. The teachers agree that the students have made progress in creative writing but have not fared very well in formulating reasonable arguments based on their own opinions. The teachers try to think about the standard, using their knowledge of multiple intelligences theory. Which intelligences are relied on to develop a valid argument? They decide that the personal intelligences—intrapersonal and interpersonal—each play an important role. To make a persuasive argument, one must be clear on one's own opinion (intrapersonal) and understand how to articulate it so others will agree (interpersonal).

The team members then ask themselves what domains other than writing require using the personal intelligences in this manner. Lillian suggests that role play and debate rely on the personal intelligences. She asks the group whether they have ever used moral dilemma activities and explains how they require students to form and defend their opinions in a fashion analogous to writing a persuasive essay.

The team decides to brainstorm the connections between writing and role-playing moral dilemma scenarios, as they did with the building and writing activity (see Figure 6.3). When they see the connections between the two, they are convinced that the moral dilemma–persuasive essay bridge is worth crossing. David volunteers to try it out. He promises to share the results at their next meeting.

The Moral Dilemma: To Tell or Not to Tell—The School Break-In. The moral dilemma involves a group of students who break into the school through an open window. One of the students feels it is wrong and immediately climbs back out, while her classmates remain and create havoc within the school. Unfortunately, a neighbor spots the girl leaving and calls the principal. The next day the principal summons the young lady to his office. The dilemma for the students in David's language arts class is to decide whether the girl should accept all the blame or reveal the names of the other students who were involved.

The students brainstorm what they would do. They then divide into groups by similar choices of action. The groups are charged with stating the three best reasons for their choice of action. They are to

Figure 6.3. Persuasive Essay and Moral Dilemma Connections

Persuasive Essay	Moral Dilemma Activity
Identify with issue	Identify with the problem
State your position	State a position
Select reasons for your position	Generate reasons for your position
Provide examples to support your reasons	Critically defend your position
Write the essay	Orally present argument

use these reasons in a convincing way to persuade their classmates to join their group.

One of the students in the class, Yvette, immediately assumes a leadership role. She organizes her group and offers critical feedback about prioritizing its reasons. After each group has shared its responses, the other groups are allowed to challenge the presenting group. Yvette listens attentively and gives thoughtful challenges to the other groups' reasoning. At the end of the reporting, the students are allowed to move to another group if they have changed their position. Many students move into Yvette's group, suggesting she made particularly persuasive arguments.

The next day the group finishes the story based on its position. The day following, each group takes another group's scenario and writes an ending. Finally, the students write individual essays about loyalty in friendship.

Reflecting on Yvette's Bridging Experience

David is especially pleased with the results of the activity. Most of the students have performed better than usual in their writing. He is most surprised with Yvette's response. She is usually a quiet student who rarely speaks up in class. Indeed, language arts is not her best subject, and when she finds an assignment difficult, she seldom completes it.

During this activity, another side of Yvette emerged. She assumed a leadership position, offered her opinion, and organized her group verbally. In addition, her essay was a great improvement over earlier assignments. She was able to organize her ideas and give good examples.

David shares Yvette's essay with the team, and together they compare it with one of her earlier pieces of writing. They can see the differences between her previous writing and the essay that resulted from purposeful bridging. Below are excerpts from both.

What Is the Best Kind of Pet?

The best kind of pet is a dog. I have a dog named Sausage and I play with him a lot. He licks my face. My mother used to have a dog when she was little. That dog's name was José. Dogs have funny names. Here are the names of

some dogs I know—Champ, Gus, Lucky, Fluffy, and Blackie.

Everyone should have a dog because dogs are fun. I think dogs make the best pets. There are many kinds of dogs. I saw the movie *Benji*. It was about a dog. You should buy one.

What It Means to Be a Friend

Friendship is very special. It can mean different things to different people. To have a friend, you need to be a friend. In my opinion, a friend should be someone who is honest, tries to be there when you need her, and likes to have fun. This essay will tell you about these three things.

First, I think to be a friend you need to tell the truth. Sometimes that is hard because your friend may not like to hear it. Once my best friend wanted to go to the movies and her parents told her that she could not go that day. She wanted to tell them she was at my house when she was really at the movies. I told her that I would not lie for her because her parents would not trust me anymore. At first she was angry with me, but then she said I was right.

The team comments that Yvette did not make any logical arguments in the pet story, but the friendship essay has specific arguments with supporting information. They agree that the moral dilemma activity provided a structure for Yvette and others to state their arguments and reasons clearly. And in Yvette's case, the activity tapped into her strengths in intrapersonal and interpersonal intelligences. After thinking about it, David admits that he should not have been surprised that Yvette responded so well to this activity. "During social studies," he comments, "Yvette can be different. She seems to have a wealth of knowledge on world issues such as hunger, child abuse, and pollution. During current events discussion, she often speaks out dramatically and passionately about social issues and how people need to care about other people. She demonstrates strengths in the personal intelligences there."

David remarks that several other students also produced better essays than usual. Upon reflection, he notes that these students regularly state their opinions during class discussions and are often determined to persuade others of their point of view. He hypothesizes that students who have strengths in both interpersonal and intrapersonal intelligences benefit by writing from a personal perspective.

The team agrees that using moral dilemmas helped all the students to form an opinion and support it—skills required in developing a persuasive essay. Students were thus able to transfer these skills from their oral arguments to their written essays. These positive results motivate the team to expand their use of bridge points to connect students' strengths to their challenge areas. Subsequently, they offer their students activities that tap into different intelligences and that address writing objectives.

PUTTING THE BRIDGING PATHWAY INTO ACTION

In the previous section, we described two ways in which you can approach this pathway. The first focuses on adapting the activity for a specific student whose particular profile of intelligences calls for alternative methods (as in the example of Chris). The second approach homes in on the learning objective itself and involves crossing into other domains or intelligences to introduce the skill area (as in the persuasive essay example).

Features of the Bridging Pathway

The major features of the Bridging pathway are:

- Targeting a literacy or math skill,
- Identifying domains and intelligences for the lesson's initiating activity, and
- Establishing the *bridge points* (initiating activity, scaffolding, and destination point).

Targeting the Skill. Bridging begins with identifying the specific skill to be addressed in the lesson. For example, if you are working on essay or story writing in your classroom, then you might identify paragraph writing as the target skill. The Lincoln Elementary team decided to target a skill that was particularly challenging for at least one student, Chris:

procedural narrative and elaboration. They also chose persuasive essay writing as a target skill, a challenging task for many of the students.

Identifying Domains and Intelligences for the Initiating Activity. This step varies according to whether you are starting with a student's intelligence strengths or with intelligences underlying the targeted skill.

Starting with Student Strengths. Identify the student strength area you will use in the initiating activity. Lillian Vega knew building was Chris's strength. She had observed him as a self-regulated, confident learner when he was building, traits absent when he was given a writing assignment. She knew that she needed to find a way to create a bridge for Chris between building and writing.

Starting with the Target Skill. In this case, the initiating activity is one that engages the target skill (or an analogous skill) through a domain distinctive from the skill's originating domain or subject area (language arts, math, etc.). Consider the skill of writing a paragraph, which involves the organization and sequencing of information. In thinking about what other domains organize and sequence information, photo journalism, filmmaking, and dance come to mind.

Establishing the Bridge Points. Once you have chosen the target skill and the approach you will take—student strength or skill—you are ready to begin building the bridge.

The Initiating Activity. How you choose or develop the initiating activity depends on whether you are starting with student strength or the skill area, as described above. In the first case, you start by identifying an activity that taps into the student's strength(s) and then identify common elements between the strength area and the targeted skill. Because Chris was a builder, the Lincoln Elementary School team sought connections between building a structure and writing. They saw many similarities or ways to connect the two processes, as shown previously in Figure 6.2. They chose the paper tower activity as the initiating activity to bridge to writing procedural narratives.

When starting with the target skill, the initiating activity should use the same elements as the target skill, but from the perspective of a different domain. The initiating activity is likely to tap into different intelligences as well. In the case of paragraph writing, for example, its basic elements of organization and sequence can be addressed through storyboarding, a technique used by filmmakers to organize a film scene by scene. Storyboarding relies on spatial intelligence and appeals to students who have difficulties finding the right words.

Through scaffolding, the teacher will point out that the process is analogous to the skill used in the domain of the initiating activity and can be applied to the targeted skill. This is how David used the moral dilemma activity to teach the writing of a persuasive essay. He understood that both activities involved stating a position and defending the position by citing arguments and examples. The role-playing aspect of the moral dilemma teaches the skill using drama and reasoning.

In short, using the Bridging pathway from a target-skill focus requires viewing literacy and numeracy skills from a multiple intelligences perspective. You must ask yourself what intelligences the skill evokes or requires, and where else those skills are tapped. Again, you will need to consider initiating activities that don't require mainly linguistic or logical–mathematical content. Integrating authentic activities from different disciplines, such as the visual and performing arts or architecture and engineering, is a reasonable starting point.

There are many instructional strategies that use alternative intelligences and represent a variety of domains. Figure 6.4 provides examples of instructional strategies that can be used as initiating activities. They include dramatic movement, improvisation, storyboarding, and deductive reasoning (See Supporting Materials for complete descriptions of the activities listed and for additional domain-specific activities.)

Scaffolding the Target Skill. Once students have been introduced to the elements through the initiating activity, they need to be carefully scaffolded to use the skill in the target domain. Scaffolding describes the structure the teacher provides, such as questioning, coaching, corroborating, and providing examples that support students' understanding of a concept or completion of a task (Wood, Bruner, & Ross, 1976).

Figure 6.4. MI-Based Initiating Strategies

Instructional Strategy	Intelligences Tapped	Example
Movement and writing	Bodily–kinesthetic	Bilingual 1st graders move to song "Monster Mash." Their monster movements generate descriptive vocabulary in English to use in writing.
Character interviews	Bodily–kinesthetic, Interpersonal, Intrapersonal	Sixth graders use improvisational techniques to develop characters for a story they are writing.
Story-boarding	Spatial	Fifth graders develop visual stories to improve their writing. They use storyboarding, filmmakers' techniques to organize and focus their ideas, and topic sentences and paragraphs.
Logic puzzles	Logical–mathematical	Third graders use a deductive reasoning puzzle to improve reading comprehension.
Music and graphing	Musical, Bodily–kinesthetic	Fourth graders practice writing music to learn and understand graphing.
Movement exercises	Bodily–kinesthetic, Spatial	Fourth graders develop their use of imagery and metaphors in writing poetry through movement exercises.

Lillian's scaffolding for Chris included providing a format for writing a procedural narrative using his building strength. She provided specific steps to guide his thinking: design and build the structure (initiating activity), draw a sketch of the model, test the model, analyze what went wrong to make the structure fall, and write a damage report (destination point). The damage report used similar cues: explain why you decided to build the tower as you did, describe what it looks like (using the sketch as an organizer), list the problems encountered, and conclude with suggestions for improving the structure. The vocabulary and ideas for the writing come out of the building experience and the accompanying discussion.

In a similar fashion, David's students learned to structure their arguments within a role-playing situation. The structure of the moral dilemma activity taught the youngsters how to present an argument. Once the skill had been learned in this context, David carefully scaffolded the process to apply the thinking to creating a piece of writing.

Creating the Destination Point. The destination point has students using the identified target skill (in our two examples-writing procedural narratives and persuasive essays). In the case of Chris, the writing skills were assessed through his damage report. This assignment not only required the use of a procedural narrative, but also tapped into his ability to analyze and elaborate on his ideas. Lillian assessed Chris's attention to detail and his explanation of the procedure to gauge his mastery and to assess what follow-up activities would be needed.

Guiding Your Journey

The Bridging Pathway Guide and the Bridging Pathway Organizer accommodate both approaches to this pathway: focus on skill or student. The Bridging Pathway Guide, shown in Figure 6.5, "guides" your development of Bridging strategies. It lists the Bridging features and includes additional questions to prompt your thinking. The Bridging Pathway Organizer lists the major questions and provides space for you to take notes and organize your ideas. Two completed organizers are presented in Figure 6.6 and Figure 6.7. The first shows how the Lincoln Elementary team designed the writing lesson for Chris. The second shows the team's outline for the persuasive writing procedure. A blank organizer appears in the Supporting Materials section of this chapter.

THOUGHT QUESTIONS AND ACTIVITIES

This section will allow you to gain a more in-depth understanding of the ideas presented in the Bridging pathway. Before moving on to the next pathway, try reflecting on the open-ended prompts offered below. You also will find additional activities to try with your colleagues or students. Conducting the activities and discussing what you observe will make the ideas within this chapter more meaningful for you. Last, review the materials included at the end of the section as they provide the forms and directions needed for activities mentioned earlier in the chapter, as well as for the activities listed here.

Thought Questions

- How do you think using MI theory can influence student motivation?
- There has been a drastic increase in the number of students identified as having an attention deficit disorder. In most cases, the disorder is manifested when these students are asked to listen, read, or write. Can MI theory help generate hypotheses about why this may be? What reasons can you give that might account for this phenomenon?
- How do you think using a multiple intelligences approach in the classroom can help to decrease behavior problems?
- The September 1995 issue of *Educational Leadership* featured the theme of strengthening student engagement. A persistent idea throughout the journal is described as follows: "Students who are engaged persist, despite challenges and obstacles, and take visible delight in accomplishing their work" (Strong, Silver, & Robinson, 1995, p.8). How do the ideas presented in the Bridging pathway help to realize this vision?

Implementation Activities

Activity 1. Using the completed Bridging Pathway Organizer in Figure 6.7, complete the blank Bridging Pathway Organizer (Figure 6.8 in the Supporting Materials section) for particular students of yours who may be having difficulty in mastering a skill targeted in the curriculum. First, identify their profiles of intelligences, and then develop strategies using those intelligences as initial activities for bridging purposes.

Activity 2. Using the "skill focus" section of the Bridging Pathway Guide (Figure 6.5), develop a lesson focusing on alternative entry points that connect to the target skill from your mathematics or language arts curriculum.

Activity 3. Implement your student plan with one youngster or the whole class and discuss with

Figure 6.5. Bridging Pathway Guide

Bridging Features	Things to Think About
Targeting the Skill *Which skill am I focusing on for this bridging experience?*	• Why have I chosen this skill? • Does it align with the literacy or math standards or outcomes for my grade level? • Am I aware of benchmarks that will help assess performance?
Selecting the Approach Student Perspective Approach: *Which student do I feel can benefit from the Bridging pathway and what are his or her strenghts?*	• When have I seen this student at his or her personal best? Which intelligences underlie those examples?
Skill Perspective Approach: *Which skill or skills can be taught more effectively using the Bridging pathway? What are the MI elements of the skill?*	• Why have I chosen this skill? • Think about the attributes of the skill and their relationship to multiple intelligences. (See Figures 6.1 and 6.2.)
Creating Bridge Points  1. Initiating Activity	• Which activity would align with the student's strengths? How can this activity be bridged to the targeted skill? • List attributes of the activity and see how it relates to the targeted skill and to the student's strengths.
2. Scaffolding	• What are the steps I will take to link the elements of the initiating experience to the targeted skill?
3. Destination Point	• How will I assess mastery or performance? • How will I use the student's performance to inform my instruction and next steps? • Will I need to develop an assessment rubric or outline benchmarks?

Figure 6.6. Sample Completed Bridging Pathway Organizer (Student Focus)

Bridging Lesson	Writing

Targeting the Skill *Which skill am I focusing on for this bridging experience?*	Narrative procedure and descriptive writing

Selecting the Approach

Student Perspective Approach: *Which student do I feel can benefit from the Bridging pathway and what are his or her strenghts?*	Chris and other students with building talents (spatial and bodily–kinesthetic intelligences)
Skill Perspective Approach: *Which skill or skills can be taught more effectively using the Bridging pathway? What are the MI elements of the skill?*	Building–Writing connections: Both building and writing need strong foundations. There is structure in architecture and a structure to a story. Both are enhanced by elaboration.

Creating Bridge Points 1. Initiating Activity 	*Implement building activity:* • Divide class into engineering teams. • Give students materials and directions. • Have them draw structure before testing its strength. • Students prepare a damage report.
2. Scaffolding	*Have students:* • Describe the structure. (Look at the picture.) • Tell what happend during testing. • Hypothesize on structural problems. • Answer the question: What could you do differently?
3. Destination Point	Check report for verbal fluency, breadth of details, and sequence of ideas. Have students evaluate their writing with me and make changes as necessary.

Figure 6.7. Sample Completed Bridging Pathway Organizer (Skill Focus)

Bridging Lesson	Writing

Targeting the Skill

Which skill am I focusing on for this bridging experience? | Persuasive writing

Selecting the Approach

Student Perspective Approach:

Which student do I feel can benefit from the Bridging pathway and what are his or her strenghts? | Yvette and other students with intra- and interpersonal talents.

Skill Perspective Approach:

Which skill or skills can be taught more effectively using the Bridging pathway? What are the MI elements of the skill? | Using moral dilemmas to teach persuasive arguments. Persuasion requires inter- and intrapersonal intelligences. You need to know your opinion and be able to convince others.

Creating Bridge Points

1. Initiating Activity | Present dilemma: "To Tell or Not to Tell."

2. Scaffolding

- Have students brainstorm options for resolving dilemma.

- Divide students into groups according to similar choices of action.

- Each group states the three best reasons for its choice of action.

- Each group presents its argument to the other groups to persuade them to its action.

- Each group can question the presentations, citing its own reasons.

3. Destination Point | Have students create an essay on an opinion backed by specific reasons. For example, loyalty in friendship, what makes a good friend.

your colleagues what you observed as a result. Address the following:

> *Attention:* To what degree was there a change in the student's ability to focus on the task?
> *Engagement in learning:* To what degree did the student remain actively engaged during the lesson?
> *Skill acquisition:* To what degree did the student show improvement in the targeted area? Was the learning objective accomplished?
> *Student attitude:* Explain any changes in the student's motivation during the activity.
> *Student confidence or self-efficacy:* What student behaviors indicated an increase in student self-efficacy during the lesson?
> *Student self-regulation:* In what ways did the student seem to be taking charge of his or her own learning?

Activity 4. Members of your study group may each select a resource to review from those listed at the end of the next section. Each of the resources describes an approach and offers instructional strategies that engage particular sets of intelligences. When you report to the group, you might want to describe the resource, explain how it could relate to your curriculum, and provide a demonstration lesson to teach others in the group how to use the ideas it presents. Perhaps the group can identify other resources to share in like manner.

SUPPORTING MATERIALS

This section includes materials needed to implement the activities within the chapter. Figure 6.8 is a blank Bridging Pathway Organizer. You also will find additional Bridging activities for your consideration and understanding.

Bridging Activity Materials

Following are directions for two activities described in the chapter: the paper tower and the moral dilemma.

Paper Tower Activity

Objective: To build a paper structure that can support a stack of books. (Using several sets of encyclopedias is a simple way to test the structures.)

Materials: 20 sheets of 8½ × 11 paper (copy paper works well). One roll of scotch tape.

Directions: Divide the class into engineering teams consisting of 4–6 students. Each team must design a structure that will support a stack of books. The structure must be 11 inches high and not exceed a base of 8½ × 11 inches. Allow at least a half hour for the teams to construct their towers. Each team then can test its structure to see how many books it will hold. Before testing, the students sketch their design for future reference. Team members observe what happens to the structure as each book is added. When the structure finally topples, the team hypothesizes what was wrong with the structure and how they might rebuild the structure to make it stronger. This information then is written as a damage report.

Moral Dilemma Activity

Objective: To have students use critical and creative thinking to make decisions and convince others of their opinion.

Materials: Moral dilemma, paper, pencil, markers.

Directions: This activity takes place over five class periods.

Day 1: Present the following dilemma to the class:

> Students broke into the school during the summer. One of the girls felt it was wrong and left. She was seen leaving the scene by a woman who lived next door. The woman informed the authorities, who confronted the young lady. To complicate the situation, the others caused damage after the girl left. The authorities accused the girl and asked her who else was involved. What should she do? Should she inform the authorities about the other girls who were with her?

Figure 6.8. Bridging Pathway Organizer (blank)

Bridging Lesson

Targeting the Skill

> *Which skill am I focusing on for this bridging experience?*

Selecting the Approach

Student Perspective Approach:

> *Which student do I feel can benefit from the Bridging pathway and what are his or her strenghts?*

Skill Perspective Approach:

> *Which skill or skills can be taught more effectively using the Bridging pathway? What are the MI elements of the skill?*

Creating Bridge Points

1. Initiating Activity

2. Scaffolding

3. Destination Point

Have the class brainstorm solutions to the dilemma and divide students into several groups by the solution chosen.

Day 2: Have each individual within a group develop reasons for his or her position. After members of the group share their arguments with one another, have the group decide on the three most compelling arguments to present. Have each group present its three most compelling arguments to the class. Field two questions per argument by the rest of the class. Ask students to change groups if they are convinced to take another position.

Day 3: Instruct each group to finish the story based on its solution.

Day 4: Have all students write a persuasive essay on what makes a good friend. Have them recall how they developed the arguments in their groups. Ask them to remember how they supported their argument and how they decided on the most compelling ideas. Discuss the essay format and how reasons must be supported. Bridge to the dilemma activity.

Day 5: Students prepare a final draft of the essay.

Additional Examples of the Bridging Pathway

These examples further illustrate the use of the Bridging pathway. The first activity, Monster Mash, uses music and movement to generate language and descriptive writing. The second employs drama and improvisation techniques as bridges to character development and analysis. The third activity presents the strategy of storyboarding as an organizational strategy for writing. This technique is particularly helpful for students who are spatial thinkers.

The Monster Mash

Skill: Descriptive writing by expanding vocabulary.

Target Audience: Children who use English as their second language.

Initiation Point: Movement (bodily–kinesthetic intelligence).

Description: This lesson was implemented by two 1st-grade teachers in an elementary school where most of the students were at risk in reading and writing. The teachers were concerned about their students' poor fluency with language and their inability to write descriptive information. Because many of these 1st graders were "active children," the teachers used movement as a strategy to teach writing.

The movement activity asked the students to become monsters. The lesson began with a warm-up activity where these 1st graders brainstormed what kind of people used movement in their careers. Their list included dancers, doctors, football players, builders, and so forth. In each case, a child was asked to pantomime the movement. The students were reminded that wild, silly movements were inappropriate for a professional. In fact, if a basketball player kept sliding along on the floor, he probably would be asked to leave the team. (When using movement activities, it is important to provide a structure. Children may tend to be wild or silly when asked to participate in a movement activity if they have not been asked previously to move creatively.)

The next activity required the students to become a monster and move to the song "Monster Mash." The students formed a circle and one at a time could volunteer to perform in the center, while the remainder of the children copied the student's movement. This gave the teacher an opportunity to identify those students who had purposeful and creative movement representations. Those students then became model monsters, and the others copied the movement. Finally, the teachers selected the most convincing monster as the model for the writing activity. The "target monster" performed her movements again, and students brainstormed words to describe the monster.

Scaffolding Bridge Point. The teachers scaffolded the experience by asking questions such as: How is the monster moving? What kind of steps is she taking? What is her personality? Is she making any noise? All the words and phrases students gave as answers were listed on the board. The next task was to incorporate all the words into a class story.

Destination Point. The teachers provided the writing purpose—an article for the newspaper about the monster seen at their school. The teachers would provide transitions as needed. Two stories are shown below.

> A ferocious monster was seen near our school. It looked scary and mean. It marched along by kicking out its long legs and stomping loudly. Its head and arms were wiggling all over. The monster had frog fingers that looked like worms. When the monster saw us coming with a big net, it ran away. If you see it, call us at 911 and ask for Monster Busters.

> We saw a monster near our school. It was scaring everybody. It stomped along quietly as it sneaked up on people just like a tiger. When it decided to scare someone, it stretched out its hairy arms and tickled the person in the stomach. At the same time, it made a loud growl like a gorilla. We are warning you to beware of the Tickle Monster.

Results. In both these cases, the teachers revealed that the model monster was the worst-behaved child in the class. The teachers also commented on how differently these students—who usually don't attend or produce very much—behaved during the activity. Not only did they have outstanding movement representations, but they also listened and provided critical feedback during the writing activity. For instance, in the first story, the class wanted to say that the monster marched along. The "actor" replied that he didn't think he was marching and demonstrated again exactly what he did. He then explained that it was a special kind of march where you kick out your legs. The class agreed to add his comment. The teachers also commented on the children's ability to read the words from the brainstormed list and again when used in the context of the story.

Character Interviews

Skill: Descriptive writing by expanding vocabulary.

Target Audience: Children who use English as their second language.

Initiation Point: Improvisation. This lesson uses the personal and bodily–kinesthetic intelligences as entry points to help students invent characters and think about the dimensions that make up complex characters in preparation for writing narrative accounts. The personal and bodily–kinesthetic intelligences predominate because "players" are acting out parts, rather than simply questioning and describing the attitudes and interests of their "characters."

Description: A teacher in a 6th-grade classroom used improvisation as an initiation point for creating complex characters as an element of narrative writing. The "character interview" also can be adapted to lessons in response to literature in order to deepen understanding of characters in literature.

Procedure: This is a chance for students to give their imaginations a workout. There can be no wrong answers. In this activity you'll see how perceptive students can be about why people think and act the way they do.

Model an interview with a student volunteer. You should take the role of the character and, if necessary, rehearse with the student volunteer before class. After this demonstration the students will take their turn, with the following directions:

1. Pair off. Decide who will be Interviewer and who will be Interviewee.
2. Each "character" to be interviewed is given a name, a job (it may be unusual), and an attitude toward life.
3. To start off, the "Interviewee" appears to be "doing something" in connection with his or her job. The "Interviewer" asks open-ended questions and "goes along" with the answers. Questions, which draw the character out, are usually around his or her likes and dislikes, family situation, work, and so forth. The goal is to offer as much detail as possible about the objective and subjective reality of the character, which in turn will generate good material for a writing exercise as well as insights into complex characters in fiction.

Sample Interview: (Interviewee is a famous expert on whales who has a nasty personality.)

Interviewer: Hello, you must be J. Whitaker, world renowned expert on whales.

Interviewee: Yes, why do you want to know? Can't you see I am busy?

Interviewer: Yes, but my viewers are fascinated about your work and would like to know more about it.

Interviewee: Let them read my book.

Interviewer: What is the name of your book? (etc.)

4. Repeat the process, switching roles from "Interviewer" to "Interviewee."

5. When the activity is over, discuss the following questions: What did you like about this activity? Did you have a preference for the role of Interviewer or the role of Interviewee? What did you dislike? Did you learn something about yourself in this activity?

Scaffolding Bridge Point. Ask students what they learned about their character. Brainstorm the kinds of questions they would have if they really wanted to get to know their character. List these questions on the board. Have children choose a character (job and attitude toward life) and use the questions to write about the character.

Destination Point. Have students start writing at the count of three. The writing piece becomes the first draft of a character description.

Storyboarding as a Bridge Point to Writing

Skill: Organizing and writing a story using more elaboration.

Target Audience: Children who had difficulty organizing their stories and adding details to the plot.

Initiation Point: Using pictures (spatial intelligence).

Description: A 5th-grade teacher noticed that her students were highly motivated when she introduced them to storyboarding. She decided to seize the moment and use the activity to organize their ideas into a written script. She could use this as an opportunity to teach her students how to use quotations and punctuation—goals in her language arts curriculum. She was especially interested in discovering how the students who developed interesting storyboards, but whose language skills were poor, would respond to the activity.

Scaffolding Bridge Point. The teacher scaffolded the experience by having the students talk about each frame of their storyboards and what its purpose was—the setting, motivation, what caused the problem, the effect of the problem, and the conclusion. They developed a frame a day. They first brainstormed words and phrases that described the frame. Sometimes they became the character and improvised conversation. They revised their writing by having the scene acted out according to their individual script.

Destination Point: The teacher was so impressed by several of the students' stories that she allowed them to be produced into videos. For each story chosen, the teacher established a film company comprising actors, set designers, camera experts, and the director. Six storyboards were selected, and the students who had their storyboards chosen became the directors of the film companies. Each company produced and directed its own movie. The students worked cooperatively, adding rich language to develop the storyboard into a production. Interestingly, the artist-directors took an active role in word selection and idea development. After all, it was their stories being told.

FOR FURTHER STUDY

_____(1982). *Photo search.* Kilder, IL: Learning Seed.
A kit with slides and posters depicting historical events. Two high-quality research questions accompany each photo. Excellent entry point for a particular period of history or a unit on research skills and sources. Grade level: 3–12.

Baum, S., Owen, S., & Oreck, B. (1997). Transferring individual self-regulation processes from arts to academics. *Arts Education Policy Review, 98,* 32–39.
This article will describe how using students' strengths can help them become more self-regulated and how these skills can transfer to other areas.

Chen, J., Krechevsky, M., & Viens, J. (with Isberg, E.). (1998). *Building on children's strengths: The experiences of Project Spectrum* (Vol. 1 in *Project Zero Frameworks for*

Early Childhood Education, H. Gardner, D. H. Feldman, & M. Krechevsky, eds.). New York: Teachers College Press.

This book describes an early childhood program where students' learning behaviors improved when the students were involved with strength-based activities.

Dunn, S., & Larson, R. (1990). *Design technology: Children's engineering.* Philadelphia: Falmer Press.

Williams, P., & Jinks, D. (1985). *Design and technology, 5–12.* Philadelphia: Falmer Press.

Both of the above provide ideas for integrating engineering projects into the curriculum, and demonstrate writing activities that can result when students design and build products. Intended for use with students 5–12 years of age.

Herman, G. (1986). *Storytelling: A triad in the arts.* Mansfield Center, CT: Creative Learning Press.

Teacher guide to introduce students to art and literature through storytelling. Students learn not only how to tell stories with the spoken word, but also how to use music, movement, and audience participation to add a new dimension. Designed to help students improve their artistic talents as well as their cognitive skills. Activities are appropriate for K–12 students.

Joyce, B., & Weil, M. (1996). *Models of teaching* (5th ed.). Boston: Allyn & Bacon.

A college-level text that is a handbook of useful instructional strategies. Most engage students in a problem-solving approach and allow for the expression of linguistic intelligence. Contains an excellent chapter on simulations.

Lipson, G. B., & Morrison, B. (1996). *Fact, fantasy, and folklore.* Carthage, IL: Good Apple Inc.

Provides teachers with moral dilemmas, simulations, and role-playing activities based on well-known fairy tales and fables. (Hansel and Gretel are put on trial for harassing a senior citizen, a town meeting is held to determine whether the Pied Piper of Hamlin is justified in taking children as compensation.) Excellent entry points for most students and especially motivating for students with strengths in personal intelligences and talent in drama. Appropriate for students in grades 5–8, but can be adapted for younger and older students.

Polland, J. (1985). *Building toothpick bridges (Math Projects Series): Grades 5–8.* Palo Alto, CA: Dale Seymour.

An engineering and accounting simulation in which a company (5 or 6 students) must build a bridge that bears a required load, within a given budget. An excellent entry point to a unit on money, geometry, and/or architecture. Writing can be integrated by setting up correspondence and record-keeping activities. Grade level 5–8.

Project WILD, a joint project of the Western Association of Fish and Wildlife Agencies (WAFWA) and the Western Regional Environmental Education Council, Inc. (WREEC). [Copyright © 2005, 2004, 2003, 2002, 1992, 1985, and 1983 by the Council for Environmental Education.]

An interdisciplinary environmental education program used by teachers of kindergarten through secondary-age students across the United States and Canada. Emphasizes our relationship to wildlife and, through the variety of teacher-tested activities, encourages students to analyze their responsibility to the ecosystem. Includes valuable background information for educators who may be unfamiliar with particular wildlife issues. Contains specific procedures for classroom use, most of which use readily available materials, and lists of valuable resources. Check with your state's department of environmental protection or fish and game office for information on Project WILD training in your area.

Reid, L. (1990). *Thinking skills resource book.* Mansfield Center, CT: Creative Learning Press.

A wonderful book with the premise that every teacher should be a teacher of thinking. Briefly describes 14 creative thinking skills and 30 critical thinking skills. Content-based independent practice activities for each skill. Grade level: K–12.

Thompson, R. (1989). *Draw and tell.* Willowdale, ON: Firefly Books.

One in a series of books that involve visual problem solving as part of the storytelling process. Students at the elementary level improve skills in listening and sequencing as they try to solve the mystery being related.

Treat, L. (1991). *You're the detective.* Boston: D.R. Godine.

One in a series of mini-mysteries. A picture containing some clues is provided for each mystery, and students use their logical–mathematical and spatial intelligences to problem solve. Contains excellent entry points for improving reading comprehension and models for students' use in writing their own picto-mysteries.

Another resource is Interact Publishing Company, which provides simulations across content areas for grades K–12. Write to

Interact Simulations
P.O. Box 997-590
Lakeside, CA 92040

CHAPTER 7

The Understanding Pathway

The Understanding pathway focuses on supporting students' understanding of the topics and concepts that make up the academic curriculum. MI theory is used as a framework to create and identify learning experiences that engage students in the academic content they must learn, invite students to explore unfamiliar ideas or disciplines in their areas of strength or comfort zones, and allow them to understand the subject matter in multifaceted and complex ways.

Understanding means taking knowledge and using it in novel ways and in new contexts. Understanding involves the ability to tap into more than one symbol system to conceptualize and solve problems and to demonstrate one's learning in more than one way. Effective and productive thinkers are able to employ different symbol systems or mental representations to conceptualize and solve problems. For example, James Watson and Francis Crick developed their intuitive (but incomplete) notion of the complex structure of DNA by interacting with a three-dimensional model, a means of problem solving outside the (mathematical) forms of mental representation generally accepted in their field. Watson (1968) explains:

> Only a little encouragement was needed to get the final soldering accomplished in the next couple of hours. The brightly shining metal plates were then immediately used to make a model in which for the first time all the DNA components were present. In about an hour I had arranged the atoms in positions which satisfied both the x-ray data and the laws of stereochemistry. The resulting helix was right handed with the two chains running in opposite directions. (p. 200)

Exploring a topic deeply so that students develop complete understandings contradicts the familiar pressure to "cover" a broad curriculum. Such in-depth exploration requires that we spend more time on fewer essential topics, ideas, and questions with which students become very involved and familiar. The Understanding pathway engages MI theory toward that end.

PATHWAY BACKGROUND

Gardner (1999a) suggests three important reasons for using an MI approach in planning curriculum and assessment for understanding: (1) individuals do not all learn in the same way, *so more individuals are reached*; (2) when they discover that they are able to represent specific content in more than one way, *students learn what it feels like to be an expert*; and (3) because understanding also can be demonstrated in more than one way, *students can display their new understandings—and misunderstandings—in ways that are comfortable for them and accessible to others.* The Understanding pathway uses Gardner's notion of entry points and exit points to guide the development of learning experiences that either promote or allow for the expression of in-depth understanding of concepts.

Using Entry Points

In the Bridging pathway, intelligences are used to create "bridge points" that connect students' strengths to literacy skills. In the Understanding pathway, Gardner's entry points provide teachers with an approach for creating multiple ways into a topic or unit. The entry points correspond only roughly to the intelligences, as they depict how the intelligences are combined and used in the real world.

With a variety of entry points available, all students, regardless of their unique blends of intelligences, experiences, and interests, can find ways to become involved with the topic and to study it from multiple perspectives (Hetland, 1998). If a topic is a room, then the entry points are many doors into the room. Giving students multiple ways to approach a topic increases the likelihood that they will be more motivated and involved in the topic—a key feature in developing understanding. At the same time, deepening their understanding through entry points supports learning success for all students. Students vary as to which entry points are most appropriate for them and which routes are most comfortable for them to follow once they have gained initial access to the "room." Awareness of these entry points can help the teacher introduce new material in ways that can be grasped easily by many students. As students explore the topic through other entry points, they have the chance to develop multiple perspectives central to genuine understanding of the topic.

Gardner explains that almost all topics have intriguing aspects that can be approached through narrative, quantitative/numerical, logical, existential, aesthetic, experiential, and social entry points (see Figure 7.1).

Figure 7.1. Gardner's Entry Points Defined

The *narrative* entry point uses a story or narrative about the concept in question and engages learners in narrative experiences.

The *quantitative/numerical* entry point invokes numerical aspects of a topic and approaches the concept through numerical considerations.

The *logical* entry point examines the logical relationships and implications of a topic and applies deductive reasoning processes.

The *foundational or existential* entry point emphasizes the philosophical and terminological aspects of the concept and focuses on life's "big questions."

The *aesthetic* entry point emphasizes sensory or surface features of the topic and involves using learning strategies that appeal to learners who favor an artistic stance.

The *experiential or hands-on* entry point approaches the hands-on aspects of a topic and involves concrete experimentation, enactment, and making products.

The *social* entry point examines the social experiences involved in the topic and uses collaborative and introspective approaches to learning experiences.

While both MI theory and the entry point approach concern the process of learning, MI theory describes different aspects of those who do the learning, while entry points describe different aspects of what is being learned. MI theory and entry points coincide at the place where the learner "meets" the content to be learned. The entry points are used to engage a range of intelligences and to tap into students' particular strengths or profiles of intelligences. Figure 7.2 provides examples of learning experiences derived from each of the entry points across two topics: light, a science topic, and the Holocaust, a social studies topic.

In similar fashion to Watson and Crick's work with a three-dimensional model of DNA, students can draw or construct models (experiential, aesthetic entry points), represent ideas with their bodies or through movement (experiential, logical entry points), and hear the stories of great scientists (narrative entry point) to support their developing understanding of a scientific concept, like DNA, molecular bonding, why there are seasons, or how neurons deliver information across synapses.

Gardner also offers the use of "telling analogies" as a more focused strategy to create understanding-centered entry point activities. Analogies that convey important aspects of a new topic are drawn from material students already understand. For example, in the case of introducing the concept of balance of nature, analogies can be found in the playground using a seesaw or balance beam as examples.

In one 5th-grade classroom, students studied the power of the ocean as both a constructive and destructive force. They worked in small groups to dramatize, sketch, and, eventually, develop narrative analogies to the power of the ocean. Of note, the curriculum and instruction were in English, a second language for most of the students in this African international school. "Mr. Pacific," one poem written by a small group of students and shown in Figure 7.3, demonstrates their exploration and developing understanding of metaphorical language and of the power of the ocean.

Understanding Assessments: Exit Points

Assessment in the Understanding pathway is focused on students' developing understandings.

Figure 7.2. Gardner's Entry Point Examples

Entry Point	Topic: Light	Topic: Holocaust
Narrative Involves stories, change over time, turning points, people's lives, myths, legends, development.	The story of the invention of the light bulb.	Read *Diary of Anne Frank* and other stories by youth set in the Holocaust. Keep a journal as a child during the Holocaust.
Quantitative/Numerical Quantitative methods, quantities, numbers and numerical relations, patterns, size, ratio, change, scope.	Measure brightness of light.	Studies of war casualties or survival rates, organized by population (Jews, gypsies, others) or location (country, region, camp).
Logical Logical propositions, relationships, and implications. Applies logical reasoning (arguments for and against, deductions, inferences, assumptions).	Compare reflective indices of different materials.	Work with moral dilemmas. Conduct debates. Have students conduct web searches.
Foundational or Existential Philosophical aspects of the topic, fundamental questions about existence.	The use of light in religious ritual.	Study of human nature, mass mentality, "How could this happen?"
Aesthetic Aesthetic aspects of the topic. Appreciation of the topic's properties through beauty, forms, and relationships. Involves expressiveness, balance, organization, color, shading, tone, ambiguity of meaning.	The ways different-colored lighting affects the audience reaction to a scene.	Study art produced during the Holocaust or art that depict relevant historical moments or themes. Study art about or representing the Holocaust: visual art, literature, music.
Experiential or Hands-On Hands-on aspects of the topic, hands-on investigation. Involves concrete experimentation, body movement, product making.	Find a method to bend light; examine the dilation of the pupil when light levels change.	Visit a Holocaust museum or exhibit. Interview a survivor. Make maps. Take a field trip to a historic site.
Social Social experience with others who are involved in the topic. Deals with people's thoughts and feelings; involves collaboration, group projects, human values, introspection.	Work in teams to design a light demonstration to teach others about light.	Role play exercises. Produce a play about an event of the Holocaust or World War II. Discuss real or hypothetical problems and solutions in small groups.

Source: Adapted from Sullivan, 1999. Used by permission of publisher.

Assessing students' understanding means asking (and answering) the question, "To what degree do students demonstrate understanding of the essential questions and ideas of the subject (unit, topic, etc.)?" Gardner has noted that during the elementary years it is especially important that students develop an accurate understanding of concepts, in order to avoid misconceptions that interfere with learning more advanced concepts. Understanding assessments can help teachers identify such misconceptions.

In the Understanding pathway, we develop and use "exit point" activities to assess student understanding. Exit points are products or performances that demonstrate whether and to what extent students can

- Demonstrate their understanding within the target discipline or subject area;
- Represent their understanding using more than one symbol system; and
- Apply their knowledge in a novel way or in a new situation.

Case in Point: Oh Deer! This example illustrates how the entry and exit point approaches can be used in a science unit. The unit is modified from an activity called *Oh Deer!* (Project WILD, 1992). The understanding goals for the unit are to

- Explore the relationship of the components of a habitat and how it influences population dynamics.
- Explain the three essential components of a habitat (food, water, shelter) and their importance to the survival of a species.
- Identify and provide examples of limiting factors to a population's growth.
- Recognize fluctuations in wildlife population as natural.
- Define *carrying capacity* and give examples.

The teacher used two entry points to engage her students in the unit. The first was the experiential entry point. Students became "deer" and components of the habitat as they simulated population dynamics. The simulation covered the changing deer population over the course of 10 years. Each round required the deer to secure elements of the environment they needed. If successful, they brought the element back to their home, and the element became another deer for the next round. As the deer population increased, the habitat became somewhat depleted. Over the course of several rounds, the habitat was no longer able to support the deer population, causing some to die off and become part of the habitat in a subsequent round. In year 5, a mountain lion was introduced as another limiting factor to the deer population. Thus, with a decrease in deer, the environment was able to replenish itself. As a result the deer population was again on the rise. By being the deer, elements of the environment, and the mountain lion, the students lived the idea of population dynamics and their understanding began to develop. They experienced the relationship between population growth and what limits or enhances it.

To further students' understanding, the teacher represented the concept numerically the next day, using a logical–mathematical entry point. The teacher had kept a running record of deer and other elements for each year. Using a chart like the one shown in Figure 7.4, she entered the data for each round. Students looked for patterns and predicted future years' changes based on the data from previous years. The numerical representation of the simulation allowed students to deepen their initial understanding as they saw through the eyes of a mathematician.

Upon completion of these experiences, the students were given reading materials from their science text, explored some websites, and viewed a video documentary of population dynamics in the animal kingdom, thus enriching their understandings of the topic. They also completed journal entries of what they were learning, including the definitions of terms *limiting factors*, *habitat*, *population dynamics*, and *carrying capacity*.

Figure 7.3. Mr. Pacific Poem

Mr. Pacific
by Patrick Bechbache, Gautam Ailani, and Toya Ebulu

My name is Mr. Pacific.
I'm as powerful as a stroke of lightning
I'm as dangerous as a Siberian tiger
My midnight waves recklessly protect the coastline
given to my charge
But I can be playful as well.
My best friends are Mr. and Mrs. Arctic
We meet up north just to create wonderful waves together
Giant peaks capped with white foam.
An artist's dangerous delight.

Figure 7.4. Oh Deer! Data Chart

Annual Record

Year	1	2	3	4	5	6	7	8	9	10	11	12
Deer												
Habitat												
Predator												

The final sessions of the unit were exit point activities designed to assess the students' understandings. Students were given a variety of choices and worked in groups to create products to share with their classmates. The choices, elaborated below, represented the use of disciplinary understandings expressed in the learning goals. The products also required the students to employ a variety of symbol systems to represent these understandings. Additionally, the choices helped students to apply the understandings to novel situations using multiple disciplinary perspectives.

Graphologists: You are working for the Bureau of Environmental Studies and are in charge of documenting the statistics of the deer population for the county. Please use the data in the chart to create line and bar graphs to explain population dynamics, carrying capacity, and limiting factors, including features of the habitat over the past 10 years.

Reporters: You are working for a major environmental organization and need to write an article for their newsletter about the growing deer population and the problems it is causing. Trace the growth from the data in the chart during the years when the population was at its maximum and discuss the issues.

Filmmakers: You are working for a major film studio and have been asked to design a documentary film on animal life. You are to create a storyboard depicting the deer population dynamics during the past 10 years using the data on the class chart. Please make sure your documentary includes information about population dynamics, carrying capacity, and limiting factors, including features of the habitat.

Social activists: You have heard that the town is planning to sell the forestland on the edge of town to developers who are planning to use the land to build a huge shopping mall. Please stage a protest using posters and speeches explaining the issue for the deer population. Include information

about population dynamics and limiting factors.

Science researchers: You are working for the state environmental agency and need to find out about the deer population in your state. Please explore the websites bookmarked for you on our computers and design a fact sheet with the following information: the number of deer in the state, problems caused by the deer population, and the laws that protect or limit the deer population.

By sharing their products, students were able to gain an in-depth understanding of the concepts. Students were given a skeletal rubric to use in evaluating their product before they presented it (see Figure 7.5). Together with their teacher, they generated specific criteria for each level of performance. Developing rubrics together enabled the students to grasp expectations and focus their efforts accordingly. In this way they were able to ensure that their products would be evaluated favorably.

After the presentations were completed, the teacher gave the students a paper-and-pencil test on the topic. The entry and exit points in which the students engaged during the unit prepared them well for the more traditional assessment.

Figure 7.5. Oh Deer! Assessment Rubric

Product Assessment Rubric

Rating	Acceptable	Good	Superior
Quality of product			
Evidence of limiting factors			
Evidence of population dynamics			
Evidence of habitat			
Evidence of carrying capacity			

Case in Point: Uncovering Misunderstandings. Sometimes having students represent their understandings in another symbol system cues us in to their misunderstandings that may not be obvious from traditional paper-and-pencil tasks. The account of Juan, a bilingual 2nd grader in a New York City public elementary school, offers a case in point. As a talented and motivated artist, Juan chose to draw his understanding of a recent lesson about the HIV virus. His drawing, shown in Figure 7.6, illustrates how this understanding assessment surfaced Juan's misconception related to the topic. It also shows how analogies—in this case metaphorical language—can be misinterpreted or confused, highlighting the care and thought with which analogies should be deployed.

Juan drew his understanding of HIV as "germ warfare." His teacher believed his metaphor showed his understanding of HIV cells attacking healthy cells in the body. But the swastikas in the drawing troubled her. Juan explained his drawing: "This is germ warfare and those bad guys are the Germans."

Juan had illustrated his misconception, perhaps caused or exacerbated by the "warfare" metaphor used to describe germs and which he associated with his prior knowledge about the Germans and World War II. Juan's teacher knew she needed to clarify this language before his—and perhaps other students'—misconceptions grew.

Steps Along the Understanding Pathway

Implementing the Understanding pathway involves deploying its three steps:

- Articulating learning goals for the topic, unit, or lesson.
- Developing and planning learning experiences that address the learning goals, using Gardner's entry point approach.

Figure 7.6. Juan's Drawing of "Germ Warfare"

- Assessing students' developing understandings and identifying any misconceptions, using exit point activities.

The steps and how they are put to work in the Understanding pathway are illustrated in Figure 7.7 and described in more detail in the Putting the Understanding Pathway into Action section of this chapter.

SNAPSHOT: ONE TEAM'S JOURNEY

Over the course of several meetings, the Lincoln Elementary School 4th-grade team considers how to better promote students' in-depth understanding of the concepts that are covered in their 4th-grade units. Fourth-grade teachers Lillian Vega, David Barnes, and Sandra Edwards are in attendance, joined by Jan Simon and Paul Evans, the art and music teachers, respectively.

The group focuses on units they are teaching, to determine ways to promote in-depth understanding as described in the Understanding Pathway. Lillian begins the discussion by revisiting the social

Figure 7.7. Understanding Pathway Graphic

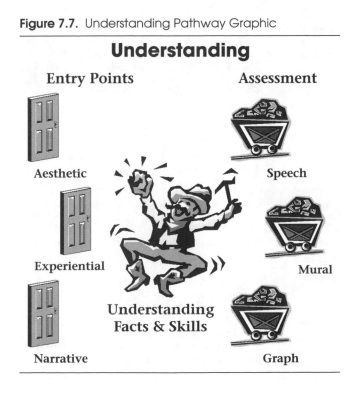

studies unit on the Middle Ages she traditionally teaches as part of the 4th-grade curriculum. In the past, she worked with Jan and Paul to create and teach an interdisciplinary unit that included the art, music, and dance of the time. The unit was enriched and the students knew many facts about the Middle Ages; in fact, for students like Chris and Yvette, the unit was particularly engaging. Students had the opportunity to build models, perform skits, and design family crests. But Lillian and the others now ask themselves what the students really understood about the Middle Ages at the conclusion of the extensive unit. They are not sure that the activities they used helped students to connect to the key concepts, generative ideas, and important issues, like fairness and justice, inherent in the study of that time period and its unique economic system.

Jan thinks that the students may come away with the idea that life during the Middle Ages was exciting and romantic. But she wonders whether they grasped the understanding that personal freedom was limited to the nobility; that distribution of wealth was unfair; and that the church held supreme power. In other words, she questions the degree to which the activities in the unit conveyed the idea of the relationship among power, freedom, and wealth.

David and Sandra agree that focusing on big ideas and major concepts or issues would be a sounder way to develop curriculum, as these ideas link across disciplines as well. The teachers acknowledge that they tended to romanticize the era of the Middle Ages and that the activities in which students participated may have led to the misconception that life in the Middle Ages was fun. The conversation turns to thinking about how they might delve more deeply into the big understandings that would guide their choice of teaching and learning activities.

At their second meeting they identify themes relating to the Middle Ages that they feel would resonate with their students. Power and fairness surfaced as matters of great concern to their students. After a lengthy discussion, the teachers decide to try out "social structures" as an overarching topic of their social studies curriculum, while highlighting the issues of power and fairness. The teachers see this theme as a valuable lens through which to understand the world and one's place in it. It is central to their students' own lives, it cuts across subject areas, and students may be unaware of its role and impact in history or in their own lives.

To assess the possible application of the concept of social structures to other topics, the team considers it for other units. They find the concept of social structures has broad and analogous applications, from the conditions that lead to civil war to the study of ants and bees, insects with their own social structures. The team decides to plan a unit on ants for the science curriculum, to extend students' developing understanding of social systems.

At their third meeting the teachers revisit their social studies unit on the Middle Ages. They explore the concept of how different social systems favor different members of society. They break down this concept into six understanding goals they feel are appropriate for 4th graders.

- What is feudalism and how does it work as a social structure? What were the advantages and disadvantages of the feudal system in the Middle Ages?
- What is the concept of "personal rights" within the feudal system, and who has them?
- What was life like in the Middle Ages for members of different feudal social classes?
- How was wealth distributed across feudal social classes?
- What was the relationship between the feudal system and power, wealth, and fairness?
- How does feudalism compare with the social structure we live in today?

They also generate a list of facts they want the students to learn over the course of the unit, such as vocabulary, dates and events of the period, and notable people of the times. In addition, they consider which skills the students should learn in the context of the unit, especially relating to historical research and communication and creative expression.

At their next session David suggests that they brainstorm ideas for how they might introduce the unit. They generate a list of entry point activities that

would engage the students meaningfully according to their strengths and interests. The ideas are displayed in Figure 7.8.

While thinking about the entry points, David suggests teaching the unit through a simulation where the students set up a medieval town and assume the roles of the people in the kingdom (e.g., artisans, entertainers, serfs, clergyman, lords, ladies, knights, king, and queen). Several times a week the students would be given a scenario to enact assuming their respective roles. For instance, one scenario might be the king's desire to build a new castle in the country. The students' focus questions might be to discuss how to finance the project, what the castle would look like, and who would need to be involved in planning and implementation.

Another situation might be to address issues within the social realm. The scenario might unfold as a lord is overseeing his land, accompanied his young son. The son makes friends with a serf child but is forbidden to play with him as there is a difference in social class. At the end of each role play, students would write in their journals about the experience. Their focus prompts could be as follows:

Figure 7.8. Middle Ages Unit Entry Point Activities

Entry point	Ideas
Narrative	Dramatize the picture book *A Medieval Feast* by Aliki to show roles in medieval society.
Aesthetic	Visit an art exhibit of knights and castles.
	View calligraphy and Gothic architecture.
	Discuss what these artifacts relate about life in the Middle Ages.
	Visit a museum with medieval fashions and distinguish among classes.
Quantitative/ Numerical	Calculate miles for Crusades and years a knight would be away on a Crusade.
	Investigate the barter system.
Experiential and Social	Do a simulation of life in a medieval kingdom.
	Visit a medieval festival.
Musical	Attend concert of Gregorian chants.
	See a demonstration of medieval instruments.
Foundational and Logical	View *Robin Hood* and discuss whether Robin Hood was justified in stealing from the rich to give to the poor. (Moral dilemma activity: Should Robin Hood be arrested?)

- What was the problem?
- Was the solution fair?
- Whom did it benefit?
- What are your feelings about the event?
- Would the same thing happen today?

By keeping and sharing journal entries, the students will develop an understanding of the feudal system in terms of its advantages and disadvantages. To assess these developing understandings of the goals of the unit, Lillian suggests that the students choose two final projects that revisit the targeted concepts. Jan thinks these projects should require the students to view the central ideas of the unit from the perspective of real-world domains. The team agrees that the project choices must be thoughtful and directly align with the understanding goals, knowledge, and skills targeted for the unit.

The team brainstorms a variety of exit points. These ideas are shown in Figure 7.9.

Paul suggests that a culminating activity could be a community service project where the whole class can work together to see injustice in terms of wealth in the local community. Lillian applauds the idea, as one of the goals is to relate social injustice to today's society. They will contact the local homeless shelters to find out what the students can do for them.

In terms of assessment, the teachers see each activity as an opportunity to gauge students' evolving understandings, as well as to uncover and address any misconceptions students may develop. The team members plan to design rubrics to assess their students' evolving understandings of the unit's central ideas, as demonstrated in their participation in the learning experiences.

In the development process, the teachers continually revisit the learning goals they have laid out and check for alignment between the goals and the learning experiences they are developing. The team believes that the activities invite the use of a range of intelligences, or symbol systems, in different ways. They are satisfied that with this initial set of entry-point-informed experiences, all their students might find comfortable and effective ways to deepen their understanding of the feudal system specifically, and social structures more generally.

Figure 7.9. Middle Ages Unit Exit Points

Disciplinary Perspective	Project
Politician	Pretend you are leading an uprising against the system. Give a speech that shows the unfairness of the feudal system.
Architectural Anthropologist	Build a model of a more just kingdom. Explain the roles of the people in the kingdom and show where they lived. Explain why you think this society is fair and just.
Economist	Prepare two budgets that show how the society's wealth ($500,000) could be redistributed if one of the following were in charge of the budget: king and queen, lords and ladies, knights, artisans and entertainers, clergy, and peasants and serfs.
Sociologist	Develop a flowchart of what would happen if the serfs went on strike and no longer produced crops. Your flowchart should show how this strike would affect each social class.
Musician	Create and perform a 3-minute composition using classroom instruments that represents the quality of life experienced by at least four social classes. Defend why you used a particular instrument for a particular social class as well as how the rhythm, tempo, and volume represent that social class.
Writer and Artists	Create a picture book about a kingdom where power and wealth are more equally distributed. What jobs would people have? How would people take care of one another?

In the Classroom

Lillian starts the unit with several entry point activities that she thinks will build on her students' strengths. She wants them to understand that there are different social classes and to that end she asks them to work together to build, draw, write, or put on a mini-skit about something that explains aspects of the different classes. They can work alone or in small groups. She tells them the information they need can be found in the materials in the Middle Ages interest center (see Supporting Materials).

Chris and his partner, Tony, decide to build a model of what they think a medieval kingdom looked like. After some preliminary research in the library and on the Internet, the boys create an elaborate model of a kingdom with blocks and building materials. The model shows serfs working in the fields, two knights' manors, and a castle with a moat and a working drawbridge, which dominates the scene. From their research and through their work with the model, Chris and Tony are able to describe who lives in the castle and how, in times of danger, all members of the kingdom could find safety within the castle walls.

At the end of the unit, Yvette chooses an exit point project that surprises the team. She does not give a speech to dramatically plead for justice, as the team might have guessed. Instead, upset that the serfs worked so hard for so little, Yvette decides to prepare budgets to show the great disparity in the distribution of wealth. Her sensitivity and concern for others motivate her to use a quantitative approach to deal with the situation.

Future Plans

At their final meeting to discuss the Understanding pathway the teachers choose to extend their students' understanding of the idea of social systems to science. They revisit their unit on the ant and bee societies and plan to rewrite the goals to align with the ones used in the unit on the Middle Ages. They also think about having the students form their own society or form a social structure by organizing a company as part of a unit in math.

PUTTING THE UNDERSTANDING PATHWAY INTO ACTION

The Understanding pathway focuses on using MI theory to develop learning experiences that give students multiple ways to explore and develop understandings of the central ideas of a topic. These learning experiences offer students opportunities to build their understanding of the targeted concepts from a variety of perspectives and to draw on their strengths and interests to do so. Assessment in the Understanding pathway focuses on gauging students' developing understandings and uncovering any misconceptions, using exit points.

The primary task of the Understanding pathway is to develop MI-informed learning experiences. However, it can be all too easy to develop fun activities using MI theory, with little or no attention to what the teacher wants students to learn about the topic. Therefore, the development of those activities should never be shorn from other aspects of curriculum planning and development: identifying the central topic(s), naming the key learning goals, and planning learning experiences and assessments that address the learning goals and gauge student understandings.

Articulate Learning Goals for the Topic, Unit, or Lesson

Typically, topics are already established by way of a school-wide or grade-level curriculum. This was true for the Lincoln Elementary teachers. But they wanted more connection across subject areas and from one unit to the next, so they decided to identify an overarching topic, "social structures." The social structures topic would weave through their required social studies units, as well as other subject areas, such as the study of insects in science.

Once a topic has been established, learning goals are identified. What do you want your students to come away with at the end of a unit? Without a clear articulation of what it is you want students to learn, MI-informed activities might lack substance and be something akin to "Eight ways to do the Middle Ages." Although students may enjoy those activities, it is less likely that they will genuinely understand the meaningful aspects of the topic.

Identify three to five learning goals related to the topic. Mentally test these out, asking:

- Are they important to the topic?
- Are they meaningful/relevant to the students?
- Are they addressable in multiple ways?

Develop and Plan Learning Experiences

Learning experiences introduce students to a topic, provide them with different ways to "mess about" with a topic, and help students build their understanding of the core ideas, concepts, and skills—or learning goals—of the topic or unit. The Understanding pathway taps Gardner's entry point approach to plan and develop fitting learning experiences throughout the unit.

Developing learning experiences involves considering each learning goal and developing or identifying activities that introduce students to the topic and then involve them in deeper inquiry of the central ideas. As with the Lincoln Elementary School teachers, establishing the unit learning experiences may entail reorganizing or "retrofitting" existing activities so that as a set they are aligned with the learning goals. Existing activities may be modified to fit new learning goals or jettisoned if found to be irrelevant to the newly structured unit. The learning goals serve as criteria for inclusion of learning experiences. The entry points help ensure a range of intelligences are invited into the learning process; or, to use Gardner's analogy, that there are several doors into the room.

Introductory Activities

The entry points are ideal for creating a set of introductory activities that allow students to explore the new topic freely. Chris and his partner began to explore the Middle Ages by conducting preliminary research on how kingdoms were physically organized and "drafting" their conception of a feudal kingdom using building materials. Introductory activities also give the teacher a chance to gauge what students know about the topic going into the unit and any obvious misconceptions.

One strategy some teachers have used to enter into a new topic is to set up interest centers, as Lillian did to provide a variety of independent activities and resource materials related to her medieval unit. (See the Supporting Materials section for sample task cards for a Middle Ages interest center.)

The Lincoln Elementary 4th-grade team developed a number of activities and modified or reorganized existing ones to introduce their students to key ideas about the feudal system in the Middle Ages. They referred to Gardner's list and descriptions of entry points to generate ideas for their unit so students could explore the topic in a range of ways that lent some comfort and familiarity to their study of a new topic. They also used analogies to help their students connect with the new topic. For example, initial discussions about the students' own "social structures" helped the 4th graders understand the idea of the feudal system.

Structured Activities

Open-ended introductory activities are followed by structured activities that invite more focused inquiry into the ideas that are particularly central to the topic and that align with the learning goals. Entry points also can be used to develop these more focused experiences. The Lincoln Elementary School team used the entry points to develop experiences that bridged a range of intelligences to the unit's learning goals. For example, the 4th graders studied hierarchy across feudal classes by participating in learning activities that allowed them to explore the different roles of the classes during the time period. Through assigned readings, interest center activities, and research opportunities, the students acquired the knowledge they would need to tackle culminating projects where knowledge, understandings, and skills would be assessed.

Plan Assessments

Understanding assessments focus on whether and how students are developing understandings related to unit learning goals. Assessments should gauge whether students are applying their learning to novel situations and can demonstrate their understanding through more than one symbol system, and whether any misconceptions emerge or persist.

Assessment is, in part, ongoing. Observing students at work, in character, or presenting their work can yield much regarding their understandings of the learning goals. For example, in the case of the Lincoln Elementary School 4th graders' simulation, Lillian might observe whether students are playing or really assuming the role based on content. Accuracy and quality of performances and products are important considerations.

Methods of observing, documenting, and assessing understanding emerge from learning activities, and they focus on signs that students are engaged in and developing understanding of the ideas represented in the learning goals. Logically, assessment approaches should align with what you want students to learn about the topic and should take place within the learning experiences as well in the form of cumulative and final performances and products.

At the end of a unit, students enhance, apply, and communicate their developing understandings through culminating activities. These culminating activities or events are more complex and typically synthesize students' understandings from a number of previous learning experiences. Culminating assessments may have an evaluative bent that ongoing assessments do not.

Cumulative or final assessments also are called exit points. As mentioned previously, activities that tap disciplinary understandings require students to represent their understandings using different symbol systems, and novel situations in which students can apply multidisciplinary perspectives ensures in-depth understanding. For the Lincoln Elementary 4th graders, the Middle Ages unit culminates in exit projects that include the community service project and reflections. Students help to design the rubric that will be used for evaluation of their projects. Written reflections in students' learning logs also can be assessed.

Additional examples of units and activities from the Understanding pathway are provided in the Supporting Materials section.

Guiding Your Journey

The Understanding Pathway Guide shown in Figure 7.10 will assist in your development of activities. Figure 7.11 is a completed Understanding Pathway Organizer used by the Lincoln Elementary team when planning their Middle Ages unit. A blank organizer for your use is found in Supporting Materials at the end of the chapter.

THOUGHT QUESTIONS AND ACTIVITIES

Thought Questions

- What does it mean to understand something?
- How can MI theory help support students' understandings of a topic and targeted learning goals?
- Conventional wisdom suggests that using MI activities will not prepare students for traditional tests. Present a counterargument.

- How can you use field trips, demonstrations, experts, and disciplinary specialists within your building to enhance curriculum that promotes in-depth understandings of topics?

Implementation Activities

Activity 1. If Yvette and Chris were in your class, how might you help them deepen their understanding of a topic? Choose a unit from your curriculum and highlight, modify, and add activities that would give Yvette and/or Chris opportunities to deepen their understandings across subjects or domains while tapping into their areas of strength. (Remember to keep a focus on your learning goals.)

Activity 2. Integrating the arts into curricular areas is one way to promote understanding. The Moving Molecules activity, in Supporting Materials, is an example of how arts processes can both engage nontraditional learners and deepen their understandings of particular concepts. Read the activity and discuss the following:

- What concept(s) are being taught?
- What connections are being made?
- How does understanding a concept in one domain strengthen understanding of it in another?
- How do movement exercises help to strengthen understanding of abstract concepts, especially for elementary students?

Activity 3. Choose a unit you already teach and use entry points to develop new activities or modify existing ones to enhance the unit's potential to build student understanding. Use the blank Understanding Pathway Organizer (in Supporting Materials) to organize your work.

Activity 4. Using the unit from Activity 3 (or another of your choice), identify learning experiences that would demonstrate understanding of central concepts. For example, how did a student's portrayal of a knight indicate his understanding of the different classes? How did a final presentation

Figure 7.10. Understanding Pathway Guide

Understanding Features	Things to Think About
Unit of Study *What is the topic or unit of study?*	• Is the topic in the curriculum? • Does it align with standards?
Articulate learning goals for the topic, unit, or lesson  *What am I trying to convey in this unit?*	• What should students know? • What big ideas or principles are central to the topic? • What should students be able to do as the result of this unit of study?
Develop and plan learning experiences that address the learning goals using Gardner's entry point approach. *What learning experiences or "doorways" can I offer that will engage my students and have them explore the topic with understanding?* *What resources can I use?* 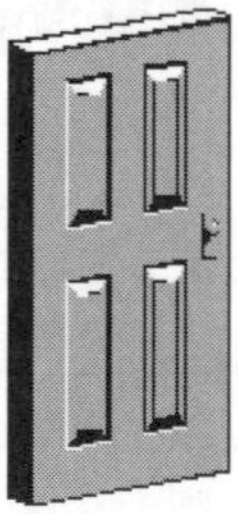	What are possible learning activities or approaches into the topic using the following entry points? • Narrative • Aesthetic • Quantitative/numerical • Logical • Experiential • Musical • Foundational • Social Are there a diversity of resources available that respond to different ways of knowing (technology, interviews, primary sources, print material, video, and film)? Which resources and activities will I actually integrate into my unit?
Assess students' developing understandings and identify misconceptions using exit point or assessment activities. *How can I provide opportunities to assess learning that align with my learning goals?* 	• Do the activities involved in the unit allow my students to apply their understandings to new situations? • Are the product choices allowing the students to represent their understandings in multiple symbol systems and from various interdisciplinary perspectives? • Are these opportunities tapping learning goals? • Have I articulated benchmarks for performances and created • Rubrics for assessment?

Figure 7.11. Sample Completed Understanding Pathway Organzier (Lincoln Elementary School Middle Ages Unit)

Unit of Study	Unit on the Middle Ages: Topic in the 4th-Grade curriculum
What is the topic or unit of study?	

Articulate learning goals for the topic, unit, or lesson	*What should students know? (facts, events, dates)*

Articulate learning goals for the topic, unit, or lesson

What am I trying to convey in this unit?

What should students know? (facts, events, dates)

Dates and places: focus on Europe

Magna Carta

Identify classes in the feudal system: nobility, clergy, knights, artisans, guildsmen, peasants, serfs

Barter system; taxation without representation

What big ideas or principles are central to the topic?

1. What is feudalism and how does it work as a social structure? What were the advantages and disadvantages of the feudal system in the Middle Ages?
2. What is the concept of "personal rights" within the feudal system, and who has them?
3. What was life like in the Middle Ages for members of different feudal classes?
4. How was wealth distributed across feudal classes?
5. What was the relationship between the feudal system and power, wealth, and fairness?
6. How does feudalism compare with the social structure we live in today?

What should students be able to do as a result of this unit of study?

1. Read a timeline.
2. Locate European countries on map.
3. Compare and contrast life-styles of social classes in the feudal system.
4. Read primary sources.
5. Express understandings through role play.

Develop and plan learning experiences that address the learning goals using Gardner's entry point approach.

What learning experiences or "doorways" can I offer that will engage my students and have them explore the topic with understanding?

What resources can I use?

Narrative: Dramatize the picture book *A Medieval Feast* by Aliki to show roles in medieval society.

Aesthetic: Visit an art exhibit of knights and castles, view calligraphy and Gothic architecture, discuss what these artifacts relate about life in the Middle Ages, visit a museum with medieval fashions and distinguish among classes.

Quantitative/Numerical: Calculate miles for Crusades and years a knight would be away on a Crusade, investigate the barter system

Experiential and Social: Do a simulation of life in a medieval kingdom, visit a medieval festival.

Musical: Attend a concert of Gregorian chants, see a demonstration of medieval instruments.

Foundational and Logical: View *Robin Hood* and discuss whether Robin Hood was justified in stealing from the rich to give to the poor. (Moral dilemma activity: Should Robin Hood be arrested?)

Figure 7.11. (continued)

Resources: Access to content that uses different ways of knowing (text, primary sources, technology, interviewing, web quests)

Web quests. These sites offer in-depth investigation into the Middle Ages and are appropriate for elementary students:

- Magnificent Medieval Times: www.thinkquest.org/library
- Web Quest—Middle Ages: www.milton.k12.vt.us/WebQuests/ SChristensen/webquest-middle_ages.htm

Textbook

Robin Hood movie

Primary sources on life in the Middle Ages

Terteling Library: www.albertson.edu/library/middleages.htm

Assess students' developing understandings and identify misconceptions using exit point or assessment activities.

How can I provide opportunities to assess learning that align with my learning goals?

Assessment opportunities and exit points:

Politician: Pretend you are leading an uprising against the system. Give a speech that shows the unfairness of the feudal system

Architectural Anthropologist: Build a model of a more just kingdom; explain the roles of the people in the kingdom; show where they lived. Explain why you think this society is fair and just.

Economist: Prepare two budgets that show how the society's wealth ($500,000) could be redistributed if one of the following were in charge of the budget: king and queen, lords and ladies, knights, artisans and entertainers, clergy, and peasants and serfs.

Sociologist: Develop a flowchart of what would happen if the serfs went on strike and no longer produced crops. Your flowchart should show how this work stoppage would affect each social class.

Musician: Create and perform a 3-minute composition using classroom instruments that represents the quality of life experienced by at least four social classes. Defend why you used a particular instrument for a particular social class, as well as how the rhythm and tempo and volume represents the class.

Writer and Artist: Create a picture book about a kingdom where power and wealth are more equally distributed. What jobs would people have? How would people take care of one another?

Assessment criteria:
- Benchmarks or rubrics that align with learning goals
- Products and performances
- Learning log journal entries.
- Evaluation of interest center activities undertaken by students
- Final test on topic

demonstrate that a student understands the connection between wealth and power in the feudal system? See the "Rubric Machine" website, *www.ThinkingGear.com*, for frameworks for developing rubrics that may be useful to you.

SUPPORTING MATERIALS

This section includes a reproducible Understanding Pathway Organizer (Figure 7.12) for your use, sample tasks cards from a Middle Ages interest center, and an additional activity, moving molecules.

Understanding Pathway Activity Materials

Sample Task Cards

The task cards below were created by teacher Kris Ollum, for use in a "Knights and Castles" Middle Ages interest center (for a full description, see McInerney, Berman, & Baum, 2005). The tasks were designed to have the students explore, create, or investigate the topic. The first card focuses on exploration. The next two require creating; and the last, investigation.

Task Card One

Hear Ye, Hear Ye: Many of the last names we hear today originated in the Middle Ages. At the beginning of the Middle Ages, people used only one name. As the towns and villages got more crowded, it was harder to tell people apart. People became known by the work that they did. So John became John the blacksmith and Mary became Mary the baker. Eventually people dropped the word *the* and were called by the two names, like John Smith and Mary Baker. What is your last name? What is its history?

Challenge: Find out about your last name. A few websites have several last names. Go to *www.clanhuston.com/name/surname*. Alternatively, type in "history of surnames" and this will lead you to several websites about last names. Several people have put their whole family history on a webpage. Is your family one of these? If you do not have access to a computer, you can look up your last name in a book. Here are three different titles you can find in your local library: *American Surnames* by Elsdon C. Smith; *A Dictionary of Surnames* by Patrick Hanks and Flavia Hodges; and *Family Name: How Our Surnames Came to America*, by J. N. Hook.

Tools of the Trade: computer books from your library, parents and grandparents.

Task Card Two

Hear Ye, Hear Ye: The Middle Ages was a time of very distinct classes: the nobles, the church officials, and the peasants. They all lived very different lives. The nobles ruled the land; they wore fine clothes, lived in castles, had servants, and ate good foods. The peasants worked very hard, had one set of clothing, lived in one-room cottages, and slept all in the same bed. The children's lives were different too. The children of nobles left home at the age of 7 and went to a relative's home to be taught what they needed to learn. The boys learned to be knights and to read and write. The girls learned to sew, run the household, and care for the sick. Peasant children had no carefree days. The boys helped their fathers in the field, while the girls learned skills in the home. When the noble children grew up, they had an easier life, with servants to take care of them. The peasants grew up to work the fields and have a very difficult life. Which would you rather be, a noble child or a peasant child? Read *Merry Ever After* to help you decide.

Challenge: Write a story about your life as either a noble child or a peasant child. You may write it in the form of a diary, sharing what your life is like on a daily basis for a month. Include illustrations in your story or diary.

Tools of the Trade: Paper, pens, pencils, and your imagination.

Task Card Three

Hear Ye, Hear Ye: Books were rare and wonderful things in the Middle Ages. Nobles might have had one or two in their homes, but peasants had none. Church officials had most of the books hidden away from the people. All books in this period were handwritten and therefore took a long time to complete. Many had beautiful lettering called calligraphy, which is a form still used today. Many of the books were decorated in gold and hand-drawn designs. Read the book *Illuminations* to study this fine art of long ago. Because there were no calendars, the nobles' books often included a book of days, with which they wrote a type of journal as a way to mark time. They also might have had a book of prayers or stories about the saints.

Challenge: Create a book of days. You might make a book that keeps track of the birthdays of your friends and family members. Alternatively, fill the book with wise sayings or your favorite poetry. Try your hand at calligraphy after reading the book *Lettering*.

Tools of the Trade: Paper, markers, pen, and calligraphy book(s).

Figure 7.12. Understanding Pathway Organizer (blank)

What is the topic or unit of study?

Articulate learning goals for the topic, unit, or lesson *What am I trying to convey in this unit?* 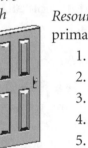	What should students know? (facts, events, dates) What big ideas or principles are central to the topic? What should students be able to do as a result of this unit of study?

Develop and plan learning experiences that address the learning goals using Gardner's entry point approach.
 	
What learning experiences or "doorways" can I offer that will engage my students and have them explore the topic with understanding?
 	
What resources can I use?
	Narrative:
	Aesthetic:
	Quantitative/Numerical:
	Experiential and Social:
	Musical:
	Foundational and Logical:
	
	Resources: Access to content that uses different ways of knowing (text, primary sources, technology, interviewing, web quests)
	   1.
	   2.
	   3.
	   4.
	   5.

Assess students' developing understandings and identify misconceptions using exit point or assessment activities.
 	
How can I provide opportunities to assess learning that align with my learning goals?

	Assessment opportunities and exit points (disciplinary perspective and project description):
	   1.
	   2.
	   3.
	   4.
	   5.
	
	Assessment criteria:
	   1.
	   2.
	   3.
	   4.
	   5.

> **Task Card Four**
>
> *Hear Ye, Hear Ye:* Tapestries were used in the Middle Ages as decoration and to keep drafts out of the castles. Sometimes, like the Unicorn Tapestries or the Bayeux Tapestry, they told stories. They were often woven by noblewomen, or by peasant women looking for work. Weaving was a useful skill to have, as it was used not only for tapestries, but for making clothes as well.
>
> *Challenge:* Use the loom to weave a scarf, a table runner, or clothes for a doll.
>
> *Tools of the Trade:* Yarn, loom, and directions found in the resource folder.

Additional Understanding Activity

The lesson below is one of a series developed by ArtsConnection in New York City as part of a federally funded Jacob Javits grant, New Horizons. Teachers worked collaboratively with professional artists to develop curriculum that integrates authentic arts processes. The lessons were designed to attract nontraditional learners, deepen their understanding of concepts in a variety of disciplines, and improve their ability to regulate their own learning.

Moving Molecules

(Note: Created by Carrie Amon, Kelly Hayes, Jessica Nicoll, and Mabel Velazquez)

I've been teaching about water molecules for years; it's a very difficult concept for 4th graders to grasp. This year I used creative dance and they know it cold. I'll never teach about water molecules again without using creative dance. (Mabel Velazquez, Teacher)

Before You Start. This lesson is part of a science unit in earth science, specifically, understanding water molecules in gas, liquid, and solid states. It will work best if students are already comfortable with the use of movement in the classroom. Students should

- Be able to move through space, working cooperatively in a small group;

- Be familiar with the use of timing in movement improvisations; and
- Have experience creating dances with a "shape, movement, shape" structure.

Several activities for developing these skills are listed in ArtsConnection's *Using the Artistic Process: Creative Dance.*

Space. You will want to arrange an open space in your classroom to allow for free movement by some or all of your students. You may choose to have only one small group move at a time, with the remainder of the class observing, or you may choose to have the entire class participate at once.

What This Lesson Will Accomplish. The students will discover the differences among water molecule bonds in gas, liquid, and solid states, using creative dance. This lesson will help students *take risks* as a self-regulatory behavior. Students will be required to explore the new and difficult concept of molecular bonding through the creative dance activity.

The Lesson

Warm-Up. Lead the students in a brief warm-up that prepares them for the dance activities. (Two examples, *Circle Time* and *Away & Back,* are described in ArtsConnection's *Using the Artistic Process: Creative Dance.*)

Improvisation: Speed. In a circle, ask for five to eight volunteers for a movement improvisation. Tell the volunteers they will have 8 counts to move away from their place on the circle and 8 counts to return. They may follow any pathway they choose as long as they don't bump into any other member of the class. Ask the students to move at a very quick pace.

Ask for five to eight volunteers from the circle for another movement improvisation. Repeat the directions above, but ask the dancers to move very slowly.

Group Discussion. Focus student observations of the dance activities by facilitating a discussion.

Sample Questions:

- In what ways did the two movement impro-visations differ? (Encourage the students to consider body, force, and space as well as time when discussing the improvisation.)
- What parts of the dancers' bodies were moving?
- Did the pathway or distance traveled differ?
- What qualities did you notice the first time? The second?

In the circle, discuss molecules. Tell the students that everything in the world is made up of millions of tiny molecules and that they will be learning about water molecules today.

Dance Activities. Divide the class into three groups. Ask the members of the first group to find a space in the room. Tell them they will be moving through space on any path they choose. The other two groups should sit down at the side.

Tell the first group that each one of them is an H_2O molecule. Ask them to move through space quickly. While they are moving, focus their movement by asking questions and side-coaching.

Sample Questions:

- Can you vary your path?
- Don't forget your torsos and arms and head as you move quickly (not just your feet and legs).
- Can you change your level or directional facing?
- Think about the different kinds of movement you can make quickly: wiggly movements, sharply flicking movement, soft, swift runs, and so on.

After the first group dances, ask the observers what they noticed about the dance.

Sample Questions:

- Describe what you saw. What did you notice about individual dancers as well as about the group as a whole?

- What parts of their bodies were moving?
- How were the dancers moving?
- What did the dance remind you of?

Record responses and observations in one column on the board.

Ask the second group to stand up. Tell them that they should all join hands in one line and must remain holding hands throughout the movement improvisation but should not be pushing or pulling each other. Tell them they will be moving through space, covering as much classroom area as they wish to and can. Focus their movements by asking questions such as the ones suggested for the first group's movement improvisation. (This group should not be able to move as quickly as the first group.) Facilitate a class discussion and note the students' observations of the dance in a second column on the board. The class should try to note the differences in the use of body, space, force, and time between the first and second groups.

The third group should stand up and all lock elbows, forming a circle. They are to remain like this for the entire movement improvisation. Focus their movements by asking questions such as the ones suggested for the first group's movement improvisation. They may travel through as much of the classroom space as they wish. This group will be forced to move even more slowly than the second, because of the limitations of the dancers' movements.

Facilitate a class discussion and note the students' observations of the dance in a third column on the board. The class should try to note the differences in the use of body, space, force, and time between the first and the third group.

Content Connection. Tell the class that each one of the movement improvisations represented water in a different state (gas, liquid, and solid). See if the class can match the movement improvisations to the different states of water. Ask them to explain their reasoning.

Once the columns have been labeled correctly, make sure the students understand and can give an example of H_2O as a gas (e.g., steam from the shower or from a pot of boiling water). Facilitate a discussion about each state of matter/movement improvisation.

Sample Questions:

- What can you tell me about the molecules of H_2O when it is a gas?
- How do the molecules move? How was this type of movement reflected in the dance improvisation?
- What is the relationship of the molecules to one another? How was this demonstrated in the dance improvisation?
- What do you think is the factor that determines the molecules' relationship to one another—whether the H_2O is a gas, liquid, or solid?

Linking Dance and Scientific Concepts. Using the experiences from this lesson, the students can now create dances inspired by water molecules. Each of the three groups will take the molecules on a journey through the three states of matter, in any order they choose. They may choose to create a story that goes along with the dance (e.g., the ice cubes came out of the freezer, melted, and evaporated, or the steam from the engines settled on the window, where it dripped down the window and froze into ice crystals). Each group should have time to create and practice its piece. (Remind students to be clear about beginnings and endings.)

The students should be encouraged to create music for the piece (with classroom instruments) or to select recorded music to accompany it. The students may wish to embellish and narrate their dances with the stories or they may choose to leave the narration out altogether. After all the groups have shared their dances, encourage the class to discuss the choices that were made by each group. You may want to see the dances again, keeping in mind what was very different. Consider prompting the discussion with these questions:

- What choices were made by each group (music, order of states of matter, with or without narration, use of space and time, etc.)?
- Did these water molecule dances remind you of anything else?

FOR FURTHER STUDY

Blythe, T., & Associates (1998). *The teaching for understanding guide.* San Francisco: Jossey-Bass.

A user-friendly guide that walks readers through the elements of the teaching for understanding framework. It includes examples and reflections from many teachers using the framework and helpful graphic organizers.

Boix Mansilla, V. (2000). *The Project Zero classroom.* Cambridge, MA: The President and Fellows of Harvard College (on behalf of Project Zero and Veronica Boix Mansilla).

Describes the ideas from Harvard's Project Zero that are the focus of its annual summer institute: teaching for understanding, assessment, thinking, and multiple intelligences theory, including an extensive entry point section.

Davis, J. (1997). *The MUSE book.* Cambridge, MA: The President and Fellows of Harvard College (on behalf of Project Zero and Jessica Davis).

Describes Project Zero's development of the entry point approach—a good introduction. The entry point approach is used in the visual arts, to inform appreciation and understanding of visual arts through the lenses offered by the entry points.

Gardner, H. (1999a). *Intelligence reframed: Multiple intelligences for the 21st century.* New York: Basic Books.

Includes a chapter on "MI for Understanding" that elaborates on the use of entry points, telling analogies and core representations. Gardner uses the Holocaust and evolution as topics through which he elaborates on the three elements.

McInerney, M., Berman, K., & Baum, S. (2005). *Differentiation through interest centers.* Mansfield Center, CT: Creative Learning Press.

A guide for effective use of interest centers in the classroom, this book includes six complete interest centers. Activities use entry and exit points based on MI theory. Topics include knights and castles, quilts, meteorology, storytelling, and heroes. See the For Further Study section in Chapter 5 of this book for more resources about interest centers.

For information and practical ideas about using simulations and social action activities to promote understanding across the curriculum, write to:
Interact Simulations
P.O. Box 997-S90
Lakeside, CA 92040

CHAPTER 8

The Authentic Problems Pathway

For many educators, multiple intelligences theory is most effectively implemented when students solve real-world problems using real-world methods of inquiry. Such authentic learning experiences bring to bear a variety of intelligences, allow students to use their particular collections of strengths, support students' developing understanding of central topics and concepts, and allow them to learn and practice basic academic skills in genuine contexts.

The purpose of the Authentic Problems pathway is to offer opportunities for students to solve authentic problems and make real products together. Basic skills are employed by students in the problem-solving process. When students are first-hand inquirers, problem-solvers, and makers of authentic products, they use their multiple intelligences as they are used in the real world.

PATHWAY BACKGROUND

Schools today are charged with producing citizens that have the knowledge and skills needed to be productive and successful. Employers complain that it is difficult to find prospective employees who are self-disciplined, can think and solve problems, are effective communicators, and can work cooperatively with others. To meet this challenge, schools must provide experiences in which students learn and apply skills in authentic situations. Such opportunities give students the chance to address problems in the same ways professionals do: using methods of inquiry, materials, and strategies specific to real-world domains.

These experiences naturally require a multiple intelligences approach, given that MI theory was developed with real-world domains in mind. Assignments should mirror the kinds of questions and tasks required by practicing professionals within and across domains.

We know that human potential is defined by the spectrum of intelligences that each individual possesses. The unique set of abilities brought to bear on specific challenges helps to explain the degree of success experienced in various domains of human endeavor.

Mahatma Gandhi, for instance, did not achieve prominence by scoring high in interpersonal intelligence, but rather by his ability to influence change and work toward the betterment of the human situation. His intellectual abilities allowed for a particular type of problem solving and leadership. Using authentic opportunities for inquiry within and across domains gives students a forum to express and apply *their* spectrum of abilities as they work together to solve problems and develop products.

Many educators argue that this kind of curriculum is essential to produce a literate and productive citizenship and is most instrumental in helping students complete their journeys from novice to expert within a particular domain. Confidence in their own abilities to solve problems and make products increases the probability that students will reach their potential. More important, academic skills become relevant when they are applied in ways that are meaningful to students. Seeing purpose in what they are doing, they often become highly self-regulated and goal directed. They demonstrate effective learning behaviors they may not have used before. Once students have become productive learners, they are likely to repeat these learning behaviors on future tasks. This pattern results in improving students' self-efficacy, self-regulation, and achievement

(Bandura, 1986; Baum, Oreck, & Owen, 1997; Baum, Renzulli, & Hébert, 1994; Zimmerman, Bonner, & Kovach, 1996).

What Is Meant by Solving Authentic Problems?

Using real-world problems and contexts is not a new idea. John Dewey (1938) argued that schools should be a reflection of the *real* world where children learn by doing. His vision of a progressive classroom was one that resembled the community institutions in which the students some day would be employed. With strategic help from adults, children set up laboratories to study nature and conduct small-scale scientific experiments. They selected workshops in which they built their own equipment and gathered materials to study different phenomena and create authentic products across different disciplines. Dewey felt that through these projects children could come to know their world, achieve a fuller understanding of themselves, and begin to develop a real sense of the skills and concepts that lay at the heart of formal disciplines.

During the Sputnik era this idea of authenticity emerged again. This time it focused on students learning the basic concepts and principles of a discipline by using authentic inquiry methods. Jerome Bruner (1960), who promoted this approach, argued that "inquiry in a third grade classroom should be no different from inquiry on the frontiers of knowledge" (p. iv). He maintained that students could become practicing professionals as they used the methods and materials of a discipline to understand existing knowledge and create new knowledge as well.

In 1977 Renzulli combined the ideas of Bruner and Dewey when he created the Enrichment Triad Model, whose major goal was to transform students from mere consumers of knowledge to producers of new knowledge (Renzulli & Reis, 1997). This model, originally designed for use with students in gifted programs, asks students to use authentic means of inquiry to confront real problems. They then communicate their solutions to a relevant audience using creative, professional-quality products. Knowledge is not an end, but a means to solving problems.

Problem-based learning involves inquiry within and across specific disciplines. In problem-based approaches students confront real-life problems that require real-life solutions. The problems are ill-defined and open-ended, and have no predetermined solution. Students must first define the issues, then formulate hypotheses, collect data, and test out their ideas in order to devise fitting solutions to the problem. Students also explain, justify, and evaluate their solutions. In the process, they challenge assumptions, recognize patterns and relationships, take risks, see things in new ways, build their knowledge, and develop real collaborative relationships with their classmates.

Using authentic problems that require teams of students with different, complementary strengths to work together is one way to optimize multiple intelligences in the classroom. Students rely on one another's contributions to solve the problem and communicate their results. As they work together, they learn from one another and grow to value one another's unique strengths.

An Example of an Authentic Problem

Members of a 5th-grade class observed the condition of a pond and surrounding site on the school grounds. They felt lucky to have a pond right on the school property, but now they took note of the crumbling structures, the overgrown flora, and the fact that it went generally unused. The students talked about it in their class. The 5th graders became determined to improve the condition of the pond and its surrounding property. The teacher saw this as a powerful teachable moment and decided to guide the students through a major project, which she called the Pond Problem. She designated the last period of each day over 6 weeks as project time. The teacher folded science and social studies objectives into the project. All students applied language and mathematical skills in their particular roles.

The teacher divided the 27 students into five research and development companies. The companies were challenged to develop plans to revitalize the pond and surrounding area.

The Pond Problem project was structured to facilitate the students' learning how to work within the pertinent domains, using real tools and methods. The tasks were set up by the teacher with student input. The teacher provided inquiry guides to help students organize and manage their work on the project, from their initial analyses of the site to the final presentation of a proposal. Sample pages of an inquiry guide are shown in Figure 8.1 on page 100.

Students were placed in their companies based on the expertise they could offer. Several areas of expertise were needed—writing, engineering and design, biological science, visual arts, and performing arts, among them. Student experts in all these areas were needed in each company in order to analyze the problem, develop a viable plan, and communicate the team's proposal to the town's Board of Education.

Company teams met to consider how they would approach the Pond Problem. Every student assumed primary responsibility for particular aspects of his or her team's work. For instance, even though all the students went to the pond to collect information, the biologists were charged with analyzing flora and fauna and conducting water tests. The engineers studied the dam and other physical structures, as well as the topography of the grounds. The visual artists made sketches and took photographs to collect data from the pond site. The writers sent letters of inquiry to town officials to trace the history of the pond and to identify who was responsible for its upkeep.

As their plans evolved, the students consulted with domain specialists. They were given access to real laboratories containing equipment and materials used by practicing professionals in the disciplines represented. Biologists from each company brought specimens to the science lab and studied them under the microscope. They discussed their hypotheses with the science teacher.

The engineers worked with a city engineer who made himself available to the students on a regular basis. They built models and scale prototypes of bridges, dams, and nature trails they envisioned. In the art studio, the visual artists created murals from the sketches of the birds and reptiles they had spent hours observing at the pond. Performing artists and others worked with the high school drama teacher to improve their verbal communication and delivery skills in preparation for their presentations to the Board of Education, the project's culminating event.

Students' presentations included illustrations, video clips, three-dimensional models, artistically embellished overhead transparencies, and dramatic performances. Each proposal included a scientific rationale, an estimated budget, and a media presentation designed to promote the plan. See Figure 8.2 on page 101 for a photo of a three-dimensional model.

Authentic Problems Assessment

Assessment along this pathway addresses how effectively students apply the methods, knowledge, and skills of a discipline to deal with the problem at hand and in the development of related products. It also permits the assessment of a variety of skills used in genuine ways to solve real problems.

Steps Along the Authentic Problems Pathway

Putting the Authentic Problems pathway into action involves implementing the following three steps:

- Identifying (selecting, generating) a problem
- Identifying the professional roles students will assume and the talents needed; assigning student roles and organizing groups
- Aligning the problem-based experiences with curricular content and basic skills

Figure 8.3 on page 101 displays the interaction of the steps.

SNAPSHOT: ONE TEAM'S JOURNEY

The Lincoln Elementary School 4th-grade team had already been thinking about creating a problem-based experience to follow up on their study of social structures. Over several sessions the team developed a problem that involved students organizing their own company. How students defined the corporate structure also would enable the teachers to assess the students' abilities to apply what they learned about social structures in their Middle Ages unit and in their study of ant societies. Some of the concepts the team wanted to target were division of labor and distribution of power and resources. Stu-

Figure 8.1. Pond Problem Inquiry Guide Pages

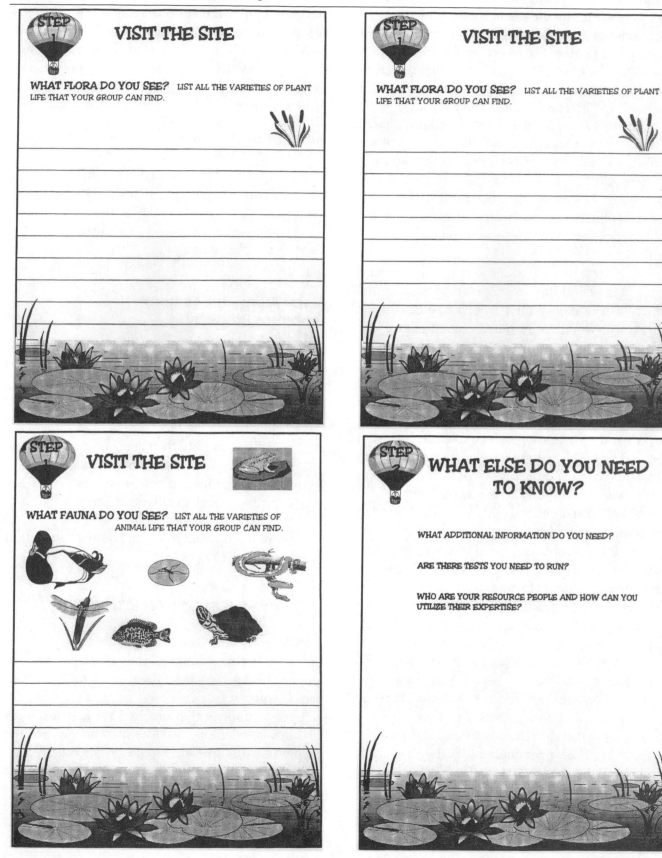

Figure 8.2. Pond Project Example

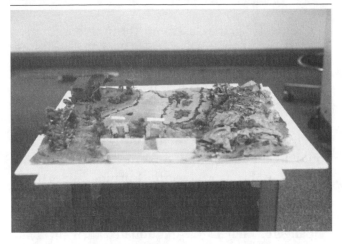

Figure 8.3. Authentic Problems Pathway Graphic

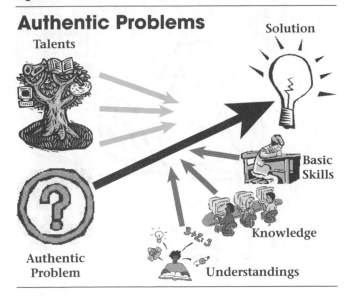

dents would be challenged to develop a company where the social structure contributed to the success of the company.

The teachers present the idea at a meeting with all the 4th graders. They invite Jan, Paul, and Carol to attend so that they are involved in the planning. The students generate many ideas and ultimately decide on establishing a computer graphics company. The teachers help their students identify the roles they will fill and talents they will need if their company is to be successful.

Management, advertising and sales, graphic art, accounting, and research and development are domains that relate to most of the intelligences and will

maximize opportunities for students to work in their areas of strengths and interests. The teachers develop job descriptions for each profession, along with the qualifications needed to get these positions. Each class member prepares a resume and applies for one or more positions for which he or she feels most qualified.

The 4th-grade team members (including the specialists) review the applications, interview the students, and select the individuals for the various positions. They also identify parents and other community members with expertise in the corporate sector or in other relevant professional roles who might share their knowledge with the students. With help from the computer teacher, Chris heads the computer graphics department. Yvette accepts a position in advertising and sales. After some research and discussion, the students opt for equal profit sharing; they all want the same number of shares of company stock.

The unit lasts 4 weeks, during which time the students design and make products, such as notecards, stationery, and book covers. Social studies, math, science, and language arts all come into play as students work together to design, market, make, and sell their products.

The students develop a brochure with descriptions and prices, which are set to yield a 10% profit. They take orders, continue to make their products, complete the transactions, and conduct a customer satisfaction survey. For his part, Chris is most engaged in product design and development. Yvette brings a concern for the customer to the company's marketing plans. While Chris works hard to make an excellent product line, Yvette works equally hard to describe the products accurately and to price them fairly.

The 4th-grade team is interested in assessing how well students apply basic skills in math, communications, and computer technology, and whether and to what extent they demonstrate understanding of concepts about social structures. The quality of the students' products also will be assessed. Most of all, the team wants to track whether the students are using professional methods and are developing abilities such as leadership, cooperation, and critical and creative thinking. The teachers share their assessment goals with the students and describe how they will document the students' work.

The team of teachers values working with the students in this way, facilitating their project work. Jan enjoys serving as the graphics art consultant. Paul is delighted with the music that students compose for advertising jingles. David comments on how engaged the students have been during the unit. He is tickled by the fact that students who never proofread or double check their work are now making sure that everything produced is spelled correctly and all calculations are accurate. Sandy remarks that the students seem to have a better understanding of fractions and percentages than they typically do after a standard math unit on the topic.

When students see a purpose to what they do, David notes, they are more inclined to make the effort. Carol is amazed that the children who have difficulty with academics seem to thrive in this authentic problem-based learning environment. She quotes one of her students, who has both learning and attention deficits: "I feel like a real businessman now. School is getting to be fun." Lillian proposes finding more opportunities over the year to use authentic problems within the curriculum.

PUTTING THE AUTHENTIC PROBLEMS PATHWAY INTO ACTION

Putting the Authentic Problems pathway into action involves identifying real problems, issues, or needs that students address collaboratively, finding real solutions or developing authentic products. Students assume the roles of practicing professionals as they use authentic methods and materials to meet their objectives. Curricular goals and basic skills are integrated into the project.

Identifying the Problem

To create a problem-based experience, start by identifying the problem. The problem can evolve from the curriculum, from a school situation, or from a real-world issue. Students might identify problems that affect them personally, or take on projects or causes that stir them to action. At Lincoln Elementary, the problem evolved from the curriculum as an extension of the social structures theme.

Forming a company was exciting and meaningful to the students.

In one 1st-grade classroom, the problem emerged from the students. One student had become fascinated by the American eagle on a camping trip with her family. Her parents told her that the eagle was in danger of becoming extinct. When she reported this to her classmates, they wanted to know more about which animals were at risk for survival and what they could do about the situation. The teacher, Terry Angelini, saw this as a powerful learning opportunity and launched the children into an authentic inquiry. As a result, they developed and sold sets of "Color Me Endangered" notecards and donated their profits to Green Peace (see Figure 8.4 for sample notecards).

Figure 8.4. Endangered Species Notecards

Scarlet Macaw

The Scarlet Macaw lives in tropical forests from Mexico to Brazil. It is endangered because of lack of habitat and illegal trade. Each bird sells for about $1,500!

Hawaiian Monk Seal

The Hawaiian Monk Seal lives in the westernmost part of the Hawaiian Islands. It is endangered because of over-hunting for its oil and fur. It looks like a chubby cigar because of a layer of fat under the skin which keeps it warm.

Identifying and Assigning Professional Roles

After you have identified the problem on which students will work, you need to identify the professional roles students will take. At that point you decide whether you wish to have the whole class work in one large group, as the teachers did at Lincoln Elementary, or form smaller companies similar to the Pond Problem scenario. Next, you decide the roles the students will play during the experience. You can either assign students to roles according to their specific strengths, or allow them to choose the roles they wish to play. At times all students will be involved in curricular tasks and at times the curriculum will be differentiated according the role assignments.

At Lincoln Elementary School the teachers let the students decide the roles that would be needed in their company. To do this the teachers invited a business-woman from the community to discuss with the 4th graders how she had started her own company, including what resources she had needed and how she had found customers. The teachers and students then brainstormed about what they needed to do to start their own company. First, they developed a business plan, objectives, and a timeline for starting the company and developing the product. They listed the roles or specialists their company would require and set the criteria for each role. The students applied for particular roles by completing an application, providing a letter of reference, and interviewing for the position.

Aligning the Problem Activities with Curriculum

The next step is to identify which areas of the curriculum will be covered through the problem exploration. In this kind of learning the acquisition and application of knowledge and skills occur within the context of solving the problem. Because the curriculum is embedded within the problem experience, students can work on the problem during the times allocated for the relevant curricular areas. In the Lincoln Elementary scenario, the teachers planned related activities to take place during math, language arts, and social studies time slots. For example, the students learned how to write a business plan and create a brochure during the language arts block. Spelling and vocabulary words for all the 4th graders came out of the project activities, while the editors of the company became particularly good proofreaders.

The teachers chose the topics of fractions, percents, and money from the 4th-grade math curriculum because these topics fit naturally with creating a business. Students would be developing a budget and discussing profits and costs. The problem-based approach opened up the opportunity to differentiate the curriculum to challenge all students. For example, while most students used calculators to work out percentages, some were able to use long division for these calculations. The company accountants learned how to use computer software to develop a spreadsheet to record expenses and income, and to create sales graphs to include in their weekly report.

Much of the work took place during the social studies block. Each social studies period began with a stockholders' meeting at which time the students made company decisions, submitted progress reports, and set up their tasks for the next day.

When the 4 weeks were over, the teachers and students used the Data Collection Matrix (Figure 8.5) to organize the kinds of data that would be used to assess the students' work. The first column of the matrix lists the specific learning outcomes targeted. The other columns indicate how these outcomes will be observed. In this case, teachers used observations, student logs, products, and student self-evaluations to assess the targeted outcomes. With student input, teachers developed rubrics with specific benchmarks aligned with the particular domain and based on three levels: novice (demonstrated some skills, was able to produce with support from teacher, etc.); emerging (few errors noted in skill areas, was able to work mostly independently, used original ideas to improve products, etc.); and expert (mastered grade- and higher-level skills, needed no assistance, attacked and solved problems eagerly and creatively, could discuss problem-solving strategies, etc.).

Guiding Your Journey

The Lincoln Elementary School teachers found the Authentic Problems Pathway Guide (shown in Figure 8.6) and the Authentic Problems Pathway Or-

Figure 8.5. Graphic Design Company Data
Collection Matrix

Learning Goal	Observation and teacher assessment	Log	Product	Self and peer assessment
Method of Documentation				
Application of social studies concepts				
Division of labor	×	×		×
Shared decision making	×	×		×
Distribution of resources			×	×
Math (accounting) skills				
Calculating percentages	×		×	
Calculating profit and loss margins	×		×	
Communication skills				
Advertising text (creativity)	×		×	×
Visual advertising				
Mechanics (grammar, punctuation, spelling in written products and advertising)	×		×	×
Computer skills				
Graphic design	×		×	
Keyboarding/ word processing	×		×	
Use of spellcheck	×			×
Product development				
Use of methods and tools	×	×	×	×
Aesthetics	×		×	×
Collaboration		×		×
Personal skills				
Leadership	×			×
Cooperation	×			×
Creativity	×		×	
Problem solving	×	×		×

ganizer very helpful in designing and implementing this learning experience. They especially liked the inclusion of how students would use their strengths and how specific skills would be integrated into the learning experience. See Figure 8.7 for their complet-

ed organizer. A reproducible blank Authentic Problems Pathway Organizer appears in the Supporting Materials section (see Figure 8.8).

Much has been written about the benefits of problem-based learning and how to align the problems with the curriculum. However, the discussion rarely focuses on students assuming authentic roles of the discipline. This exciting aspect of using problem-based curriculum ensures that students use their multiple intelligences in realistic ways. Two additional examples of authentic problems are given in the Supporting Materials section at the end of the chapter.

THOUGHT QUESTIONS AND ACTIVITIES

Thought Questions

- When authentic problems are used in the classroom, students have the opportunity to assume the role of the practicing professional. How does MI theory support this kind of authentic role play?
- Gardner defines intelligence as a way to solve a problem and develop a product. How does this definition relate to using authentic problems in the classroom?
- How did the team's understanding of MI theory enhance its initial effort in using this pathway? How did the experience contribute to Chris's and Yvette's development?
- What are the challenges and obstacles you foresee along this pathway? How might you address them?

Implementation Activities

Activity 1. In the Supporting Materials section of this chapter you will find an example of how the principal of Wolcott Elementary School initiated a school-wide use of authentic problems. As noted in the Request for Proposal (RFP), the principal devised the problem so that students would work like practicing professionals. He also encouraged students to use a variety of intelligences during the various aspects of the project.

Figure 8.6. Authentic Problems Pathway Guide

Authentic Problems Features	Things to Think About

Identify (select, generate) a problem.

Is there an issue or problem that will intrigue my students into inquiry, problem solving, and action?

- Is the issue current and does it have no clear solution?

- How might the problem or issue relate to the curriculum?

- Does the issue or problem invite the application of multiple talents and skills?

- How can the problem lead to projects and action?

Identify the professional roles students will assume and the talents needed. Assign student roles and organize groups.

What talents are needed to solve the problem?

- What are the unique talents of my students?

- How can I use their talents in setting up the authentic problem experience?

- How can I group the students so each student can contribute her talent to the solution?

Align the problem-based experiences with curricular content and basic skills.

How can I cover basic skills in my yearly curriculum through problem-based learning?

- What skills will be needed as the students pursue the problem?

- Where do these skills fit in my math, language arts, science, social studies, arts, and inquiry goals and objectives?

- How can I integrate skills into problem-solving experience?

Figure 8.7. Sample Completed Authentic Problems Pathway Organizer

Identify (select, generate) a problem.

Is there an issue or problem that will intrigue my students into inquiry, problem solving, and action?

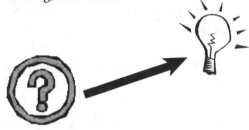

Problem: *Establishing a computer graphics company*

Purpose: *There is a need for computers for publications and posters and projects.*

Audience: *All classes and school personnel.*

Identify the professional roles students will assume and the talents needed. Assign student roles and organize groups.

What talents are needed to solve the problem? Which roles will the students assume?

Roles	Talents
Management	Math/logical, interpersonal
Advertising and sales	Interpersonal, artistic, creativity, performing arts
Graphics	Technology and visual arts
Accounting	Math
Research and development	Scientific data collectors

Align the problem-based experiences with curricular content and basic skills.

How can I cover basic skills in my yearly curriculum through problem-based learning?

Curricular areas/ activities	Targeted concepts and skills
Computer technology	Graphic design
Math	Percent and profit and gain; data analysis
Communications	Communication skills: design, product development, designing a survey
Social studies	How social structures enhance operations and production

- How does this activity allow students to use authentic problem solving and product development?
- Which intelligences were highlighted by the RFP? How did the administrator encourage teachers to participate?
- How can this idea be applied to create authentic problem-solving opportunities for the students in your school?

Activity 2. Current events and social or local (the playground) issues can be used as a starting point for authentic problem solving. Use a copy of the blank Authentic Problems Pathway Organizer provided in Supporting Materials to develop an authentic learning experience from a real problem identified by your students.

Activity 3. As illustrated by the Pond Problem and Lincoln Elementary School example, the use of authentic problems as an instructional strategy works well when the students have uninterrupted time to work on them. Discuss the pros and cons of reserving 1 week during a marking period when students can fully engage in solving an authentic problem. Explain how basic skills can be integrated into the learning experience. Plan how you can use school specialists and other experts within the school to work with the students.

Activity 4. With your colleagues, brainstorm curriculum topics through which you might offer students the opportunity to use their intellectual strengths to solve real problems and make real products. Identify experts or key people within your school who could act as mentors for the students for specific roles or domains.

SUPPORTING MATERIALS

Figure 8.8 is a reproducible blank Authentic Problems Pathway Organizer for your use. Two additional examples of authentic problem-based curricula are included in this section.

Developing Authentic Problems from Literature

In early childhood classrooms much of the curriculum revolves around a whole-language literacy approach, so creating problems from literature becomes particularly appealing. With their sophisticated themes, picture books today offer challenging possibilities from which to develop a problem-based curriculum emphasizing student inquiry in elementary and middle schools.

A team of 2nd-grade teachers we worked with used a favorite picture book of theirs, *Thunder Cake* (Polacco, 1990), to develop problem-based activities for their students. *Thunder Cake* uses colorful folk art to acquaint students with Russian culture. Using the oral history method of handing down stories to younger generations about situations that occurred in the past, the author assures young learners that, throughout the course of time, approaching storms with thunder and lightning have frightened people everywhere.

In *Thunder Cake*, a grandmother relates the story of how her own grandmother helped her overcome her fear of thunderstorms by baking a special thunder cake before a storm arrived. The grandmother artfully describes the challenge of collecting the ingredients while anticipating the closeness of the storm by counting the seconds between the flashes of lightning and the thunder claps that followed. Included is a recipe for a chocolate cake that uses tomatoes as an ingredient.

Why is *Thunder Cake* such an outstanding example of a book that can help teachers nurture the multiple intelligences of their students and structure problem-based experiences? First, the book's use of descriptive language and rich illustrations provides children with information and complex ideas. Truisms like, "Brave people can't be afraid of sounds," can lead to a lively discussion. Also, ways to overcome unfounded fears offer avenues to critical and creative thinking, and vocabulary words like *babushka*, *samovar*, *wood stove*, *dry shed*, and *trellis* will nurture linguistic potential in all youngsters.

In addition, the author's verbal descriptions of the sound of thunder introduce the idea of onomatopoeia to the youngsters, and her artistry reveals intricate visual patterns in the quilts and woven tablecloths. Embedded within the story are several disciplines—quilt making, meteorology, chemistry, psychology, and agriculture, to name a few.

Developing Possibilities. This book offered the team of teachers sufficient complexity to initiate prob-

Figure 8.8. Authentic Problems Pathway Organizer (blank)

Identify (select, generate) a problem.

Is there an issue or problem that will intrigue my students into inquiry, problem solving, and action?

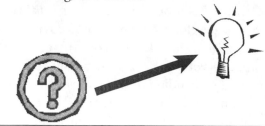

Problem:

Purpose:

Audience:

Identify the professional roles students will assume and the talents needed. Assign student roles and organize groups.

What talents are needed to solve the problem? Which roles will the students assume?

Roles	Talents

Align the problem-based experiences with curricular content and basic skills.

How can I cover basic skills in my yearly curriculum through problem-based learning?

Curricular areas/ activities	Targeted concepts and skills

lem-based learning. To think of ideas, the teachers first listed possible problems for consideration. Some of their ideas included having their students design a quilt to tell a story or to commemorate an event; become social scientists by examining fears students have in the primary grades; develop a school weather station to investigate weather patterns; and form a kitchen chemistry group to investigate how tomatoes and other ingredients affect the thunder cake.

Storytelling across generations was another point of entry for anthropology and sociology, as was examining the relationships between youngsters and their grandparents. The teachers agreed that these themes could be developed into problem-based activities for young quilt makers, psychologists, meteorologists, kitchen chemists, and anthropologists in their rooms. Each of these domains requires a different spectrum of intelligences as the children engage in authentic inquiry and develop real-world products to communicate their results.

Each teacher decided which of these ideas to develop, presented the following problems to the children, and documented in what ways these opportunities would involve authentic processes and inquiry.

Problem 1: The Quilting Society of America is commissioning the production of an original quilt to honor grandparents. To be considered, the quilt must have original symbols and patterns to portray the importance of the role grandparents play in the lives of their grandchildren.

In this problem the students assume the role of historians and quilters. The presentation of the finished quilt also may involve those students who can plan and implement such an event. This will depend on how the students plan to approach the problem.

Problem 2: Students want to know whether a person can predict how close a storm is by the lapse of time between the thunder and lightning, as indicated in the story. Can they create a weather station to detect weather patterns and develop theories to help predict the weather?

In this problem the young naturalists and scientists work with classroom engineers to de-sign instruments, observe patterns, and develop formulas for predicting the weather.

Problem 3: The Commission on the Study of Fears in Children has hired you. They want to know what students your age are afraid of and how to let other children know that they are not alone in their fears.

This problem may be appealing to children who are high in both interpersonal and intrapersonal intelligence. Further, it can offer opportunities for data collection and reporting results using creative graphs for mathematical and spatial thinkers. Writers can help report the findings. Students can assume different responsibilities in their research and development team.

Developing the Plan. Figure 8.9 is a completed organizer for Problem 3 of the *Thunder Cake* literature example. The teacher hoped to have the students report the results of their inquiry by writing an article to submit to *Creative Kids,* a journal by kids for kids. In the article the students would share their findings with other students who read the journal—just as social scientists communicate the results of their studies in the real world. The organizer shown in Figure 8.9 illustrates how all the components of this kind of learning interact to offer students an opportunity to use their strengths and apply basic skills to solve problems and develop products.

A Schoolwide Authentic Problem: W.E.I.R.D

At Wolcott Elementary School in the suburban community of West Hartford, Connecticut, a sign greets visitors as they enter: "Welcome to Wolcott Elementary School—a community of authors, visual and performing artists, and scientists and mathematicians." Here the students are given opportunities to work as practicing professionals and are expected to solve problems and create original products.

To engage students in this kind of learning, the school's principal, Plato Karafelis, issued to all teachers a Request for Proposal (see Figure 8.10) for a research project that needed undertaking. Students completed their proposals and applications (see Figure 8.11) with their teachers and peers in their classrooms.

Figure 8.9. Sample Completed Authentic Problems Pathway Organizer (Fear Study)

Identify (select, generate) a problem.

Is there an issue or problem that will intrigue my students into inquiry, problem solving, and action?

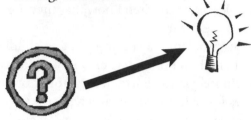

Problem: What are children afraid of and how can they overcome their fears?

Purpose: To help all kids realize that we all have fears and that there are ways to overcome them.

Audience: Article to be published in Creative Kids

Identify the professional roles students will assume and the talents needed. Assign student roles and organize groups.

What talents are needed to solve the problem? Which roles will the students assume?

Roles	Talents
Writers	Technical writing (linguistic)
Interviewers	Acting (Inter- and intrapersonal, linguistic)
Instrument developers	(interpersonal, linguistic)
Artists to illustrate and design charts and graphs	Visual artists (spatial, bodily–kinesthetic)
Statisticians	Mathematics (logical–mathematical)
Psychologists to develop fear-reduction strategies	Personal/social problem solvers (inter- and intrapersonal)

Align the problem-based experiences with curricular content and basic skills.

How can I cover basic skills in my yearly curriculum through problem-based learning?

Curricular areas/ activities	Targeted concepts and skills
Mathematics	*Designing a survey:* Collecting, organizing, and interpreting data. *Creating graphs and charts:* Graphing data. Using fractions.
Language Arts	*Designing a survey:* Formulating questions. Using spelling and punctuation. *Writing an article:* Vocabulary and spelling. Organizing an article. Proofreading. *Conducting a focus group:* Interviewing skills
Social Studies	*Understanding others*

Figure 8.10. W.E.I.R.D. Request for Proposal

W.E.I.R.D.
GATHER , ANALYZE, AND PRESENT REQUEST FOR PROPOSAL

The Problem: W.E.I.R.D. is interested in knowing every piece of data about people who enter and exit Wolcott School through the front door. How many people enter and exit? What are their ages? Are they male or female? Do more people enter and exit on Monday or Tuesday? Is there a time of day that is busiest? Why have they come to Wolcott? Did they accomplish their goal? W.E.I.R.D wants to know the answers to these and other questions you can think of.

The Application: (see attached) This is a competitive grant. Any classroom in the school may apply for this opportunity. Only one classroom will be chosen. Final selections will be determined by a committee of parents, teachers, and central office personnel. Students must be involved in the application process. Parents *may* be involved in the application process. If no applications meet W.E.I.R.D standards, no class will be chosen.

Criteria of Selection: Thoroughness of application; neatness of application; breadth and depth of questions to be addressed; plans for final presentation of data; description of process; proposed budget: parental involvement in the process; integration with math and writing curricula.

Procedure: Submit application by the due date. Upon selection, begin planning the project with the whole class. Submit to periodic review on the first of each month.

Resources: The classroom that is selected to receive the W.E.I.R.D grant will receive the following resources:

1. $500.00 for the purchase of classroom learning materials to be used for this project. Materials may include resource books, charts, markers, manipulatives, etc.
2. Two professional days for the teacher to visit other schools or attend related conferences.
3. A classroom pizza party.
4. Teaching assistant assigned to your class for 5 days.
5. Bus money for a field trip.
6. The students may choose a book which Dr. K. [principal] will read to the class.

Presentation of Findings: At the completion of the project, the researchers will present their findings to a panel of experts. The presentation will be open to the public. Data must be complete, accurate, clearly presented, and neat. We would like to see problem statements, predictions, charts, writing, a short play or song, pieces of art based on your experience, and conclusions.

Master of Research: Upon completion, each researcher (students and teacher) will be honored as a Master of Research. This honor will be presented at a formal evening ceremony that will include parents and distinguished guests. Each researcher will receive a medal, a certificate, and a T-shirt. Masters of Research will be formally presented at a "town meeting." The Master of Research distinction is intended to be the highest mathematics and science honor bestowed by the school. Students who receive this distinction may thereafter sign their names followed by the initials, M.R., e.g., Robert Hawkins, M.R.

Figure 8.11. W.E.I.R.D. Application

W.E.I.R.D. APPLICATION

Teacher:

Date:

1. List all the questions you plan to answer about the problem.
2. Select three questions from the above list and make predictions based on some kind of logic.
3. Who will be involved in this project and how?
4. How and when will you gather data?
5. For the teacher: How will you integrate this project into your math and writing curriculum?
6. Why should your class be selected for this project?

Note: Applications must be received by 9:00 A.M. on March 1. Neatness counts.

FOR FURTHER STUDY

Eberle, B., & Standish, B. (1980). *CPS (Creative problem solving) for kids.* Buffalo, NY: D.O.K.

Introduces students to a six-step strategy for solving authentic problems.

IMSA Center for Problem-Based Learning. *http://www. imsa.edu/team/cpbl/cpbl.html*

Established by the Illinois Math and Science Academy to engage in problem-based learning research, information exchange, teacher training, and curriculum development in K–16 educational settings.

Renzulli, J. S. (1977). *The enrichment triad model.* Mansfield Center, CT: Creative Learning Press.

Explains how to move students from being just lesson learners to creators of new knowledge.

Steippen, W. (1991). *Case studies involving legal issues* (*Wall Street Journal* classroom ed.). New York: Wall Street Journal.

Examines complicated issues of real legal cases. Provides excellent topics with which to launch student inquiry projects.

Steippen, W. (1995). *A guide for designing problem-based instructional materials.* Geneva, IL: Human Learning Resources.

A thorough and practical guide for developing problem-based learning opportunities in the classroom. Outlines a ten-step procedure to develop instructional units.

Wigginton, E. (1982). *A Foxfire Christmas: Appalachian memories and traditions.* Chapel Hill: University of North Carolina Press.

> One in a series of books with students as anthropologists immersing themselves in the Appalachian culture. Inquiry projects integrate all areas of the curriculum and are models for authentic problems and projects at the secondary level.

Materials that allow students to solve problems by using authentic methods of a discipline include:

Lewis, B. (1991). *The kid's guide to social action.* Minneapolis, MN: Free Spirit.

Lewis, B. (1995). *Kids with courage: True stories about young people making a difference.* Minneapolis, MN: Free Spirit.

Miles, B. (1991). *Save the earth: An action handbook for kids.* Madison, WI: Demco Media.

Wiggers, R. (1996). *The amateur geologist.* Missoula, MT: Mountain Press.

CHAPTER 9

The Talent Development Pathway

What happens when a teacher recognizes a special talent in a student? That teacher may want to support the youngster but feel stymied and frustrated by her lack of time, resources, and sufficient familiarity with the domain. This pathway supports the creation of different kinds of talent development activities—classroom-based and school-wide—for all students to explore and develop their special talents. It also suggests more rigorous opportunities for students in need of higher levels of challenge.

PATHWAY BACKGROUND

Talent development opportunities traditionally are offered to students who have been identified as "gifted." Who these students are often is dictated by a school district's definition of giftedness and by what is valued by the school community. For the most part, conceptions of giftedness applied today restrict gifted education services to a select few, typically those who score high on an IQ test. Conceptions of giftedness that are broad in nature, however, allow for the development of talents in many areas for many students.

The concept of giftedness emerged in this country early in the 20th century with the work of Lewis Terman. As discussed in Chapter 2, Terman was largely responsible for the advent of wide-scale IQ testing in this country. Interested in understanding the characteristics of students who scored at the high extreme on his *Stanford-Binet Test of Intelligence*, Terman instituted a longitudinal study of 1,528 children who had scored in the top 3–5% (over 135 IQ) on the Stanford-Binet test. His conception of giftedness as a high IQ score continues to influence who is considered gifted and how gifted education is implemented today.

In the 1970s, however, growing dissatisfaction with this definition led to the introduction of some broader views of gifted and talented, including the U.S. Department of Education's federal definition (1975, 1978, 1991, and 1993). The federal definition identified multiple areas in which one could be gifted: general intelligence, specific aptitude, creativity, leadership, and the visual and performing arts. The latest version defines giftedness as occurring when

> . . . children and youth of outstanding ability or talent perform or show the potential for performing at remarkably high levels of accomplishments when compared with others of their age, experience or environment. (Office of Educational Research and Improvement, 1993, p. 26)

Other researchers in education and psychology also advanced more expansive conceptions of giftedness. Siegler and Kotoszsky (1986) found that most fall into two categories: those that rely solely on IQ and those that involve multiple qualities, including social, motivational, and creative factors (see Figure 9.1 for examples of different conceptions of giftedness).

Joseph Renzulli, Director of the National Research Center on the Gifted and Talented, refers to these two conceptions of giftedness as "schoolhouse giftedness" and "creative productive giftedness." The first is characterized by high intelligence on traditional measures of giftedness in one or more academic domains. Students who are schoolhouse gifted are extraordinary learners in formal educational settings and need more advanced or accelerated educational programs. Such precocity does not predict achievement in life, however (Renzulli, 1986).

Conceptions of creative productive giftedness, on the other hand, describe those individuals who are

Figure 9.1. Conceptions of Giftedness

IQ as Major Consideration	
Theory	Key Features
Terman (1926) Longitudinal studies of genius	Extraordinary intellectual ability as measured on traditional test of intelligence. Top 1–3% of population.
Silverman (1997) Psychological needs of gifted individuals	High-IQ students who exhibit early signs of giftedness: unusual alertness in infancy, long attention span, high activity level, extraordinary memory, sense of humor, enjoyment and speed of learning, early language development.
Stanley (1997), Bembow & Lubinski (1997) Mathematically precocious youth	High aptitude in a domain and in need of acceleration.

Multifaceted Approach	
Theory	Key Features
Renzulli (1985) Three ring conception of giftedness	Developmental model for encouraging gifted behavior, defined as confluence of average ability, task commitment, and creativity brought to bear on specific domains or specific areas of interest or talent.
Tannenbaum (1997) Intellective and nonintellective factors: general ability, special aptitude, environmental supports, chance	Giftedness is the potential for becoming critically acclaimed performers or exemplary producers of ideas in spheres of activity that enhance the moral, social, intellectual, or aesthetic life of humanity.
Sternberg, (1997) Triarchic theory of intelligence	Giftedness is a blend of analytic, synthetic, and practical abilities.

not merely consumers of knowledge but producers of new knowledge in particular domains. IQ scores alone are not valid measures of creative productive giftedness. Rather, measures of talent, interest, and creativity within a particular domain uncover creative productive giftedness (Renzulli, 1986).

Renzulli for many decades has promoted a more inclusive definition of giftedness. The first researcher to challenge the traditional definitions, Renzulli (1978) argued that scoring in the top 3–5% on measures of aptitude or achievement does not predict

adult giftedness. Renzulli offered the *three-ring conception of giftedness* (Figure 9.2) in place of what he perceived as an inappropriate, exclusive definition.

Renzulli maintained that creative, productive people who make significant contributions to society possess a relatively well-defined set of three interlocking clusters of traits: above average (not necessarily superior) ability, task commitment (or passion), and creativity. No single cluster makes giftedness; rather, it is the interaction of these traits that underlies creative productivity in specific areas and domains. In other words, individuals are gifted in real-world endeavors and are not just able test takers. It is this productivity that Renzulli defines as gifted behavior.

Given that multiple intelligences theory rejects a unitary view of intelligence, it similarly rejects a unitary definition of giftedness. Unlike traditional definitions based on IQ measures or standardized achievement test scores, multiple intelligences theory supports the view that students exhibit a diversity of talents in which they can be gifted.

Like Renzulli, Gardner (1999b) defines the truly talented person, or to use his term, *creator*, as possessing similar traits. These individuals master a domain, are willing to experiment and not deterred by failure, and demonstrate "a potential to solve problems, create products or raise issues in a domain in a way that is initially novel but is eventually accepted in one of more cultural settings" (p. 116).

In developing his theory of multiple intelligences, Gardner studied a variety of creators who were especially talented in particular domains. From their contributions he inferred which specific abilities or intelligences were needed to explain such high levels of performance. For instance, Gardner attributed Picasso's artistic talent to his high levels of spatial intelligence. Gardner suggests that talented individuals are drawn to and maintain a high degree of attraction to a particular quality or feature of a domain.

MI theory is not "anti-gifted," as has been claimed. In fact, Gardner (1999b) readily admits that "people are not created equal, nor are all intelligences" (p.115). He describes gifted and talented youngsters as those who perform particular tasks in specific domains earlier than their peers, causing them to stand out and be noticed. Some possess extraordinary talents at young ages and can be regard-

Figure 9.2. Graphic Representation of the Three-Ring Conception of Giftedness

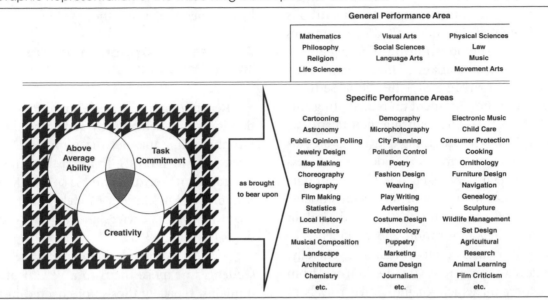

ed as child prodigies. MI theory, in essence, widens the lens on how giftedness is identified and nurtured. While each individual has potential in all intelligences, some have above average strength in particular intelligences or domains. For Gardner (1993b), this proclivity, together with a great interest or passion in the domain, often suggests a special talent.

Renzulli (1978) describes two kinds of abilities: general (traditional measures of ability and achievement) and, more important, specific. Analogous to Gardner's conception of intelligence, he claims ability as manifested in activities that represent the ways in which human beings express themselves in real-life domains, such as chemistry, ballet, mathematics, musical composition, and sculpture. Renzulli's conception of giftedness also is based on real-world problem solving and the development of creative products.

What Is Talent Development?

The future of any society depends on the development of its most precious resources—the gifts, talents, and interests of its students. According to a 1993 report by the Office of Educational Research and Improvement (OERI), the United States is failing to recognize and develop the potential of many students. That so many students do not actualize their potential may be the fault of an educational system that fails to meet the diverse needs of today's students.

As Linda Darling-Hammond (1996) argues, what is needed is an education

> that seeks competence as well as community, that enables all people to find and act on who they are, what their passions, gifts, and talents may be, what they care about, and how they want to make a contribution to each other and the world. (p. 2)

Gardner (1993d), too, thinks schools should recognize and develop potential strengths and talents.

> In my view the purpose of school should be to develop intelligences and to help people reach vocational and avocational goals that are appropriate to their particular spectrum of intelligences. People who are helped to do so, I believe, feel more engaged and competent and therefore more inclined to serve society in a constructive way. (p. 9)

In other words, talent development should be a major educational goal.

Unfortunately, too few students are identified and served by the traditional definitions of gifted education that underlie most gifted and talented programs. As noted in OERI's 1993 report, a variety of factors interfere with our ability to recognize potential talent in more students, especially those whose talents lie in areas outside of linguistic and mathematical domains.

Chief among the factors that prevent recognition of talent in more students is conservative definitions of gifted and talented. Second, limited opportunities exist for students to demonstrate outstanding potential across a variety of domains. Third, talent development is not a priority in most educational settings. More time and money are spent on remediating students' weaknesses than on nurturing their talents.

In reality, however, programs that focus on student weaknesses have not met with widespread success (Hopfenberg & Levin, 1993; Renzulli, 1994). Not only do these factors lead to lost opportunities for students to develop their talents, but they may indeed result in students' diminished motivation and confidence in their ability to learn and be successful more generally.

Talent development refers to the journey from novice to expert on which an individual travels in his/her area of talent. Gardner (1993b) studied this development by tracking the individual journeys of seven "creators" in different domains. He was able to discern particular benchmarks in their development as well as environmental influences.

Indeed, whether or not a potential is actualized depends on a variety of factors, including family influence, supportive environment, talent development opportunities, and cultural receptivity. These factors are addressed when adults identify specific talent or potential in students and provide opportunities that move the individual from novice stages to expert performances within a domain. Talent represents abilities *within a domain* and programs should be designed to develop those talents.

Services and Opportunities for Talent Development

Renzulli and Reis (1997) maintain that we can develop gifted behavior by arranging the school environment in a manner that capitalizes on students' strengths and interests. To foster this kind of learning environment, Renzulli and his colleagues created the Schoolwide Enrichment Model (SEM), which offers a continuum of services and opportunities for students (see Figure 9.3).

At the beginning levels, services are offered to all students to expose them to a wealth of topics and domains, typically those not covered in the regular curriculum. When particular students are ready for more challenging experiences, they may be identified for more advanced talent development opportunities. These opportunities may include modifications or additions to the curriculum or specialized programs for which students may be identified or choose to participate.

Exposure and Enrichment Activities for All Students

Identifying talents creates the need to provide exposure activities for all students across a diversity

Figure 9.3. Continuum of Services for Talent Development

Service	Implementation	Sample opportunities for talent development	Entrance requirements
Exposure and enrichment activities (Offered to all students)	Classroom Exploration activities within and outside of the regular curriculum	• Exploration activities • Differentiation based on interests and strengths (entry and destination points) • Interest centers	• Informal observations • Choice
	Enrichment opportunities outside of the regular classroom	• Speakers, mini-courses • Enrichment clusters	• Interests, strengths • Nominations, self-selection
Talent Development Programs (Offered to some students who show readiness for advanced opportunities)	Modification of the regular curriculum	• Individual or small-group investigation of a real-world problem	• Student's in-depth interest
	Rigorous talent development within a domain	• Advanced placement classes • Talent development classes taught by professionals within the domain • Mentorships and apprenticeships • Specialized schools	• Formal assessment of talent within a domain

of domains or intelligences. Initial exposure may include beginning instruction in talent areas to ascertain students' potential. Enriched experiences within the classroom provide the platform from which to launch talent development opportunities. (Moreover, students feel like valued members of the classroom community and can become highly motivated when they are given opportunities to work in their areas of strength and interest.)

Work in the other pathways can set the stage for talent development. The Exploration pathway (Chapter 5) focuses on creating or arranging the environment to expose students to diverse experiences and provides opportunities to observe and identify students' abilities. Starting with exploration activities we can identify those kinds of experience that show students at their personal best and begin to recognize talent potential. We can use these observations to shape and organize later talent development opportunities.

Alternative entry and exit points from the Bridging, Understanding, and Authentic Problems pathways give students the chance to use their strengths and interests in meaningful ways. These differentiated learning experiences would likely reveal students' talents as well. Any learning event may present itself as an opportunity to observe student talent in action.

An enriched classroom environment is the setting for initial exposure activities and for observing students' talents. However, daily classroom fare alone generally is not sufficient to develop talents, for several reasons. Classroom activities focus on the prescribed curriculum, which is sure to leave out many potential talents. Moreover, talent development requires grouping students with others of similar talents and interests so that they can work together and challenge one another. Powerful talent development experiences also rely on adult mentors who model the skills, methods, dispositions, and attitudes of the practicing professional.

The Talent Development pathway supports the creation of experiences purposefully designed to identify and nurture talent in its own right, as shown in the continuum of services in Figure 9.3. The Schoolwide Enrichment Model has several components that can be used in and outside of the classroom for talent development purposes. Especially germane to our discussion is the model's "enrichment cluster" component.

Enrichment clusters are "non-graded groups of students who share common interests and come together during specially designed time blocks to pursue these interests" (Renzulli & Reis, 1997, p. 296). In a cluster, children decide with their mentor or teacher-facilitator which product or service they will produce. The curriculum for the cluster is guided by three questions.

1. What do people with an interest in this area do?
2. What knowledge, materials, and other resources do individuals need to perform authentic activities in this area?
3. In what ways can individuals use the product or service to affect the intended audience?

A puppet-theater group, for example, might include puppet makers, directors, actors, writers, and set and costume designers. The students join because of their common interest but contribute to the group using their different talents. "Every child is special if educators create conditions in which that child can be a specialist within a specialized group" (Renzulli, personal communication, August 2, 2004).

Talent Development Programs

Talent development opportunities described thus far are somewhat informal and include all children. There are occasions, however, when certain youngsters demonstrate outstanding abilities within a domain and require even more challenging opportunities. Some of these opportunities require modification of the regular curriculum so that students can engage in more advanced or independent work. The most rigorous are programs specifically designed for talent development.

Although talent development programs vary depending on the domain and the approach that is adopted, most have several components in common (Bloom, 1985; Csikszentmihalyi, Rathunde, & Whalen, 1993; Renzulli & Reis, 1997). First, there is a formal identification process closely linked to the features and behaviors of the domain or talent area. Once students are identified, they work with knowledgeable adults to develop expertise and creative productivity within their talent area. Other types of specialized programs may include accelerated classes, specialized schools, and mentorship opportunities with experts or professionals. See the Supporting Materials section for descriptions of three different talent development programs.

Talent Development Assessment

Assessment comes in two forms in the Talent Development pathway: identifying talent in students and assessing the development of a student's talent from novice to expert.

Talent identification at the initial stage involves making informal observations. Rather than search for high-level skill only, which may or may not be present at this point, look for other behaviors as well (see Figure 5.3, in Chapter 5). Students tell us a lot about themselves in their expressions of interest and enthusiasm and with their initial forays into new domains.

Identifying talent should include methods that are authentic to the domain. For a 4-year-old, that might mean playing a board game to observe and assess her mathematical abilities, such as Project Spectrum's Dinosaur Game and the Bus Game (Chen, Krechevsky, & Viens, 1998). As students get older, identifying their talents can look more like the Authentic Problems pathway (Chapter 8), where students participate in—and are assessed using—real domain-specific projects.

In order to assess talent, criteria or indicators of ability are required. The need for efficient and systematic means to assess talent invites the use of checklists, rubrics, and portfolios to organize and make sense of observations and student work from a talent identification standpoint.

Multiple intelligences theory frames the identification and clustering of abilities. Recognizing the intelligences that contribute to a talent in a particular domain will help to set identification criteria. The criteria can be used as an observational or postobservational checklist to describe and assess students' problem solving and talent within a particular domain (see Figure 9.4). In the case of

Project Spectrum, key abilities of each intelligence (see The Eight Intelligences section in Chapter 2) were used to organize more open-ended observation notes (Chen et al., 1998). Patterns of students' high-level use of particular intelligences were identified in the observations across disparate domain activities.

Figure 9.4 is a checklist for the identification of science talent in 4th and 5th graders. Students participate in a series of talent discovery activities over several weeks. Observations of the students help identify those who are ready for more challenging opportunities. The criteria on the checklist indicate strengths in logical–mathematical and spatial intelligences within the domain of science.

Steps Along the Talent Development Pathway

The steps of the Talent Development pathway are:

- Establishing or clarifying your vision and goals for talent development.
- Identifying existing talent development opportunities.
- Investigating other possibilities for talent development.
- Developing a Talent Development action plan.

Figure 9.5 provides a visual representation of the Talent Development pathway.

SNAPSHOT: ONE TEAM'S JOURNEY

Currently Lincoln Elementary School has no gifted and talented program. However, many of the faculty and administration are keenly interested in providing talent development opportunities to their students. A committee has been formed to investigate existing programs. Lillian Vega and other members of the 4th-grade team sit on the committee.

Each of the committee members has volunteered to study one program model, and those who can will visit programs in the area. The group meets monthly to share and discuss the models and their suitability for Lincoln Elementary. The committee's goal is to

Figure 9.4. Science Talent Checklist

Talent Discovery Checklist

Rater: _____ Date: _____ Science Area: _____

Directions: For each student listed, mark a "+" in the appropriate space when you first observe the student exhibiting any of the behaviors listed in the first column.

Student Behaviors	Student Name									
Displays curiosity by asking relevant questions.										
Shows a lot of knowledge related to today's topics.										
Actively manipulates materials.										
Communicates clearly the results of the project.										
Systematically tests hypothesis.										
Tries to predict outcomes.										
Represents ideas in the form of a model.										
Finds means of overcoming obstacles in problem-solving.										

Following the team's discussion concerning student behaviors observed, each rater should assign a holistic score for each student based upon the following key:

3 = Place student in talent development class
2 = Defer judgment
1 = Placement in talent development class not appropriate at this time

Student Name										
Holistic Score										

submit an action plan to the principal by the end of the current school year.

At the first meeting of the committee, Lillian talks about how the Pathways Model has resulted in opportunities for her to observe and nurture some of her students' special talents within the classroom. Lillian adds that since she started using MI theory to organize her practices, she is seeing her students in a new way. MI theory and the eight intelligences act like a "strengths-based lens" through which she sees each child's special talents and interests.

David Barnes, another member of the 4th-grade team, joins Lillian in describing Chris's engineering abilities and Yvette's sensitivity to people and her flair for drama. Through classroom activities informed by multiple intelligences, both Lillian and David ad-

mit that they are more attuned to and are becoming better at identifying their students' strengths and interests.

The two share some ideas they have for incorporating students' strength areas into the regular curriculum. Their motivation comes from Chris and Yvette who, since the teachers' implementation of an MI approach, have become active learners and enthusiastic participants, especially when they get to build and act.

At the second meeting, Laura Finestein, a 3rd-grade teacher, presents the Schoolwide Enrichment Model (SEM) to her colleagues (see Figure 9.3). She proposes that Lincoln Elementary offer enrichment clusters. In enrichment clusters, part of the SEM, cross-grade groups of students work together to

Figure 9.5. Talent Development Pathway Graphic

Talent Development

Specialized Opportunities

School-Wide Enrichment
(clubs, clusters, teams)

In-Class Enrichment
and Choices

**Vision:
All students have a right
to have talent development.
Some need advanced opportunities.**

solve problems, make products, or deliver a service (Renzulli, Gentry, & Reis, 2003). Students join clusters according to their interests and contribute according to their talents. One school Laura visited had expanded its traditional academic gifted program to offer a variety of enrichment clusters for all children (see Supporting Materials).

The committee members like this idea, especially when it comes to providing opportunities for students in areas the teachers themselves feel ill-equipped to support. For example, David and Lillian understand that an acting coach could nurture Yvette and other promising actors more professionally. Chris and other budding engineers would progress in leaps and bounds if they were offered the chance to work with a practicing engineer. Enrichment clusters led by adults with domain expertise would provide the types of experiences and modeling to support the development of the students' talents.

At the next meeting, Jennifer Todd, the assistant principal, reports that she has read two interesting books: *The Enrichment Triad Model* (Renzulli, 1977) and *Developing the Gifts and Talents of All Students in the Regular Classroom* (Beecher, 1996). She explains that, according to these books, talent development involves helping students with advanced abilities become "creative producers."

The Enrichment Triad Model exposes students to various topics of interest and fields of study. Its focus is to support students' use of "advanced-content, process-training skills and methodology" in their areas of interest (see Supporting Materials for a description of this model).

David and Lillian are intrigued by this model and plan to consult with the 4th-grade team to determine whether and how to use it in their classrooms. Both already use interest centers in their classrooms as part of other pathways. Now they are considering using them as a vehicle for students' independent investigations.

Over the next few weeks David and Lillian—in consultation with the 4th-grade team—think about developing a research interest center as a means to stimulate students' curiosity about research. If an individual or a small group of students becomes excited about a topic, the teachers agree that they will find a way for the students to investigate it independently, even if it is outside of the regular curriculum.

The team sees the research interest center as a way to introduce students to research in different disciplines through a variety of exploratory, skill-building, and independent project activities. The teachers decide to place the center in the hallway and allow students to work at it on a fixed schedule or during their free time. The teachers gather and organize activities that will serve as entry points into learning about research and that will provide them the opportunity to observe students in different research-related activities.

David once again observes Yvette's concern and curiosity about people in her center activities. Yvette has become intrigued with an old photo album that, in effect, traces the history of an unknown family. Yvette is drawn to the details in the photographs, and her curiosity is piqued. She generates interesting questions about the family portrayed in the album. She applies her spatial and interpersonal intelligences once again, this time in the domain of history. Yvette tells David that she wants to become a historian so that she can understand people from different times in history.

Team members identify Yvette's response as a teachable moment that should not be lost. They meet to figure out how to give Yvette—and other students in the future—an opportunity to pursue her own investigation. But how can they focus on Yvette with many other students in their charge? And how can they make time for Yvette to conduct a special project above and beyond the regular curriculum?

As part of their language arts program, David arranges a field trip to the Noah Webster House so that students can understand how biographers gather data for their books. The curator tells the class about Jerusha Webster, Noah Webster's older sister. Yvette is fascinated and asks if she can come back to learn more about Jerusha.

David decides that he will help Yvette conduct an independent study that also will address parts of the social studies and language arts curricula. In his mind, one in-depth experience will benefit Yvette more than rushing through the topics to be covered in the curriculum. However, he is still challenged to integrate some of the 4th-grade curriculum goals into the project.

When David discusses the idea with the 4th-grade team, Jan, the art teacher, says that an acquaintance of hers, a recently retired history buff, Frank Olsen, would make a great mentor for Yvette. She thinks he would be happy to work with Yvette. For her part, Yvette loves the idea and can hardly wait to begin.

The next week Frank meets with David and Yvette to outline a plan for the investigation. Because very few people know about Jerusha Webster, they decide that Yvette can address this state of affairs by developing a slide show to be presented at the local historical museum.

With the support of Frank and David, Yvette conducts her project like a real historian. She collects and reviews multiple sources of data through interviews, an examination of artifacts, and original documents at the Noah Webster House. Her show is entitled "A Day in the Life of Jerusha Webster." In it she becomes Jerusha Webster, dressed in costume and speaking dramatically about her life in colonial times. Yvette's slide show is put on display in the museum.

Through her historical research, Yvette has worked on several pieces of the 4th-grade language arts and social studies curricula. She also has developed technical skills in the process. David is very satisfied with the extent to which Yvette was able to nurture her talent while working on some of her academic requirements. He and the other team members are thrilled to observe Yvette becoming increasingly confident and independent, the telltale signs of a creative producer, over the 10-week project.

Lillian describes Yvette's independent study at the next meeting of the team studying gifted programs. She reports that her team's use of the Exploration pathway, which entailed adding new types of experiences in their classrooms and observing their students in action, was the perfect starting place for identifying their students' talents. She notes that an enrichment specialist within the school could facilitate this kind of learning for many students. They wonder whether existing faculty at the school could share the role for the near future, using the Exploration pathway as a launching pad.

Jennifer raises the idea of instituting a more formal gifted program. She describes some interesting talent development programs that had been funded as part of the Jacob Javits Gifted and Talented Program. The Javits program was designed to identify and nurture gifts in students who are typically not represented in traditional gifted and talented programs. Javits-funded programs generally focus on specific domains, also typically underrepresented in gifted education programs, such as performing arts, science, engineering, and writing.

Eve Hodet, the Lincoln Elementary School principal, describes one such program in the arts developed by ArtsConnection in New York City (see Supporting Materials). Talent Beyond Words identifies and serves inner-city students with talents in the arts. Eve wonders whether there is a similar resource their school might be able to tap into to support arts domains in their talent development initiative.

Carol, the resource teacher, suggests investigating some programs that would serve students like Chris. She has noticed that more than a few students with learning disabilities have engineering talent or above average spatial and bodily–kinesthetic intelligences. These abilities are evident in art classes, especially when the students are working on three-dimensional projects.

Carol proposes that the committee explore funding sources to develop an engineering or advanced art program that could serve as a pilot for a larger-scale, domain-specific gifted program in the future. Eve, the principal, suggests checking out ArtConnection's Javits-funded arts talent development program in New York City as a model.

After hearing the reports from its members, the committee on gifted education gathers to make its recommendations. In terms of their available resources—time, money, and personnel—starting a pilot enrichment cluster program appears to be the most practical first step. After discussing the idea with Eve, the committee decides to try the approach with 3rd-, 4th-, and 5th-grade students and their teachers in the fall.

Postscript

In late September of the following year the teachers plan for Friday afternoon clusters that will meet for a 6-week trial, October through December. They design offerings based on a combination of students' interests and the talents of teachers who will be leading the clusters. As with any given group of adults, a range of intelligences is represented across the options. Students will choose a cluster based on their interests and contribute to it according to their particular spectrums of strengths. The pilot offerings are shown in Figure 9.6.

Thinking back to the interest inventories her students completed the first week of school, Lillian Vega is confident that each of her students will find a cluster that aligns with his or her interests. She thinks about Chris and Yvette, now in 5th grade, and wonders which clusters they will choose. Chris may tap his engineering abilities in the puppetry or paper engineering cluster. Yvette might become a puppeteer

Figure 9.6. Pilot Enrichment Cluster Offerings

Domain	Cluster
Dramatic Arts	Puppetry Players
Zoology	Society for the Prevention of Cruelty to Snakes
Anthropology	Cultural Travel Club
Design Technology	Paper Engineering Guild
Visual Arts	Animators Inc.
Language Arts	Comedy Club
Ecology	Recyclables and More
Mathematics	Surveys Unlimited

or, more likely, join the cultural travel club to pursue her intrigue with understanding people.

PUTTING THE TALENT DEVELOPMENT PATHWAY INTO ACTION

This pathway requires a dedicated group of school members to carefully plan how to provide opportunities for talent development. There are many opportunities both within the classroom and in the wider community. These decisions should consider the student population and the available resources. It is always advisable to start small and pilot some ideas, expanding as you learn what works best. The following sections provide information to guide your efforts. Outlined below is a review of the major features that define the activities of the Talent Development pathway.

Establishing or Clarifying Your Vision and Goals for Talent Development

The first step of this process is to formulate a vision or philosophy for talent development as an important aspect of your school's mission. When teachers at Lincoln Elementary witnessed the positive effects of focusing on students' strengths, interests, and talents, they embraced the idea of adding talent development to their school's mission statement. Once talent development became a school-wide goal, they felt they could develop a systematic approach for providing talent development activities. To accomplish this they formed a committee to investigate the approach that would suit the needs of their students.

Identifying Existing Talent Development Opportunities

The next step is to determine the opportunities that already exist for talent recognition and nurturance. The most common programs can be found in the area of athletics. These programs are excellent opportunities for talent development. Other opportunities may include advanced classes within the school, mentorship, or independent study options. Some schools support an artists-in-residence program, chorus, or student government. Assessing the kinds of activities already in place will help you decide what else needs to be done.

Assessing what has already been done also includes looking at the regular curriculum. Questions such as these can guide your thinking: Is the Exploration pathway used to support initial talent development efforts? Do teachers use the information they notice about students to differentiate the curriculum in the classroom (Bridging, Understanding, and Authentic Problems pathways)?

Any existing programs can support talent development and serve as the foundation for a more wide-scale program. The teachers at Lincoln Elementary School felt they were using the pathways to accommodate the needs of many students in their classroom, but felt inadequate to foster talent development as a major commitment. In short, they agreed that a more formal school-wide program might better serve the talent development needs of their students.

Investigating Other Possibilities for Talent Development

Once you decide to expand the talent development accommodations in your school, you must determine which approach will best meet your students' needs. Reading about program models, visiting ongoing programs, and hiring a consultant to help are all viable strategies. The Lincoln Elementary School committee decided to both read about models for talent development and visit local programs. The members of the committee volunteered to undertake specific tasks and report their findings to the committee.

Developing a Talent Development Action Plan

The final step is to evaluate the possibilities that exist and decide which ones you wish to put into action. Develop a specific timeline and responsibilities for putting your plan into action. As in the case of Lincoln Elementary, the committee decided that their school's needs would be best met by piloting an enrichment cluster program for the following fall. They chose to begin with grades 3, 4 and 5.

Guiding Your Journey

The Lincoln Elementary teachers used the Talent Development Pathway Guide (see Figure 9.7) to complete the Talent Development Pathway Organizer (Figure 9.8) to help them plan talent development opportunities for their students. A blank organizer (Figure 9.9 in the Supporting Materials section) can help you identify those opportunities that are appropriate for your context and meet the needs of your particular student population.

There are many ways to provide opportunities for talent development. The essential components of talent development are recognizing the talent and providing opportunities to develop that talent, preferably with help from a knowledgeable adult facilitator or mentor.

When students are at the initial stages of talent development, opportunities can be informal and used as a way to identify the level of potential talent, interest, and commitment shown by the students. As their talents develop, they will need increasingly challenging opportunities to help them become creative producers. When the students—and the school—are ready for a rigorous program, a more formal identification procedure may be implemented, coupled with talent development experiences conducted by experts within a domain.

THOUGHT QUESTIONS AND ACTIVITIES

Group discussions of the questions that follow as well as participation in the activities will enhance your understanding of the major ideas presented in the Talent Development pathway.

Thought Questions

- Should talent development be a priority for education? Defend your position.
- What are the implications of MI theory for gifted education?
- Think about your school's priorities and practices. Is the climate ripe for talent development? In what ways is talent development supported and in what ways is it inhibited?

Figure 9.7. Talent Development Pathway Guide

Talent Development Feature	Things to Think About
Establish or clarify your vision and goals for talent development.  *In what ways should the school be committed to developing the talents of its students?*	• What is my philosophy about the role of school in developing talents in students? • How do I define talent? • Which services should we offer and to whom?
Identify existing talent development opportunities. *Existing Opportunities:* • *In-class enrichment and choices* • *School-wide enrichment (clubs, clusters, teams)* • *Specialized programs* 	• What kinds of in-class activities do I use to help students identify, develop, and apply their talents? • How has my use of MI pathways (exploration, bridging, understanding, and authentic problems) nurtured students' talents? • What school-wide opportunities are already in place for enrichment, nurturing student interests, and developing student talent and advanced abilities?
Investigate other possibilities for talent development. *What opportunities exist in other districts, in your school's community, or online for talent development?* *Search for new ideas:* • *In-class enrichment and choices* • *School-wide enrichment (clubs, clusters, teams)* • *Specialized programs* 	• Are our most advanced students in need of more challenge? • What opportunities do I wish to add in my classroom for talent development? • Are there model programs we could visit? • Do we need a school-wide enrichment committee to identify talent development opportunities?
Develop a Talent Development Action Plan *Steps To Action* 1. 2. 3.	• Where should we begin? • Can we set some deadlines? • Can we find resources?

Figure 9.8. Sample Completed Talent Development Pathway Organizer (Lincoln Elementary School)

Establish or clarify your vision and goals for talent development.

In what ways should the school be committed to developing the talents of its students?

Vision: Systematic approach to providing talent development activities that focus on students' strengths, interests, and talents.

Identify existing talent development opportunities.

Existing Opportunities:

- *In-class enrichment and choices*
- *School-wide enrichment (clubs, clusters, teams)*
- *Specialized programs*

4th-grade team notes:

- Pathways model allows us to observe and nurture talents within the classroom.
- MI has helped to view students in new ways. We have found special talents and interests.
- Art and music classes.
- Use of interest centers.

Investigate other possibilities for talent development.

What opportunities exist in other districts, in your school's community, or online for talent development?

Search for new ideas:

- *In-class enrichment and choices*
- *School-wide enrichment (clubs, clusters, teams)*
- *Specialized programs*

School visits by the Lincoln School's gifted and talented education committee resulted in these findings:

1. Schoolwide Enrichment Model/enrichment clusters.
2. Kids with talents need opportunities to work with practicing professionals and mentors for talent development.
3. Students wtih advanced talents and interests should have opportunities to become creative producers. Students can do independent studies.
4. Use of mentors and community resources.
5. Enrichment specialist within a school.
6. Formal gifted programs with indentification of specific strengths and talents (ArtsConnection, engineering programs, grant sources).

Develop a Talent Development Action Plan

Ideas and needs:

- Look for funding for talent development program.
- Need opportunities for formal talent development and perhaps hiring an enrichment specialist.
- Offering independent study options.
- Integrate arts into talent development.
- Start an enrichment cluster program.

In classroom:

- Continue to use MI approach for options within the curriculum based on students' strengths, interests, and talents.
- Develop a research interest center.
- Allow for independent study operations.
- Use community resources to help students develop their talents.

Outside of classroom:

- Establish a pilot enrichment cluster program for next year.
- Investigate funding for specialized talent development opportunities for domain-specific talents.

- How can you use MI theory to broaden your definition of giftedness?

Implementation Activities

Activity 1. If your school were to decide to adopt talent development as a goal, finding resource people in the community would become essential. Playing People Bingo is a creative way to begin to identify talent and interests. Try playing it with your faculty, your parent organization, and other groups within the community. The directions and Bingo Card are in Supporting Materials.

You also need to identify students with similar talents and interests. Find ways to match them by setting up lunch dates, email opportunities, or enrichment clusters. You can generate new categories of talent based on the strengths and interests of the students. Ideally, all of the intelligences eventually would be represented more than once in different domains.

Activity 2. Some schools allow specialists like art, computer, music, and science teachers to work with a multiaged group of students talented in their particular domains. Meet with the specialists in your school to discuss this idea. How might these specialists be given time to work with the students? How might they identify which students would participate? Is the idea feasible in your school?

Activity 3. Investigate gifted programs in your area. Explore their definitions of giftedness and talent development. How many and what talents do these programs nurture? How are students selected for these programs? What are the strengths and weaknesses of the programs?

SUPPORTING MATERIALS

This section includes materials that you need to implement the activities within the chapter, such as the planning guide and organizer. A blank reproducible Talent Development Pathway Organizer is presented (see Figure 9.9).

Activity Materials

People Bingo

Distribute a bingo card (see Figure 9.10 on page 128) to each student. Tell students that they are to circulate around the room and get others to sign their cards. Signers may write their name in any box that applies to them, but can sign a single box only once. This part of the activity is complete when the first person who collects five signed boxes across, down, or diagonally calls out "Bingo." (You might want to have an inexpensive prize available for the winner.) Discuss the relationship of individuals' strengths (where they signed) and the intelligences they use for those activities.

Information About Programs

In this section you will find a description of the Enrichment Triad Model. Following are overviews of three talent development programs. The first vignette describes an enrichment cluster program implemented by Southampton Elementary School in Long Island, New York. The second program, Talent Beyond Words, was implemented in New York City by ArtsConnection. This program identified and nurtured visual and performing arts talents (music, dance, and theater) in economically disadvantaged students. Evaluation of the program showed positive effects in achievement. The final description is a talent development opportunity offered at the Island School in New York City, where students became the school historians.

Enrichment Triad Model

The Schoolwide Enrichment Model (Renzulli & Reis, 1997) incorporates the *Enrichment Triad Model,* a talent development model originally developed by Renzulli in 1977 as a means to transform students from consumers of knowledge to producers of new knowledge. This model consists of three types of activities: general exploratory; process or skill development; and individual or small-group investigations of real-world problems. More specifically, Type I activities are designed to introduce topics to students

Figure 9.9. Talent Development Pathway Organizer (blank)

Establish or clarify your vision and goals for talent development.

In what ways should the school be committed to developing the talents of its students?

Vision:

Identify existing talent development opportunities.

Existing Opportunities:
- *In-class enrichment and choices*
- *School-wide enrichment (clubs, clusters, teams)*
- *Specialized programs*

1.

2.

3.

4.

5.

Investigate other possibilities for talent development.

What opportunities exist in other districts, in your school's community, or online for talent development?

Search for new ideas:
- *In-class enrichment and choices*
- *School-wide enrichment (clubs, clusters, teams)*
- *Specialized programs*

1.

2.

3.

4.

5.

Develop a Talent Development Action Plan

1.

2.

3.

4.

5.

Figure 9.10. People Bingo Card

Draw or paint	Study maps	Play musical instrument	Keep a diary	Crossword puzzle fan
Speak in public	Dance	Take photos	Give advice and support	Read biographies
Do logic puzzles	Garden/ farm	Read/ write poetry	Act in theatrical productions	Sing
Do volunteer work in the community	Sculpt or carve	Build/ renovate	Write songs	Spend time outdoors
Take care of kids	Athlete/ play sports	Do crafts	Can say "no"	Family "accountant"

as a means of generating excitement in new areas of interest. Named general exploratory activities, they are offered in the form of field trips, films, visits, interviews, television documentaries, professional magazines or journals, and guest speakers who may be experts on specific topics. It is important to note that students are not evaluated on these experiences. Instead, the teacher is to observe the students' levels of interest in the topic area.

Type II enrichment, process or skill development, involves group-training activities. They are used to enhance students' skills within a discipline, including how to solve problems in that discipline and create like the practicing professionals in the discipline. In addition, general skills involved in thinking and creativity are offered. These abilities are categorized as thinking process skills, learning how to learn skills, advanced researching skills, and communication skills, and are necessary for students to develop their creative products.

Type III enrichment is the major focus of the model because Type III experiences encourage students to assume the role of the practicing professional or first-hand inquirer in their pursuit of a problem or issue. They use authentic methods and instruments to develop products or solutions, and, like adult creative producers, they share their results with concerned audiences. This type of problem solving was mentioned in the discussion of the Authentic Problems pathway and is related to it. The major difference is that the focus is on student interests, not on the prescribed curriculum. Indeed, the activities discussed in this pathway are intended to go beyond the regular curriculum and focus on the talent development needs of students.

This model is used in gifted programs throughout the country. Recently, schools have adopted SEM as a means to differentiate curriculum within the regular classroom according to students' varying levels of readiness, interest, and strengths (Beecher, 1996).

Talent Development Programs. We offer the following three examples as food for thought as your team begins to think about instituting talent development opportunities for the students in your setting. They describe how some districts provided talent development opportunities for their students. The first example demonstrates how extending the district's narrow gifted program to school-wide enrichment was successful in developing diverse talents and interests of all students. The second example describes a domain-specific program in music. The third explains how one principal created talent development experiences for particular students as their talents and interests began to emerge.

Enrichment Clusters: Southampton Elementary School

Southampton Elementary School, located in suburban Long Island, decided to nurture talents in all students by offering enrichment clusters, as described in the Schoolwide Enrichment Model (Renzulli & Reis, 1997). In this model, all students participate in enrichment activities based on their strengths and interests. These clusters were taught by adults who had talents in those areas themselves.

Children from the Shinnicock Indian Reservation, children of immigrant workers, as well as affluent residents contribute to the school's multicultural population of over 700 students. The school, organized in heterogeneous classes, had a traditional program for academically gifted students for many years. Participation in this program was determined

by a team of psychologists and school personnel who identified approximately 60 students a year based on their performance on standardized achievement and IQ tests. Identified students participated in a 1-day-a-week enrichment program held in the gifted center where they engaged in challenging and enriched curriculum.

This approach appeared to provide rigorous learning opportunities for these students. It did not, however, support the vision of identifying and nurturing the broad range of talents of the entire school population. Opportunities were provided for the staff to explore multiple intelligences theory as a means for broadening the school's capacity to develop talent. The Schoolwide Enrichment Model was introduced as a practical plan for implementing expanded services. MI theory provided support for the expanded range of talents that would be encompassed.

With leadership from the school principal, Celia Dominich, and Gifted and Talented coordinator Kathy Goebel, the school began an initiative to expand talent opportunities for all students. Beginning the school year with the theme of honoring a diversity of talents, each class developed products that related to a range of student interests and abilities. Through displays, books, and assembly presentation this theme of honoring talents was enhanced. Student interest inventories as well as staff, parent, and community inventories provided the data for a computerized talent database developed at the school.

Classroom teachers, parents and community members were trained to participate in an enrichment cluster program called "The Success Express." A series of high-interest enrichment clusters were developed and offered to students. At the beginning stages, a train whistle over the loudspeaker system signaled the students to take their tickets, leave their regular classrooms, and attend their enrichment cluster. In the first cycle, a variety of 12 clusters, including gardening, environmental education, poetry, and foreign language instruction, were offered. Careful attention to the design of the offerings ensured that all intelligences could be expressed through these clusters. This initiative has expanded to over 40 diverse offerings. The success of this approach has led the Southampton School District to plan a Middle

School Component and to offer highly motivating opportunities during the summer months.

Formal Domain-Specific Programs: Talent Beyond Words

Formal domain-specific programs are by design more rigorous and sophisticated. Students gain entry by showing their readiness for advanced challenges through formal identification. The programs are geared to developing high levels of multiple potentials in young people by providing resources, opportunities, and encouragement to support the continuous escalation of student involvement in both required and self-selected activities. An example of one such program is Talent Beyond Words, developed by ArtsConnection, a New York City arts-in-education organization, in collaboration with several schools in Brooklyn, New York. The purpose of the program, funded by the Jacob Javits Gifted and Talented Program, was to identify and develop artistic talents of inner-city youth. During the first year, 24 3rd-grade students from one school were identified as musically talented through a 7-week identification process designed for the project. Both classroom teachers and artists observed the students during the audition process. They documented how students performed based on certain behaviors deemed indicative of musical talent. The students participated in a rigorous talent development program (Baum, Owen, & Oreck, 1996).

The curriculum developed for this program was highly challenging and sophisticated based on polyrhythmic percussion and voice using complex arrangements of jazz and traditional music from around the world. Within the arrangements the students were given opportunities for self-expression through improvisation. The students had to learn and play interlocking parts that constantly challenged their listening as well as their technical skills. From the start of the instructional program there were frequent public performances. These performances expanded from school assemblies to public venues, including citywide festivals, President Clinton's inauguration, and teacher conferences. The more challenging the curriculum became, the more effort the students exerted. As their musical competence grew, they desired even more difficult challenges.

The students are currently in high school, and of this group six have emerged as highly gifted musicians and are part of a professional performing ensemble with their teacher mentor. Two plan to study music in college, and the others will continue to keep music in their lives but have selected other fields of study.

Island School and Historical Research

Our final example comes from the Island School, where co-author Barbara Slatin is principal. For Dr. Slatin, the heart of MI theory rests in giving her students opportunities to work across a diversity of domains in order to discover their strengths and interests, and then, subsequently, to nurture their talents further. She feels strongly that the Talent Development pathway can be the starting point in addressing the school's overarching mission of higher expectations and improved student achievement. She argues that giving the students many opportunities to engage in something they love to do and at which they are capable will develop their competence, self-confidence, and abilities as learners. Such engagement will make all students feel like valued (and valuable) members of the learning community.

While the Talent Development pathway finds a home in enrichment and after-school activities at the Island School, Dr. Slatin also infuses a talent development perspective—identifying and nurturing student talents—into students' everyday academic experiences. This means that there is no distinct separation between talent development opportunities and the academic curriculum at the Island School. Every learning opportunity is seen as an occasion to identify and develop students' talents. Because talent development is integrated with the school's lessons and programs at the Island School, students have continuous talent development opportunities across a range of domains—tapping all the intelligences in a variety of ways. Below we describe how Dr. Slatin and her staff integrate the Talent Development pathway into the school's academic, after-school, and summer programs.

Technology. Opportunities for exploration in technology are available to all Island School upper-elementary students as a part of their standard curriculum. Furthermore, technology-related enrichment clusters and the school's summer program offer more in-depth experiences for students who want to pursue them. Within the curriculum, Island

School students learn to create websites and to use tool-based project development software. Other Island School technology programs include: Lego and Roamer robotics, Lego Logo, MicroWorlds, and Duplo engineering. An intensive Lego Logo experience is offered as part of the Island School's summer program. The school librarian-technologist facilitates student-developed video projects (using digital camera and computer-based editing software).

English-Language Learning. The Island School also makes use of CALLA (Cognitive Academic Language Learning Approach), a constructivist and technology-enhanced approach to teaching and learning English as a Second Language. It was instituted as a step toward making the Island School a fully Dual Language school. Dr. Slatin brought in CALLA as a way to develop English-language learners' talents in technology while supporting their language learning needs.

Social Sciences. Then and Now is the name of a school-wide interdisciplinary unit that integrates social studies, English Language Arts (ELA), and technology. Students in kindergarten through 6th grade explore the concept of change—a concept central to the New York State Social Studies Core Curriculum—using a problem-based approach where the students take on the roles of researchers and historians and attempt to discover what life was like at the time their school was built (1902). Students become critical thinkers as they compare their lives in their community today with life in that same community many years ago.

The multiple intelligences framework used by the school ensures the integration of various media and arts (e.g., music, dance, theater, photography, robotics, journalism, and poetry) in the project. Practicing professionals, such as archivists, architects, and oral historians, work directly with students and teachers in the classroom and model the professional roles involved in this type of historical research.

The Then and Now curriculum aligns with state standards in English Language Arts, Social Studies, and Technology. For Dr. Slatin, this project provides an excellent opportunity to develop her students' talents in the disciplines that are integrated into the project. Her young artists, technologists, photographers, and poets, to name only a few, have authentic opportunities to explore and develop their disciplin-

ary talents through Then and Now and other Social Studies projects undertaken at the school.

Peer Mediators. The Island School Peer Mediation Program identifies the social mediators and leaders at the Island School and offers them the training necessary to become the school's peer mediators. This program allows students with strengths in the intra- and interpersonal intelligences to experience a high degree of success in their talent area while also providing the school community with peer mediation services; helping to find nonviolent, peer-mediated solutions to inter-student fights; and other solutions to social problems.

Natural and Physical Sciences. Local scientists, such as Dr. Terry Neu (Sacred Heart University), work directly with Island School students to nurture their proclivities in the science domains. Dr. Neu uses an environmental education, or naturalist framework, to work with students on grade-appropriate content. In addition, the Island School connects students with summer experiences to further develop their interests, understanding, and skills in the natural and physical sciences.

The Arts. Many of the newly-integrated programs at the Island School serve a dual purpose of addressing academic goals as well as providing a context to observe students across a range of activities and domains, opening the opportunity for them and their teachers to identify their personal strengths. In the past, the Island School's academic programs did not address the artistic domains. In order to provide those types of opportunities for students, Dr. Slatin and her staff instituted a number of arts programs both within the standard curriculum and as part of the after-school program. Weekly music, dance, and theater improvisation sessions are now offered; 3rd Street Music comes into the school to offer violin lessons and chorus to interested students; and percussion lessons are offered, including an "anger management through drumming" counseling approach.

Other arts offerings include a visual arts enrichment group led by the Island School art teacher and visiting artists. One visiting artist worked with 3rd graders studying South Africa through crafts. One 5th-grade teacher worked with the school art teacher on teaching landscape art techniques, including a trip to the Met to study Hudson River paintings. These are examples of the type of short-term arts projects that infuse the Island School curriculum throughout the school year. Through both the ongoing and short-term programs, students have the opportunity to explore art domains in order to discover and nurture their talents in the arts.

After-School and Summer Enrichment Programs. The Island School maintains a rich and fully-enrolled after-school program. Students are offered many opportunities in a number of domains, such as tap dance, photojournalism, visual arts, poetry/creative writing, and technology/computers. The Island School also hosts a Saturday program, including a performing arts program entitled "Say it, Sing it, Shout it" that allows student participation in a variety of ways, including music composition, sound effects creation, dance, vocal, and theater arts.

Dr. Slatin also instituted a comprehensive summer camp and summer school. A variety of programs are offered to students throughout the summer months, including a week-long environmental summer camp in the Adirondacks.

With Dr. Slatin at the helm, the Island School continues to develop and enhance the talent development opportunities available to its students, as well as integrate a talent development mindset across its academic programs. Through its talent development focus, the school is successfully meeting its goals of maintaining high expectations for all its students and increased academic achievement, confirmed by significant increases in its test scores.

FOR FURTHER STUDY

To find out about existing talent development programs, consult the following:

National Association for Gifted Students (NAGC)
1701 L. Street NW, Site 550
Washington, DC 20036
202 785-4268, *www.nagc.org*

National Research Center on the Gifted and Talented (NRCGT)
University of Connecticut
362 Fairfield Road, U-7
Storrs, CT 06269-2007
(860) 486-4826, *www.gifted.uconn.edu*

Resources for more in-depth information about talent development include the following:

Bloom, B. (Ed.). (1985). *Developing talent in young people.* New York: Ballantine.

Csikszentmihalyi, M., Rathunde, K., & Whalen, S. (1993). *Talented teenagers: The roots of success and failure.* New York: Cambridge University Press.

Renzulli, J. S. (1994). *Schools for talent development: A practical plan for total school improvement.* Mansfield Center, CT: Creative Learning Press.

Renzulli, J. S., & Reis, S. M. (1997). The *schoolwide enrichment model: A how-to-guide for educational excellence* (2nd ed.). Mansfield Center, CT: Creative Learning Press.

Winner, E. (1997). Gifted children: Myths and realities. New York: Basic Books.

CHAPTER 10

Conclusion:
A Case for the Pathways

Diversity in students and high expectations that all our children deserve to learn make our task as teachers daunting. In response to this challenge we offered you the Pathways Model. The pathways will introduce you to the many ways MI-informed instruction can be used to engage students in their learning. We are confident that implementation of the Pathways Model will energize classrooms and provide opportunities for all students to achieve.

We recognize that teachers are somewhat frustrated in today's educational climate, peppered with state and national standards and high-stakes testing. With the emphasis on teacher accountability and student achievement, many teachers are hesitant to try new ideas unless they can be sure that the approach will enhance student learning. The ideas presented in this book have been shown to be highly effective in improving students' achievement and self-efficacy.

Many of the practices described in each pathway were field tested in both urban and suburban settings. In fact, several federally funded projects were designed around the elements of the Pathways Model. Systematic evaluation of these projects have revealed highly positive results in student achievement, especially among students at risk. As a final offering, we present these results to you in an effort to provide a research-based rationale supporting your efforts to implement the Pathways Model.

RESEARCH SUPPORTING THE PATHWAYS MODEL

In large part, the Pathways Model is a synthesis of practices gleaned from three former Javits projects, two of which showed significant gains in student achievement as measured by standardized achieve-

ment tests Project CUE and Talent Beyond Words/New Horizons. The third project, Project High Hopes, focusing on students with severe learning, behavioral and attention difficulties, resulted in extraordinary student performances. As a result of these research projects, we know that using a strengths-based MI approach is particularly successful in addressing the needs of students who are at risk (Baum, Cooper, & Neu, 2001; Delcourt, 2000; Oreck, Baum, & McCartney, 2000). These MI-informed experiences allowed students to feel smart, develop a positive identity, and increase self-regulation skills.

While each of these three projects was based on MI theory, they used different pathways to improve students' achievement and to develop their strengths, interests, and talents both within and outside of the regular curriculum. All of the projects implemented authentic and valid procedures for identifying specific talents and gifts in underrepresented groups and provided talent development experiences in specific domains for identified students. In addition to their similarities, the three projects had some unique aspects. These features included a summer problem-solving program, differentiation for all students within the regular classroom, and an intense professional development component for teachers that focused on improving individual talents and strengths of all students.

Examples of these elements are reflected in the five pathways of the model, as shown in Figure 10.1. A brief description of each program will show the different ways the model was applied.

Talent Beyond Words/New Horizons

This project had two phases—the Talent Beyond Words phase and New Horizons phase. Tal-

Figure 10.1. Pathways Model and Research Projects

Pathway	Former Research Projects Example
Exploration Providing resources and materials that allow for the expression of students' unique profiles of intelligences.	Creating interest centers to expose students to a variety of disciplines and domains (Project CUE).
Bridging Using strength-based approach to initiate instruction to literacy goals and basic skills.	Developing storyboards to initiate writing (Project CUE). Using movement exercises to express imagery in poetry (Talent Beyond Words/New Horizons).
Understanding Using a variety of entry and exit points to promote understanding of concepts and "big" ideas.	Dissecting owl pellets to initiate a unit on the food chain (Project High Hopes). Using movement activities to assess understanding of molecular bonding (Talent Beyond Words/New Horizons). Constructing geodesic domes to introduce formulas for areas of a triangle, rectangle, etc. (Project CUE).
Authentic Problems Integrating basic skills to solve a real-world problem.	Working in interdisciplinary teams during a 1-week summer residential program to address the problems of a deteriorating pond (Project High Hopes).
Talent Development Using authentic methods to assess talent in particular domains and provide talent development.	Combining audition activities with observational data to identify students with talent in the arts and sciences (all projects). Providing intensive talent develop–ment activities with domain-specific mentors (all projects).

ent Beyond Words focused on identifying students who were talented in music, dance, and theater, and then providing these students with special classes designed to develop these talents. The instructors were professionals from the particular discipline of talent. The majority of students identified were at great risk academically due to economic or family issues and were performing significantly below grade level in reading and math. New Horizons emphasized curriculum development and classroom instruction based on students' MI strengths (arts integration) to improve achievement, especially in reading. Teachers were included in helping select students for talent experiences and participated in workshops where they

learned how to use the arts to promote literacy and develop in-depth understanding of concepts across the curriculum. The most at-risk students received supplemental instruction through the MAGIC curriculum (Merging Artistic Gifts into the Curriculum) to support their academics. MAGIC implemented an arts-integrated MI approach.

The research focused on how well the project helped to close the achievement gap between the at-risk talented youngsters and two comparison groups. Figure 10.2 displays standardized National Curve Equivalent reading scores from the Talent Beyond Words/New Horizons population. The groups shown were two treatment groups and one comparison group. MAGIC, the first treatment group, consisted of talented students in the arts who were at risk academically. They received both talent development (Talent Development pathway) and academic support using MI arts-integrated activities (Bridging pathway). The second treatment group, Young Talent, consisted of talented students in the arts who were not at academic risk. They received talent development opportunities with some arts-integrated curriculum in the classroom (Understanding pathway). The comparison group consisted of students neither identified as talented in the arts nor at academic risk. They received no treatment of any kind. After 3 years, the talented at-risk students (MAGIC group) were significantly closing the achievement

Figure 10.2. National Curve Equivalent

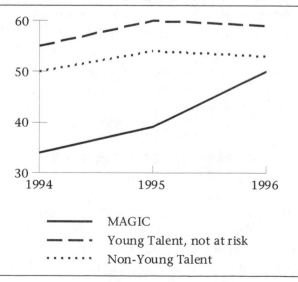

gap in reading; their performance was approaching that of the other two groups.

Project CUE

A New York City elementary school in the Bronx designed and implemented this project to improve achievement using a talent development approach. This K–5 elementary school housed a student body of primarily Latino and African American students, all of whom qualified for the free and reduced-price lunch program. Prior to the start of the project, the school was identified as at risk or a "school under review." Project CUE, funded under the Jacob Javits program, first centered on improving classroom environments and instruction. It also had a strong talent development program. Teachers learned how to create learning environments that exposed students to many areas where their unique MI profiles could be observed, to use students' strengths to promote literacy, and to develop ways to implement project-based instruction.

Each year an increasing number of students were identified as having strengths and talents in at least one of many domains: technology, mathematics, theater, writing, science, music, and art. Identified students received talent development activities daily from teacher specialists. The target population for the research component was students identified

as talented in one or more of the domains. The vast majority of these youngsters were achieving below grade level. The identified students showed significant gains in both reading and math.

For a summary of the statistical findings for both Project CUE and Talent Beyond Words/New Horizons, see Figure 10.3.

Project High Hopes

Project High Hopes was designed to identify and nurture talent in the domains of engineering, performing arts, the sciences, and visual arts in students with disabilities. The project served disabled students in grades 5 through 8 at nine sites in Connecticut and Rhode Island, including six public schools, a private school for the learning disabled, and two schools for the deaf. A major goal was to uncover the ways in which these students learn best. All students with individual educational plans from each site participated in activities designed to uncover their talents in specific domains and expose their underlying MI profiles.

Using all five pathways, the researchers were able to identify practices that enhance learning in this special population of students. Most of the students had strengths in spatial, bodily kinesthetic, naturalist, and personal intelligences. These strengths were expressed in the domains of science, visual arts, per-

Figure 10.3. Statistical Findings: Project CUE and Talent Beyond Words/New Horizons

Study	Sample Size	Focus	Comparison Group	Significant Difference
Project CUE	900 (for all of Project CUE)	Math	Site A—treatment group Site B—partial Site C—matched comparison group	No significant differences between site A ($m = 47.01$) and site B ($m = 46.2$). A and B means were significantly higher then C ($m = 39.73$; $p < .05$).
		Reading	Same as above	Site A ($m = 41.61$) showed significantly higher improvement over site B ($m = 38.64$; $p < .05$) and site C ($m = 34.25$; $p < .01$). Site B had significantly higher gains over site C ($p < .01$).
		Science	Site A—treatment Site B—comparison group	Site A ($m = 2.73$) showed significantly higher gain scores in science process skills over site B ($m = 1.85$; $F = 9.47$; $p = .003$).
Talent Beyond Words New Horizons	131	Reading	Group 1—comparison group Treatment Groups: G2—students at grade level G3—students below grade level	All groups showed gains. Significant interaction ($F = 3.24$; $p = .013$) where students in group 3 closed achievement gap between their talented peers in group 2 and students in group 1 by year 3 (see Figure 10.2).

forming arts, and engineering and design. The best learning for these students developed from the use of alternative entry and exit points that did not rely on language, as well the use of problem-based learning.

Through these methods, these youngsters began to achieve in a similar fashion to their nondisabled gifted peers. Over the course of 3 years, these students improved dramatically in their core areas aligned with their talents. For example, several students won state-wide competitions in science and engineering, others qualified for honors programs in high school, and still others were chosen for leading roles in their schools' drama activities. Figure 10.4 outlines these successes.

ADDITIONAL SUPPORT FOR THE PATHWAYS MODEL

Additional research has used instructional strategies supported by the Pathways Model. In a recent publication, Robert Marzano, Debra Pikering, and Jane Pollock (2001) identified instructional strategies that have a positive impact on student achievement. Some of the strategies mentioned incorporate a multiple intelligences approach. For example, verbal instruction (linguistic intelligence), visual instruction using organizers and other nonlinguistic representations of knowledge (naturalist, spatial intelligences), and dramatic instruction (bodily kinesthetic and personal intelligences). In short, their findings support the use of multiple intelligences theory to enhance student learning.

A FINAL WORD

We hope that these research findings will help you to follow the pathway of your choice with confidence and conviction. We hope your pathway brings you to a place where all children feel smart and no child is left behind.

Figure 10.4. Project High Hopes Successes

Domain	Opportunity	Results
Engineering	Odyssey of the Mind Competition	Five teams participated in CT, resulting in 2 second-place awards and 1 third-place award.
Engineering	Egg-Drop Competition	Two students had award-winning entries in the school's egg-drop contest.
Performing arts	Auditions for school plays	Five students were selected by an audition process for leading roles in their schools productions
Visual arts	Student regional juried art shows	Ten students had artwork selected in juried competitions in MA, RI, and CT.
Visual arts	District gifted art program	Three students were selected for advanced art class.
Science	Science fair competitions	Seven students entered science fairs and one received a written commendation for high quality.
Science	Physics Day Competition	Twelve students participated in district science competition. Nine received recognition for their problem-solving ability.
Science	Acceptance to advanced science classes	Two students accepted into the district's advanced science class for gifted students.

References

___(1982). *Photo search.* Kilder, IL: Learning Seed Company.

Aliki. (1983). *A medieval feast.* New York: Thomas Y. Cromwell.

Armstrong, T. (1994). *Multiple intelligences in the classroom.* Alexandria, VA: Association for Supervision and Curriculum Development.

Bandura, A. (1986). *Social foundations of thought and action: A social cognitive theory.* Englewood Cliffs, NJ: Prentice-Hall.

Baum, S. (1994). Novice/expert simulation. In S. Baum & T. Hébert, *Discovering and nurturing talent in children: A staff developer's guide for teacher training.* Brooklyn, NY: Community School District 22.

Baum, S., Cooper, C., & Neu, T. (2001). Dual differentiation: An approach for meeting the curricular needs of talented students with learning disabilities. *Psychology in the Schools, 38*(5), 477–490.

Baum, S., & Hébert, T. (1994). *Discovering and nuturing talent in children: A staff developer's guide for teacher training.* Brooklyn, NY: Community School District 22.

Baum, S., & Owen, S. (2003). *To be gifted and learning disabled: Strategies for helping bright students with LD, ADHD, & more.* Mansfield Center, CT: Creative Learning Press.

Baum, S., Owen, S., & Oreck, B. (1997). Transferring individual self-regulation processes from arts to academics. *Arts Education Policy Review, 98,* 32–39.

Baum, S., Renzulli, J., & Hébert, T. (1994). Reversing underachievement: Stories of success. *Educational Leadership, 52*(3), 48–54.

Beall, S. (2000). *Functional melodies: Finding mathematical relationships in music.* Emeryville, CA: Key Curriculum Press.

Beecher, M. (1996). *Developing gifts and talents of all students in the regular classroom.* Mansfield Center, CT: Creative Learning Press.

Bembow, C., & Lubinski, D. (1997). Intellectually talented children: How can we best meet their needs? In N. Colangelo & G. Davis, *Handbook of gifted education.* Boston: Allyn & Bacon.

Binet, A., & Simon, T. (1916). *The development of intelligence in children (the Binet-Simon Scale).* (E. S. Kite, Trans.). Baltimore, MD: Williams & Wilkins.

Bloom, B. (Ed.). (1985). *Developing talent in young people.* New York: Ballantine.

Blythe, T., & Associates. (1998). *The teaching for understanding guide.* San Francisco: Jossey-Bass.

Boix Mansilla, V. (2000). *The Project Zero classroom.* Cambridge, MA: The President and Fellows and Harvard College (on behalf of Project Zero and Veronica Boix Mansilla).

Bornstein, M. H., & Sigman, M. D. (1986). Continuity in mental development from infancy. *Child Development, 57,* 251–274.

Bruner, J. (1960). *The process of education.* Cambridge, MA: Harvard University Press.

Bunchman, J., & Briggs, S. (1994). *Activities for creating pictures and poetry.* Mansfield Center, CT: Creative Learning Press.

Campbell, B. (1994). *The multiple intelligences handbook: Lesson plans and more.* Stanwood, WA: Campbell & Associates.

Carroll, J. (1993). *Human cognitive abilities: A survey of factor-analytic studies.* Cambridge, England: Cambridge University Press.

Case, R. (1985). *Intellectual development: Birth to adulthood.* New York: Academic Press.

Case, R. (1986). The new stage theories in intellectual development: Why we need them, what they assert. In M. Perlmutter (Ed.), *Perspectives on intellectual development: Minnesota symposia on child psychology, Vol. 19.* (pp. 57–95). Hillsdale, NJ: Erlbaum.

Cattell, R. (1987). *Intelligence: Its structure, growth, and action.* New York: Elsevier Science.

Ceci, S. (1990). *On intelligence . . . more or less.* Englewood Cliffs, NJ: Prentice-Hall.

Ceci, S. J. & Liker, J. (1986). A day at the races: A study of IQ, expertise, and cognitive complexity. *Journal of Experimental Psychology: General, 115,* 255–266.

Chen, J., Isberg, E., & Krechevsky, M. (Eds.) (1998). *Project Spectrum: Early learning activities* (Vol. 2 in *Project Zero Frameworks for Early Childhood Education,* H. Gardner, D. H. Feldman, & M. Krechevsky, eds.). New York: Teachers College Press.

Chen, J., Krechevsky, M., & Viens, J., with E. Isberg. (1998). *Building on children's strengths: The experiences of Project Spectrum.* (Vol. 1 in *Project Zero Frameworks for Early Childhood Education,* H. Gardner, D. H. Feldman, & M. Krechevsky, eds.). New York: Teachers College Press.

Corbo, M. (1997). Reading styles times twenty. *Educational Leadership, 54,* 38–42.

Csikszentmihalyi, M., Rathunde, K., & Whalen, S. (1993). *Talented teenagers: The roots of success and failure.* New York: Cambridge University Press.

Darling-Hammond, L. (1996). The right to learn and the advancement of teaching: Research policy and practice for democratic education. *Educational Researcher, 25,* 2–12.

Davis, J. (1997). *The Muse Book.* Cambridge, MA: The President and Fellows of Harvard College (on behalf of Project Zero and Jessica Davis).

Delcourt, M. A. B. (2000). *An evaluation of Project CUE: Creating urban excellence through talent development.* Washington, DC: Office of Educational Research and Improvement, U. S. Department of Education.

Dewey, J. (1938). *Logic: The theory of inquiry.* New York: H. Holt & Company.

Dunn, S., & Larson, R. (1990). *Design technology: Children's engineering.* Philadelphia: Falmer Press.

Eberle, B., & Stanish, B. (1980). *CPS for kids: A resource book for teaching creative problem solving to kids.* Buffalo, NY: D.O.K.

Faculty of New City School. (1994). *Celebrating multiple intelligences: Teaching for success.* St. Louis, MO: New City School.

Fraser, S. (Ed.). (1995). *The bell curve wars: Race, intelligence and the future of America.* New York: Basic Books.

Gardner, H. (1993a, Fall). Choice points as multiple intelligences enter the school. *Intelligence Connections, 3*(91), 1,3,7–8.

Gardner, H. (1993b). *Creating minds.* New York: Basic Books.

Gardner, H. (1993c). *Frames of mind: The theory of multiple intelligences* (10th Anniversary ed.). New York: Basic Books.

Gardner, H. (1993d). *Multiple intelligences: Theory into practice.* New York: Basic Books.

Gardner, H. (1996). Reflections on multiple intelligences: Myths and messages. *Kappan, 77*(3), pp. 201–209.

Gardner, H. (1999a). *The disciplined mind: What all students should know.* New York: Simon & Schuster.

Gardner, H. (1999b). *Intelligence reframed: Multiple intelligences for the 21st century.* New York: Basic Books.

Gardner, H., & Checkley, K. (1997). The first seven . . . and the eighth: A conversation with Howard Gardner. *Educational Leadership, 55*(1), 8–13.

Gould, S. J. (1981). *The mismeasure of man.* New York: Norton.

Gray, J., & Viens, J. (1994). The theory of multiple intelligences: Understanding cognitive diversity in school. *National Forum, 74*(1), 22–25.

Guilford, J. P. (1967). *The nature of human intelligence.* New York: McGraw Hill.

Hatch, T. (1997). Getting specific about multiple intelligences. *Educational Leadership, 54*(6), pp. 26–29.

Herman, G. (1986). *Storytelling: A triad in the arts.* Mansfield Center, CT: Creative Learning Press.

Herrnstein, R. J., & Murray, C. (1994). *The bell curve: Intelligence and class structure in American life.* New York: Free Press.

Hetland, L. (1998). Views on understanding. Cambridge, MA: The President and Fellows of Harvard College (on behalf of Project Zero and Lois Hetland).

Hopfenberg, W., & Levin, H., and Associates. (1993). *The accelerated schools resource guide.* San Francisco: Jossey-Bass Inc.

Horn, J. (1986). Some thoughts about intelligence. In R. Sternberg & D. Detterman (Eds.), *What is intelligence? Contemporary viewpoints on its nature and definition* (pp. 91–96). Norwood, NJ: Ablex.

Johmann, C. A., & Rieth, E. J. (1999). *Bridges! Amazing Structures to Design, Build, and Test.* Charlotte, VT: Williamson.

Joyce, B., & Weil, M. (1996). *Models of teaching* (5th ed.). Boston: Allyn & Bacon.

Kallenbach, S., & Viens, J. (2002). *Open to interpretation: Multiple intelligences theory in adult literacy education. Findings from the Adult Multiple Intelligences Study* (NCSALL Reports #21). Cambridge, MA: National Center for the Study of Adult Learning and Literacy.

Kettle, K., Renzulli, J. S., & Rizza, M. G. (1998). Products of mind: Exploring student preferences for product development using My Way . . . An Expression Style Instrument. *Gifted Child Quarterly, 42*(1), 49–60.

Kornhaber, M., Fierros, E., & Veenema, S. (2004). *Multiple intelligences: Best ideas from research and practice.* Boston: Pearson Education.

Kornhaber, M., & Krechevsky, M. (1995). Expanding definitions of learning and teaching: Notes from the MI underground. In P. Cookson & B. Schneider (Eds.), *Transforming schools* (pp. 181–208). New York: Garland.

Krechevsky, M. (1991). Project Spectrum: An innovative assessment alternative. *Educational Leadership, 48*(5), 43–48.

Krechevsky, M. (1998). *Project Spectrum: Preschool assessment handbook* (Vol. 3 in *Project Zero Frameworks for Early Childhood Education,* H. Gardner, D. H. Feldman, & M. Krechevsky, eds.). New York: Teachers College Press.

Krechevsky, M., & Seidel, S. (1998). Minds at work: Applying multiple intelligences in the classroom. In R. J. Sternberg & W. M. Williams (Eds.), *Intelligence, instruction, and assessment* (pp. 17–42). Mahwah, NJ: Lawrence Erlbaum.

Lewis, B. (1991). *The kid's guide to social action.* Minneapolis, MN: Free Spirit Publishing.

Lewis, B. (1995). *Kids with courage: True stories about young people making a difference.* Minneapolis, MN: Free Spirit Publishing.

Lipson, G. B., & Morrison, B. (1996). *Fact, fantasy, and folklore.* Carthage, IL: Good Apple.

Marzano, R. J., Pickering, D. J., & Pollock, J. E. (2002). *Classroom instruction that works: Research-based strategies for increasing student achievement.* Alexandria, VA: ASCD.

McGreevy, Ann (1982). *My book of things and stuff.* Mansfield Center, CT: Creative Learning Press.

McInerney, M., Berman, K., & Baum, S. (2005). *Interest development centers: Opportunities for choice, challenge, and differentiation.* Mansfield Center, CT: Creative Learning Press.

McLaughlin, M. (1996). *Teacher learning: New policies, new practices.* New York: Teachers College Press.

Miles, B., (1991). *Save the Earth: An action handbook for kids.* Madison, WI: Demco Media.

Multiple intelligences: Theory to practice in New York City schools [manual and video guide]. (1999). New York: New York City Board of Education.

Office of Educational Research and Improvement, U.S. Department of Education. (1993). *National excellence: A case for developing America's talent.* Washington, DC: Author.

Oreck, B., Baum, S., & McCartney, H. (2000). *Artistic talent development for urban youth: The promise and the challenge.* Storrs, CT: National Research Center on the Gifted and Talented.

Polacco, P. (1990). *Thunder cake.* New York: Philomel Books.

Polland, J. (1985). *Building toothpick bridges (Math Projects Series): Grades 5–8.* Palo Alto, CA: Dale Seymour.

Project WILD, a joint project of the Western Association of Fish and Wildlife Agencies (WAFWA) and the Western Regional Environmental Education Council, Inc. (WREEC). [Copyright © 2005, 2004, 2003, 2002, 2001, 2000, 1992, 1985, and 1983 by the council for Environmental Education.]

Reid, L. (1990). *Thinking skills resource book.* Mansfield Center, CT: Creative Learning Press.

Renzulli, J. S. (1977). *The enrichment triad model: A guide for developing defensible programs for gifted and talented.* Mansfield Center, CT: Creative Learning Press.

Renzulli, J. S. (1978). What makes giftedness? Reexamining a definition. *Kappan, 60,* 180–184, 261.

Renzulli, J. S. (1985). The three-ring conception of giftedness: A developmental model for creative productivity. *South African Journal of Education, 5*(1), 1–18.

Renzulli, J. S. (Ed.) (1986). *Systems and models for developing programs for the gifted and talented.* Mansfield Center, CT: Creative Learning Press.

Renzulli, J. S. (1994). *Schools for talent development: A practical plan for total school improvement.* Mansfield Center, CT: Creative Learning Press.

Renzulli, J. S. (1997a). *Interest-A-Lyzer family of instruments, grades K–12: A manual for teachers.* Mansfield Center, CT: Creative Learning Press.

Renzulli, J. S. (1997b). *The Interest-A-Lyzer.* Mansfield Center, CT: Creative Learning Press.

Renzulli, J., & Reis, S. (1997). *The schoolwide enrichment model: A how-to-guide for educational excellence* (2nd ed.). Mansfield Center, CT: Creative Learning Press.

Renzulli, J., Gentry, M., & Reis, S. (2003). *Enrichment cluster: A practical plan for real-world, student-driven learning.* Mansfield Center, CT: Creative Learning Press.

Sabbeth, A. (1997). *Rubber band banjos and a java jive bass: Projects and activities on the science of music and sound.* Mansfield Center, CT: Creative Learning Press.

Salvadori, M. (1990). *The art of construction: Projects and principles for beginning engineers and architects.* Mansfield Center, CT: Creative Learning Press.

Siegler R.S., & Kotoszsky, K. (1986). Two types of giftedness: Shall ever the twain shall meet. In R. Sternberg & J. E. Davidson (Eds.). *Conceptions of giftedness* (p. 417–435) New York: Cambridge University Press.

Silverman, L. K. (1997). Family counseling with the gifted. In N. Colangelo & G. Davis. *Handbook of gifted education.* Boston: Allyn & Bacon

Spearman, C. (1927). *The abilities of man.* New York: Macmillan.

Stanley, J. C. (1997). Rationale of the study of mathematically precocious youth (SMPY) during its first five years of promoting educational acceleration. In J. C. Stanley, W. C. Georg, & C. H. Solano (Eds.), *The gifted and the creative: A fifty year perspective* (pp. 73–112). Baltimore, MD: Johns Hopkins University Press.

Stefanakis, E. (2002). *Multiple intelligences and portfolios: A window into the learner's mind.* Portsmouth, NH: Heinemann.

Steippen, W. (1991). *Case studies involving legal issues* (*Wall Street Journal* classroom ed.). New York: Wall Street Journal.

Steippen, W. (1995). *A guide for designing problem-based instructional materials.* Geneva, IL: Human Learning Resources.

Sternberg, R. J. (1985). Cognitive approaches to intelligence. In B. B. Wolman (Ed.), *Handbook of intelligence: Theories, measurements, and application* (pp. 59–118). New York: Wiley and Sons.

Sternberg, R. J. (1988). *The triarchic mind: A new theory of human intelligence.* New York: Viking.

Sternberg, R. J. (1995). For whom the Bell Curve tolls? A review of the Bell Curve. *Psychological Science, 6,* 257–261.

Sternberg, R. J. (1997). The concept of intelligence and its role in lifelong learning and success. *American Psychologist, 52*(10), 1030–1037.

Strong, R., Silver, H., & Robinson, A., (1995). What do students want? *Educational Leadership, 53*(1), 8–12.

Tannenbaum, A. (1997). The meaning and making of giftedness. In N. Colangelo & G. Davis. *Handbook of gifted education.* Boston: Allyn & Bacon.

Terman, L. (1916). *The measurement of intelligence.* Boston: Houghton Mifflin.

Terman, L. (1926). *Genetic studies of genius.* Stamford, CT: Stamford University Press.

Thompson, R. (1989). *Draw and tell.* Willowdale, ON: Firefly Books.

Thurstone, L. L. (1938). *Primary mental abilities.* Chicago: University of Chicago Press.

Treat, L. (1991). *You're the detective.* Boston: D.R. Godine.

Vernon, P. E. (1971). *The structure of human abilities.* London: Methuen.

Viens, J., Chen, J., & Gardner, H. (1997). Theories of

intelligence and critiques. In J. Paul, M. Churton, H. Rosselli-Kostoryz, W. Morse, K. Marfo, C. Lavely, & D. Thomas (Eds.). *Foundations of special education: Basic knowledge informing research and practice in special education* (pp. 122–156). Pacific Grove, CA: Brooks/Cole Publishing Company.

Viens, J., & Kallenbach, S. (2004). *Multiple intelligences and adult literacy: A source book for practitioners.* New York: Teachers College Press.

Waterfall, M., & Grusin, S. (1998). *Where's the me in museum? Going to museums with children.* Arlington, VA: Vandamere Press.

Watson, J. (1968). *The double helix: A personal account of the discovery of the structure of DNA.* New York: Atheneum.

Wiggers, R. (1996). *The amateur geologist.* Missoula, MT: Mountain Press.

Wigginton, E. (Ed.). (1996). *A Foxfire Christmas: Appalachian memories and traditions.* Chapel Hill: University Of North Carolina Press.

Williams, P., & Jinks, D. (1985). *Design and technology, 5–12.* Philadelphia: Falmer Press.

Winner, E. (1997). *Gifted children: Myths and realities.* New York: Basic Books.

Wood, B., Bruner, J. S., & Ross, G. (1976). The role of tutoring in problem solving. *Journal of Child Psychology and Psychiatry, 17*(2), 89–100.

Zimmerman, B., Bonner, S., & Kovach, R. (1996). *Developing self-regulated learners: Beyond achievement to self-efficacy.* Washington, DC: American Psychological Association.

Index

About the Authors

Susan Baum, Ph.D., University of Connecticut, is a professor at the College of New Rochelle where she directs the Center for Talent Development. She also directs and teaches in the elementary and gifted education masters degree programs. She has taught in elementary, special, and gifted education, is an international consultant on curriculum and instruction, and is an expert on the exceptional child.

Julie Viens, Ed.M., is a senior researcher at Project Zero at the Harvard Graduate School of Education. She has worked on several projects researching and implementing multiple intelligences theory in varied settings, ranging from preschool through adult education. Currently she is the Education Manager for the WIDE World project, a distance education initiative at the Harvard Graduate School of Education. She continues to work with educators applying multiple intelligences theory in the United States and abroad.

Barbara Slatin, Ed.D., Fordham University, is currently an elementary school principal in New York City. She has held educational positions from classroom teacher to Director of Gifted Education for the New York City Public Schools. Over the past several years, she has focused her efforts on helping her school and others use multiple intelligences theory to improve teaching and learning.

Howard Gardner, Ph.D., Harvard University, is Hobbs Professor of Cognition and Education and Senior Director of Project Zero at the Harvard Graduate School of Education, and adjunct professor of neurology at the Boston University School of Medicine. Dr. Gardner introduced multiple intelligences theory more than 20 years ago. He is the author of 18 books, including *Frames of Mind, The Disciplined Mind, and Intelligence Reframed.* Dr. Gardner served as a reader and consultant to the authors throughout the writing of this book.